Advances in Behaviour Analysis

Advances in Behaviour Analysis

edited by

**Karola Dillenburger
Mark F. O'Reilly
Michael Keenan**

Foreword by Donald M. Baer

University College Dublin Press
Preas Choláiste Ollscoile Bhaile Átha Cliath

First published 1997 by University College Dublin Press,
Newman House, St Stephen's Green, Dublin 2, Ireland

Cataloguing in publication data available from the British Library

Index by Helen Litton
Typeset in Ireland by Seton Music Graphics, Bantry
Printed in Ireland by Colour Books Dublin

Contents

Foreword

Donald M. Baer

The book that follows this foreword occurs at a special moment in the history of behaviour analysis, and reflects that specialness almost perfectly.

We have seen at least seven decades of an interaction between conceptualisation, research, and application. The initial conceptualisation was little more than that behaviour might be studied wholly in the traditions of natural science, and as a subject matter in its own right. That was a short, simple idea, but it was also revolutionary. Most prior accounts of behaviour saw it as only the occasional, imperfect token of what our inner lives must be at that moment; that made it a matter of philosophy, which was adept at inventing minds to explain what we did or ought to do, rather than a matter of natural science. Other accounts saw behaviour as only the occasional, imperfect token of what our physiology must be at that moment. The new notion was that behaviour might be studied as physiology was studied – experimentally, functionally, producing propositions always subject to proof or disproof. But at the same time, it could be studied as itself, not as the result of physiology; indeed, physiology would now be seen as merely part of behaviour – and sometimes as a result of behaviour. That idea upset many people of the day; indeed, it still does, and probably always will, as subsequent chapters will show.

That conceptualisation of behaviour may have been revolutionary, but it was also quite limited. It did not provide a strategy of *how* to study behaviour in its own right. That strategy was found in the subsequent development of the Skinner box. Natural science will not tell you that if behaviour is to be studied, the Skinner box is the way to do it; but once we see a Skinner box in operation, we see immediately that this is a natural-science way to pursue our problem.

The Skinner box yielded a sudden spate of results that proved remarkably consistent, powerful, and easy to summarise. Those summaries became more than summaries; they became conceptualisations of how behaviour works. That behaviour works is the routine assumption of natural science; actual, proven knowledge of *how* it works made the assumption good. Summarising that knowledge as a three-term contingency began a science of behaviour generalisable to any future case, even if at that moment it encompassed little more than rats pressing bars and pigeons pecking keys. The major point was that their bar-pressing and key-pecking were under our experimental control, and that thinking in terms of three-term contingencies showed us systematically how to make – not discover, but *make* – virtually any pattern of bar-pressing or key-pecking we could imagine.

The subsequent pursuit of a science of behaviour, in retrospect, appears seamless. Primitive conceptualisation that behaviour *could* be analysed experimentally led to a strategy of research; the results allowed a sophisticated conceptualisation of *how* behaviour works, which in turn suggested further research, increasingly outside the animal-laboratory Skinner box, the results of which required not revision but only elaboration of the previous conceptualisation; that in turn led to new research, some of it in application to increasingly important human problems; etc.

Meanwhile, the sociology of science placed the initial work in a small corner of psychology, and called it *operant* psychology. That label subsequently gave way to one recognising the true determinant of what was emerging, *the experimental analysis of behaviour*. As that experimental analysis grew in facts and apparent power, its true power was tested by trying its application to human problems; that proved powerful, and terms such as *behaviour modification* emerged as well. As breadth and depth of conceptualisation grew, and as elaborations rather than revisions, a disciplinary name emerged, *behaviour analysis*.

The modern discipline of behaviour analysis has three divisions, as any modern discipline should: the experimental analysis of behaviour, the conceptual analysis of behaviour, and applied behaviour analysis. The evaluation of any scientific discipline should ask the corresponding three classes of questions: (1) To what extent does the discipline display clear, powerful experimental control over its entire subject matter? (2) To what extent has the discipline refined the breadth, internal cohesion, factual backing, and predictive power of its conceptualisations? How readily taught are those conceptualisations and the techniques married to them? (3) To what extent has the discipline shown that its experimental techniques and conceptualisations give it the ability to solve or improve human problems, including an understanding of and, if merited, an improvement of its place in its society?

The chapters that follow reflect exactly that tripartite concern with the modern discipline as such. But their distinctive character, their embodiment of the modern discipline, is that they were not written as if to convince the reader that something new is at hand, something exciting, something perhaps powerful, something to be tried out, and, especially, something to be explained fully once again from its very starting point. These chapters know behaviour analysis as an established discipline, and they assume their readers know that too; this book is not concerned with establishing the discipline, as were so many of its predecessors, but with evaluating where it is and where it needs to be next.

Thus the reader will find, not the laws of behaviour, but the operation of those laws in human development. The reader will find an enduring concern with the relation of the discipline to its very large neighbour, cognitive science. That concern sometimes focuses on maintaining behaviour analysis as a natural science when its major, socially powerful competitor is not. A central issue in that struggle is how we will talk about our private, inner behaviour: Our critics (and, indeed, some of us) doubt that we can talk about it at all and remain married to experimental method. Our 'radical' component insists that we can and should talk about private events, but in behavioural ways: at least, that will rob them of their mystical status as causes in cognitive science; and at best, it may show us how to achieve some degree of experimental control over them (see the 'W-ing' chapter). If that latter goal can be achieved, private-events analysts will not seem so radical, after all. (Nor had they ever wished to be outrageous; the 'radical' they intended was the dictionary's first meaning: going to the fundamental, essential, basic root of the matter.)

Similarly, the reader will not find a primer of how to apply behavioural laws to the solution of important human problems; instead, this book offers current examples of that problem-solving, and more behaviour-analytic discussion of how behaviour-analytic application relates to its neighbours. That last topic includes a behaviour-analytic discussion of how applied behaviour analysis sometimes fails to relate to its society (see 'Bye-bye Behaviour Modification'). It is a chapter that could be about any important modern discipline, simply by changing the name of the discipline and some detailed content accordingly; in our society, *no* important approach goes without some distortion, criticism, and rejection. One point served by this chapter is that applied behaviour analysis must have achieved that kind of importance, to be worth distortion, criticism, and rejection.

Finally, the reader will not find a primer of experimental analysis, but instead a sophisticated analysis of some of the problems of fundamental importance in the modern field. We need to see the fundamental role of context in any analysis, including behaviour analysis. On the face of it, we suppose we want to find behavioural principles of the greatest possible generality. But with more experience in experimental analysis, we begin to see that the generality of almost any principle is always qualified. No behavioural principle is true and applicable to all behaviours, to all organisms, at all times, and in all settings.

Once, for example, we were delighted to conclude that behaviour is sensitive to its consequences, as if that would always be true. With more experimental analysis, we found we had to say that behaviour is sensitive to its consequences, except when it isn't. That begins a useful catechism of contextualism: Given any generalisation of the form, 'A affects B', always say, 'Except when it doesn't'. Then ask, 'When doesn't it?' Usually we can answer that question, because, if we think about it, we do know some conditions when our generalisation is not true. (In the case of 'Behaviour is sensitive to its consequences', if we say, 'Except when it isn't', and then ask, 'When isn't it?' we will remember that it isn't when the organism is satiated for the consequence in question, when the organism is ill, when the organism's history has established a contrary rule such as 'Never take candy from strangers!', and the like.) Listing those exceptions to our generalisation instantly makes it a more accurate, less misleading generalisation. It also tells us to ask what, if anything, the exceptions have in common – perhaps there is a second general principle that explains when the first general principle is not perfectly general. If we find such a second principle, we should then restate it by adding, 'except when it isn't', and then ask, 'When isn't it?' and then try to answer that question. We will become more and more accurate in our generalisations, principles, laws, etc., and perhaps more quickly, more systematically, than any other way.

And when we cannot answer the question, When isn't/doesn't it?, the next and final response in the catechism should be, 'There must be some exceptions; look for them'. If we take that seriously, we will again learn more, and perhaps more quickly and systematically than any other way.

Relational-frame theory is only a way to recognise and formalise context; the point of that chapter is not that sexual response is one of the two most important issues facing the discipline, but that it makes an excellent case in point to illustrate contextual thinking about the analysis of behaviour.

And as for the final chapter: if the concept of self-control has a reality, rule-governance is at its base and is of its essence. Need we argue that importance of understanding self-control, especially in a context of behavioural science?

So, reader, you are about to read not an advertisement for a discipline, but a consumer-evaluation of it. At the end of the book, you will know better whether you want to buy.

Preface

Behaviour Analysis in Ireland

Throughout the 1990s publications in behaviour analysis (Baum, 1994; Chiesa, 1995; Nye, 1992; Newman, 1992; Martin & Pear, 1996; Grant & Evans, 1994; Poling, Schlinger, Starin & Blakely, 1990) have born witness to an ever increasing popularity of the discipline. Behaviour analysis has contributed greatly to the knowledge base now available in areas such as social psychology (Guerin, 1993), developmental psychology (Bijou, 1993; Schlinger, 1995), research methods (Poling, Methot & LeSage, 1995; Sulzer-Azaroff & Mayer, 1991), ethics (Hayes, Hayes, Moore & Ghezzi, 1994; Kimmel, 1996), social work (Hudson & McDonald, 1991), to name but a few. Increasingly behaviour analysis is dealing with issues previously thought of as the prerogative of other disciplines in psychology and its contributions are generally welcomed within academic as well as applied fields. In this preface we will outline briefly some of the fundamental characteristics of this approach and then present a short history of the discipline within Ireland.

Essentially, behavioural analysis is a natural science approach to the study of the behaviour of organisms. It shares the epistemologies and methodologies of other natural science disciplines (physics, chemistry, etc.) as well as the philosophy of science in general. Some of the properties of this natural science approach include determinism, empiricism, and parsimony.

Determinism is a philosophical position which proposes that all physical phenomena in the universe are caused by other physical events. The causal physical events themselves are also amenable to a causal analysis in terms of other physical events. While this philosophical principle cannot lend itself to empirical proof it is the essential premise underlying all scientific investigations. The alternative to holding such a position would be to conclude that some or all physical events occur accidentally. In order to understand a phenomenon, based on the principle of determinism, a scientist must systematically control for the presence and absence of hypothetical causal events. The scientist predicts that the phenomena of interest will occur when the hypothesised causal event is present and conversely that it will not occur when the event is absent. The operations of prediction and control are therefore fundamental to the task of achieving scientific understanding. The use of the term 'control' in behavioural analysis differs from that in everyday speech (i.e., to use; to hold sway over). In behaviour analysis, being in control refers to being in control of independent variables.

The final outcome of a scientific investigation is to define the phenomenon of interest as a function of the operations of the external phenomena that were manipulated. Science is ultimately interested in establishing general functional relations between phenomena. Behaviour analysis, therefore, examines functional relations between behaviour and environmental events. Behaviour analysis is fundamentally not about behaviour per se. It seeks to establish general laws about how behaviour enters into functional relations with environmental stimuli.

Empiricism is a theoretical position that identifies the essential criteria for the practice of scientific investigations. A scientific investigation must abide by these empirical criteria to produce a believable demonstration of the variables that predict and control the phenomenon of interest. In essence, empiricism requires the practice of objective observation. Hypothesised variables must be thoroughly described and precisely quantified prior to their systematic manipulation. Empiricism therefore requires that the subject matter be limited to observable phenomena. B. F. Skinner (1953, 1974) argued that behaviour analysis, like other physical sciences, must deal also with events that are not publicly observable. Private behaviour, or behaviour that occurs within the skin of the individual, is directly observable to that individual and is therefore a legitimate topic for empirical investigation. Private behaviour differs from publicly observable behaviour (i.e., behaviour that is inter-subjectively verifiable) only in terms of its magnitude and limited accessibility. Behaviours that have traditionally been conceptualised as mental are therefore potentially amenable to a behavioural analysis. The chapters by Keenan and Taylor and O'Reilly in this book address the issue of private behaviour in greater depth.

Finally, the *Law of Parsimony* requires a scientist to explain the subject matter and the outcomes of scientific manipulations in terms of necessary and sufficient causes. Science should not seek elaborate and sophisticated explanations if simpler logical explanations can adequately describe the subject matter. Behaviour analysis attempts to explain the diversity of behavioural topographies of organisms in terms of a set of empirically derived principles or laws of behaviour (for example, reinforcement, punishment). Like all natural sciences, behaviour analysis must be consistently vigilant against superfluous and extraneous explanations because they undermine the clarity and veracity of the scientific endeavour.

While originally behaviour analysis emerged from the United States of America, there has always been an interest in the discipline in Europe. This book is the result of an initiative to collate what is best in the discipline in one European country, namely Ireland. To tell the story of behaviour analysis in Ireland we turn to Leo Baker and Julian Leslie, the two founding fathers of a group called Behaviour Analysis in Ireland.

Leo Baker writes about the beginnings of behaviour analysis in Dublin:

An Italian sea captain and an ex-social psychologist led me in the direction of operant conditioning, a theoretical and research interest in experimental psychology which was to dominate my career and lead to the psychology department in Trinity College, Dublin being known, incorrectly, in Ireland and further afield, as a behaviourist stronghold. That reputation, I suspect, owed more to the undergraduate Keller-plan courses in learning that I ran in the 1970s rather than to research output.

Giorgio Santori, a fellow psychology undergraduate at University College, London (UCL) in the early 1960s and captain of the Egyptian royal yacht, approached me one day at the college library waving a book. With enthusiasm he said that he had found a psychology textbook which was like no other and that it really explained what learning was all about. I borrowed it and soon realised that its approach to understanding behaviour was well worth following up. The book was Keller and Schoenfeld's *Principles of Psychology* (1950), the first textbook on operant conditioning.

Ian Russell had started with an interest in social psychology but by the time I was his tutorial student in my final undergraduate year at UCL he was conducting split-brain research using operant methods. My visits to his laboratory introduced me to the mysteries of the Skinner box and electromagnetic programming for running animal experiments but I was unable to accept his offer of a job in the lab when I graduated and went instead to work for SIGMA, a management consultancy in Croydon run by Stafford Beer.

There I worked on various projects as a team member but I soon realised that my knowledge as a practical psychologist was lacking with only my BSc degree so I decided to go back to university. The one I chose was Trinity College Dublin (TCD). Although appointed to teach social psychology, I soon began teaching learning and operant conditioning, the term 'behaviour analysis' not being used until many years later. With the teaching and the undergraduate laboratory classes in learning I began what became the operant laboratory.

My first attempt to condition my first project student to condition my first rat started off as a failure. However, it, she and I all learned slowly and so, gradually, the necessary knowledge and skills were acquired. A welcome supporter at this time was Ingo Fischer who had his own clinical operant laboratory at St James's Hospital for work with child autistic patients. Brian Glanville's master's degree was awarded for work done there under the joint supervision of Ingo and myself. In the TCD laboratory, Susan Willoughby spent a summer's vacation from University College, Cork, learning to conduct animal research. She proceeded to gain her Master's degree for DRL research with rats in 1972 and earned the first PhD in operant research in the republic in 1978 for her work on the transitivity of reinforcers in children (Willoughby, 1978).

During all this time I was receiving support and encouragement from farther afield also. Firstly, regular meetings of the Experimental Analysis of Behaviour Group

(EABG) in the UK became a must and I attended them twice a year from the time that I began working in the mid-1960s at SIGMA. There I made those important contacts in the field and listened to presentations by researchers who had not had to teach themselves but had been supervised in their postgraduate research by experienced scientists who knew what they were doing. Derek Blackman, then a postgraduate researcher, was one of these and became a staunch ally. He even provided rat pellets from the laboratory in Belfast in times of need until the practice was forbidden.

The other big boost was sabbatical visits to the psychology department at Colorado College, Colorado Springs initiated by Don Shearn. He was (and is) an operant physiological psychologist who discovered me and my lab by dropping into the department on Westland Row and reading the hall notice board. Seeing the outline for my course in behaviour theory, he went on up to the staff room where he introduced himself. I went twice to Colorado College on sabbaticals to replace Don or Carl Roberts and teach behaviour analysis, behaviour theory and statistics. There I discovered myself in a behavioural heaven as the majority of staff there taught operant learning, even if it was only Psych 101. My experience in the States combined with that at EABG meetings provided the basis of a network which a working scientist needs and which I have had ever since.

Jock Millenson also features in this story. Besides a mutual interest in operant psychology we were both interested in flying, as also is Don Shearn. It was during a visit to my lab that Jock and I flew in an Auster of the Irish Aero Club at Dublin. His lasting impression seemed to be that Irish phones didn't work and that the cost of flying was too high. I adopted Jock's textbook, *Principles of Behavioral Analysis* (1967), for my learning course and it was through Jock and the EABG that I got to know Julian Leslie who was then a postgraduate student of Jock's at Oxford. Julian went on to revise and rewrite Jock's text in two further editions (Milleson & Leslie, 1979; Leslie, 1996). It was Julian who brought behaviour analysis to Ireland in a big way with his appointment to the University of Ulster and his important moves in establishing the Behaviour Analysis in Ireland group, but that's his story.

Working in isolation as a behaviour analyst in Dublin was lonely and difficult at times. For example, it took me years to realise that I did not have to justify my position to all and sundry as a behaviourist and a disciple of B. F. Skinner. I think what was important in that realisation was Skinner's visit to TCD in the 1960s. He delivered a number of talks including a hugely attended one to the Psychological Society, a draft from his forthcoming book *About Behaviorism* (1974). Skinner also influenced my undergraduates, one of whom was Fergus Lowe. Fergus became a student in Peter Harzem's lab in Bangor, North Wales which I visited regularly for EABG meetings and to seek support and encouragement from Peter and his growing band of doctoral and postdoctoral workers. Fergus, of course, had joined them after graduating from TCD where he began his interest in human operant research (Lowe, Richelle & Blackman, 1985) and he went on to take over the lab when Peter Harzem left and later the department.

The Behaviour Analysis in Ireland (BAI) group (a derivative of earlier attempts to start such a group by myself, Fergus and Des Poole such as the Behavioural Engineering Group) which I ran for many years, provided the sort of venue and support group for behaviour analytic researchers in Ireland which the EABG did in the UK. I kept attending the latter but in many ways the BAI meetings had an extra appeal. Not only did it run three meetings a year for some years but it encouraged applied behaviour analysts, mostly but not exclusively in the clinical area, to present papers and this added a further dimension. It ensured that the small band of Irish behaviour analysts, both pure and applied, stayed in touch and were aware of each other's work. With its success

I began to feel that behaviour analysis had found its place within the scientific psychological community in Ireland and BAI's move under the umbrella of the Psychological Society of Ireland, like the establishment of Division 25 of the American Psychological Association, confirmed that in a way which had never happened in the UK with the EABG and the British Psychological Society. It is rewarding to have been part of that history.

Julian Leslie writes about the efforts to bring together behaviour analysts in Ireland:

My interest in behaviour analysis began at Oxford University where I took a course taught by Jock Millenson. The course was actually called 'Conditioning and Emotion', and Jock presented his ideas about how emotion and motivation could be incorporated into a behavioural-analysis framework. I then did a final-year project in Jock's lab on 'positive conditioned suppression', that is the procedure where a Conditioned Stimulus (CS) followed by an appetitive Unconditioned Stimulus (US) is superimposed on a positively reinforced operant baseline, and following graduation I began a research degree in the same lab studying conditioned suppression procedures. Unfortunately, Jock left Oxford about a year after I started the research, but by then I had benefited a great deal from a few years of intense interaction with him. Earlier in his career, Jock had been working with Harry Hurwitz in London when they established the first British behaviour analysis group, now called the Experimental Analysis of Behaviour Group (EABG). In a sense, he was involved in the origin of the Behaviour Analysis in Ireland group as well because of an introduction he made in 1970. In that summer, Jock and I attended a conference of the Behavioural Engineering Association, in Kilkenny. That was the first time I had visited Ireland and *en route* we met Leo Baker at Trinity College Dublin. As a result of that meeting I contacted Leo when I took up a post at the New University of Ulster, Coleraine, in 1974, and we began to discuss ways of supporting behaviour analysis in the Irish context. We had an advantage in that the number of people working in psychology in Ireland was small in the mid-1970s, but we also knew that behavioural approaches were not regarded very sympathetically, at least in the colleges in the 'South', the Republic of Ireland. After an initial trawl for support, we had an initial planning meeting in 1977 and Leo undertook to run the group. He did this most effectively for a number of years. Our aspiration was always to provide a location where those developing an interest in behavioural analysis, often undergraduates who had carried out final-year projects as part of their degree studies or research students in the early stages of their work, were able to present their ideas and findings in a supportive environment. We tried to meet several times a year, and also had an explicit policy of holding our meetings all over Ireland, North and South. This led to 'expeditionary forces', in the early days almost entirely from Coleraine and Dublin, setting out to 'uncharted' parts of the South and West of Ireland. Sometimes the resulting meeting was attended by relatively few locals, but it allowed us to support those who were in the area, and gave the regulars a working knowledge of the menus of Chinese restaurants all over Ireland! It gives me great pleasure to note that, in the mid-1990s, by contrast, we have strong links with University College Cork, University of Limerick, Queen's University of Belfast, University of Ulster at Jordanstown and University College Dublin, as well as University of Ulster at Coleraine and Trinity College Dublin. We also have links with professional psychologists, who, like the academics, are much greater in numbers than twenty years ago. Our objective in the next twenty years will be to establish as strong a network in Ireland for the support of applied behavioural analysis as we have for behavioural analysis in general. We have moved a long way in this direction, with human and applied studies forming an increasing proportion of the content of more recent meetings.

Things have come a long way since those early beginnings and in this book authors from North and South of the border in Ireland have come together to develop a text that is suitable not only for undergraduate and postgraduate students, but also for those working in applied settings (such as agencies working with people with developmental disabilities, child care settings). The text provides the reader with advanced knowledge and is considered complementary to introductory text books.

The book is structured in three parts covering the major issues with which behaviour analysis is concerned today. These are broadly categorised as conceptual, applied and experimental issues. Part 1, dealing with conceptual issues, starts with Karola Dillenburger's and Michael Keenan's discussion of the relation between the structure and function of behaviour in the context of human development. Chapter 2 is the first of two chapters detailing the debate concerning the study of private events in behaviour analysis. Ian Taylor and Mark F. O'Reilly discuss the neglected and misunderstood construct of private events within radical behaviourism. This chapter is followed by Micheal Keenan's teaching exercises for radical behaviourists. He argues that psychologists who misrepresent behaviour analysis do so because they were not exposed to appropriate teaching exercises. In Chapter 4 Kevin Tierney and John Smith pursue the theme of misrepresentation as it applies to recent interest in cognitive-behaviour modification. They argue that the precision associated with the natural science of behaviour analysis decays when practitioners work in environments where cognitivism is unchallenged. Their search for the reinforcers for cognitivism in behaviour therapy offers a useful backdrop for part 2 of the book which is devoted to applied issues.

The first two chapters of part 2 are devoted to a more theoretical introduction to applied behaviour analysis. Peter Walsh in Chapter 5 argues that in terms of behavioural intervention we should disband the traditional notions of behaviour modification and instead turn our attention to the more rigorous approach of applied behaviour analysis. In Chapter 6 Julian Leslie elaborates on this theme, taking the debate about the utility of behaviour analysis into the area of general applied psychology. The following four chapters deal with actual applied behaviour analytic research. A review of studies of behavioural self-control in third-level students is reported by Samuel Cromie and Leo Baker who take the issue of the analysis of private behaviour into applied settings. In Chapter 8 Dermot O'Reilly and Karola Dillenburger present behaviour analytic family intervention with conduct disordered children. Chapter 9 concentrates on work within the area of developmental disability. Mark F. O'Reilly reports on current issues in the assessment and treatment of severe behaviour disorders. In Chapter 10 Janet O'Connell and Finola Leonard apply knowledge gained through the analysis of behaviour to dairy cattle and analyse how winter housing systems could be improved.

The final part of this book (part 3) concentrates on experimental issues. In Chapter 11 Dermot Barnes and Bryan Roche introduce relational frame theory and apply it to their work in the experimental analysis of human sexual arousal. In Chapter 12 Ken Kerr and Michael Keenan conclude the book by discussing how the experimental analysis of rules and rule-governance can lead to new directions in the theoretical and experimental analysis of human behaviour.

Karola Dillenburger

Mark F. O'Reilly

Michael Keenan

References

Baum, W. (1994). *Understanding behaviorism*. USA: HarperCollins.

Bijou, S. (1993). *Behavior analysis of child development*. Reno: Context Press.

Chiesa, M. (1995). *Radical behaviorism: The philosophy and the science*. Authors Cooperative.

Grant, L. & Evans, A. (1994). *Principles of behavior analysis*. New York: HarperCollins.

Guerin, B. (1993). *The analysis of social behavior*. Reno: Context Press.

Hayes, L. J., Hayes, G. J., Moore, S. C., & Ghezzi, P. M. (Eds) (1994). *Ethical issues in developmental disabilities*. Reno: Context Press.

Hudson, B. L. & McDonald, G. M. (1991). *Behavioural social work: An introduction*. Basingstake: Macmillan Education.

Keller, F. S. & Schoenfeld, W. N. (1950). *Principles of psychology: A systematic text in the science of behavior*. New York: Appleton-Century-Crofts.

Kimmel, A. (1996). *Ethical Issues in behavioral research*. Oxford: Blackwell.

Leslie, J. C. (1996). *Principles of behavioral analysis*. Amsterdam: Harwood.

Lowe, C. F., Richelle, M., & Blackman, D. E. (Eds) (1985). *Behaviour analysis and contemporary psychology*. London: Lawrence Erlbaum.

Martin, G. & Pear, J. (1996). *Behavior modification: What it is and how to do it* (5th ed.). New Jersey: Prentice Hall.

Millenson, J. R. (1967). *Principles of behavioral analysis*. New York: Macmillan.

Millenson, J. R. & Leslie, J. C. (1979). *Principles of behavioral analysis* (2nd ed.). New York: Macmillan.

Newman, B. (1992). *The reluctant alliance: Humanism and behaviorism*. U.S.A.: Prometheus Books.

Nye, R. D. (1992). *The Legacy of B. F. Skinner: Concepts and perspectives, controversies and misunderstandings*. California: Brooks/Cole.

Poling, A., Methot L. L., & LeSage, M. G. (1995). *Fundamentals of behavior analytic research*. New York: Plenum.

Poling, A., Schlinger, H., Starin, S., & Blakely, E. (1990). *Psychology: A behavioral overview*. New York: Plenum.

Schlinger, H. jr (1995). *A behavior analytic view of child development*. New York: Plenum.

Skinner, B. F. (1953). *Science and human behavior*. New York: Macmillan.

Skinner, B. F. (1974). *About behaviorism*. New York: Knopf.

Sulzer-Azaroff, B. & Mayer, G. R. (1991), *Behavior analysis for lasting Change* New York: Holt, Rinehart & Winston.
Watson, J. B. (1924). *Behaviorism*. New York: Norton.
Willoughby, S. A. (1978) A study of human choice behaviour on concurrent variable-interval schedules: Transitivity, matching, and reinforcer value. Unpublished doctoral thesis, Trinity College Dublin.

PART 1

CONCEPTUAL ISSUES

1

Human development: A question of structure and function[1]

Karola Dillenburger and Michael Keenan

Abstract

Generally psychologists study selective aspects of human behaviour. Developmental psychologists, for example, study aspects of human development, such as physical, social, cognitive, language, sexual, or moral development. The majority of developmental psychologists devote their time to the study of the behaviour of children and they relate the age of a child to changes in the behaviour of that child. Not surprisingly the broad spectrum encompassed by developmental psychologists in this endeavour has led to a plethora of developmental concepts and theories. This is problematic for a number of reasons, but primarily because it has led to a fragmented view of the process underpinning development. In this chapter we will discuss traditional interpretations of developmental phenomena in the framework provided by issues germane to the role of structure and function of behaviour. We also expose the inherent limitations of circular reasoning that characterises theory in developmental psychology. We conclude with the prospect of an integrated and unifying concept of human development.

Introduction

The promise of the last century that psychology could develop into an integrated science has not yet been fulfilled (Catania, 1974). Today psychology is still characterised by a plethora of theories, each endeavouring to explain a

---

[1] An earlier draft of this paper was presented at the 30th Annual Conference of the British Psychological Society (Northern Ireland Branch), Dunfanaghy, Republic of Ireland, 26–28 April 1996.

different psychological phenomenon. Developmental psychology has been particularly plagued by this general problem, in that it has spawned an especially
large number of theories. Crain (1992), for example, describes seventeen such
theories in one book alone. Vasta (1992) pointed out, that '. . . one of the
clearest manifestations of a science in its infancy is the presence of a number of
competing theoretical models existing side by side' (p. ix). He proposes that in
time '. . . the number of these competing theories [will reduce] to two or three
– with several perhaps failing to adequately account for new findings and thus
falling by the wayside, and others (perhaps with further revision of incorpo-
ration of now-competing concepts) maintaining their organizing and guiding
functions' (p. x). On the downside, he feels that it may take another hundred
years or so before this may happen in developmental psychology.

   We may be closer, however, to the maturing of the science of developmental
psychology than predicted. Mussen (1992), in his foreword to Vasta's book,
recognises that there are many important commonalties in present-day developmental psychology, such as the recognition of the inherent complexity of
developmental phenomena and the rejection of simplistic explanatory notions.
Mussen states that theorists today '. . . are less concerned than earlier theorists
with parsimony and the formal aspects of theory building . . . [instead they] are
guided by meticulous analysis of possible influences on thought and behavior,
by new insights, and by findings of empirical studies' (p. xii).

   In this paper we will draw on the heritage of traditional developmental
theories and offer an insight into some aspects of commonality, such as the
direct observation of child behaviours and the debate regarding the distinction
between the structure and function of development. We will then expose some
of the major limitations of traditional developmental psychology, such as the
use of fictitious explanations, cultural insensitivity and utility. Finally, we
conclude with the prospect of an integrated and unifying concept of human
development.

Subject matter

The first unequivocal step in any science should be to agree on a common
interpretation of what constitutes the subject matter. For developmental
psychology, this could not be more beautifully expressed than by Johnston
(1989), who wrote:

My emergence as a unique individual with my own identity began in the ovaries and
testes of my parents when they themselves were embryos in the grandparental womb.
The events occurring then were in themselves linked via a thread back through successive ancestral germ lines to the emergence of humanity itself. Just as anthropologists
cannot define an exact and absolute point during evolutionary time when our ancient
ancestors became human, so I cannot define any single developmental transition at

which I became an individual with a clear identity. The evolution of humans and the development of my identity are both continuous processes. (p. 41)

With this notion of process in mind, we will look now at some examples of a developing child and examine how these observations are dealt with by traditional theorists.

One thing developmental theories have in common is that they all started with direct observations of behaviour, usually children's behaviour. We will therefore start with some observations from the development of our 11-month-old baby boy, called Tara. We join him on a Sunday morning playing in the midst of a floor full of toys in our living room. We will use our observations to illustrate briefly how traditional theorists might explain different aspects of the process that is observed.

Observation 1: *Tara puts toys into his mouth.*
Sigmund Freud (1976), for example, might state that this is part of his sexual development and that he is doing this because he is in the oral phase.

Observation 2: *Tara shakes the rattle repeatedly.*
Jean Piaget (1977) might propose that this is part of Tara's cognitive development and that he does this because he is in the sensori-motor stage.

Observation 3: *Tara turns towards the toy that fell behind the flower pot, reaches out and grabs it.*
Piaget might state that he does this as part of his cognitive development because he has developed the concept of object permanence. (Piaget & Inhelder, 1967)

Observation 4: *Tara snatches his bottle from anyone attempting to take it away from him, lies back on the floor and drinks from it.*
Lawrence Kohlberg (1964) might suggest that this is an early part of his moral development and that he is doing this because he is at the stage of pre-conventional morality with pleasure/pain orientation.

Observation 5: *Tara crawls over towards us and smiles at us.*
Erik Erikson (1963) might propose that this is part of his psycho-social development and that Tara is doing this because he is solving the conflict between trust versus mistrust adequately.

Observation 6: *Tara crawls towards us and smiles when we enter the room.*
John Bowlby (1973) might state that this is part of the development of attachment and that Tara is doing this because of the attachment he has formed with us.

Obviously many more of Tara's behaviours could have been observed that morning and many more theories could have been employed to categorise his behaviour and to offer an explanation for why he did the things he did (Crain, 1992). Given the statement by Johnston (1989) earlier, though, it is remarkable that developmental psychology seems to need such a range of disparate theories to explain what was in fact one whole individual human in the continuous process of interacting with his environment. Admittedly, Tara's behaviours were complex but the question remains why they are analysed as distinctively different rather than as part of a continuous process or 'stream of behaviour' (Keenan, 1993).

The tradition of separately analysing developmental phenomena stems from the fact that most categories of behaviour are distinguished mainly by their structure rather than by their function (Schlinger, 1995). A hundred years ago, in 1898, Titchner drew attention to this distinction between structural and functional approaches in psychology and he pointed towards the analogy with other sciences (Catania, 1973). For example,

. . . in biology, the distinction between structure and function was so well established that it supported a division of the field into such separate departments as anatomy and physiology . . . it is clearly recognised that studies of biological structure and studies of biological function are concerned with different empirical questions. To say what an organism does, it may help to know how it is constructed; yet its function is not studied in the same way as its structure. (Catania, 1973, p. 435)

An illustration of this distinction between structure and function in developmental psychology can be seen if we take, for example, a relatively simple behaviour such as a child eating her breakfast. A structural account '. . . primarily consists of a description of the organism's postural activities and bodily movements' (Howard & Keenan, 1993, p. 195). In this case a structural account would describe the topographically different actions necessary for a child eating her breakfast, such as clenching the spoon in her hand, dipping the spoon into the bowl of cereal, manoeuvring cereal onto the spoon, lifting the spoon up to the mouth, opening the mouth, manoeuvring the spoon into the mouth, closing the mouth, pulling the spoon out and chewing the food before swallowing it.

In contrast, a functional account concentrates on '. . . the contextual changes which precede, accompany, and follow [behaviour] in a predictable manner' (Howard & Keenan, 1993, p. 195). Thus a functional account of a child eating her breakfast would concentrate on variables that define the context called 'having breakfast'. Is she alone or are her parents present? Is there a bowl of cereal and a spoon? What is the child's level of food deprivation i.e., is she hungry? What is the child's previous experience with this particular type of cereal i.e., does she like it? What is the learning history of the child i.e., can she feed herself? Are there any features of the current situation which affect the likelihood that she will eat by herself? Are there any consequences which follow her behaviour that affect the likelihood that she will eat by herself?

In traditional developmental psychology the structural account usually prevails. Due to the rapid succession of structurally distinct behaviours, especially in early childhood, most developmental theories are based on structurally distinct stages of child behaviour which can usually be correlated with the age of the child. Piaget's theory of cognitive development is a case in point (Piaget, 1977). Piaget's stage theory is based on structurally different behaviour patterns that he observed in children of differing ages. He interpreted these observations with little or no reference to functional or contextual aspects of the observed behaviour. Take, for example, his conservation experiments. Piaget presented children under seven years of age with two separate lots of objects/liquids of the same size, number, or amount. He used two bits of string of the same length, two glasses filled with the same amount of liquid, two equally large balls of clay, or two piles of sweets or biscuits of equal number. One lot was arranged so as to make it appear smaller, while the other was arranged so as to make it appear larger. In the case of Piaget's famous liquid conservation experiment, the same amount of liquid was filled into one narrow, tall glass and one broad, low glass. When Piaget asked the children to point to the glass that had more liquid the children invariably pointed towards the narrow, tall glass. Based solely on the structural observation of this bodily movement (i.e., pointing) and with no further reference to contextual or functional variables, Piaget concluded that children under the age of seven had not yet developed a 'concept of conservation' (Piaget & Inhelder, 1967).

There are a range of problems with such conclusions and we will come to these later. For the moment let us concentrate on the problems that arise from a purely structural account. Schlinger (1995) observed, that '. . . [t]his structural approach in developmental psychology is based on the assumption that classes of behavior, which are distinguished primarily on the basis of structural properties, are separate functional classes requiring different explanations' (p. 18). Similarly, the assumption that behaviours with structurally similar properties should be considered in the same functional class can be mistaken. In relation to Piaget's conservation experiments, for example, observations of our own nearly five-year-old daughter showed that the structurally similar behaviour of 'pointing' should be considered a function of the prevailing contingencies. Faced with two lots of eight chocolate biscuits (one lot piled on top of each other, the other lot spread widely on the table) our daughter pointed to one lot of biscuits when asked Piaget's original question, however, she pointed to the other lot when asked which ones she wanted to eat. In other words, while the structural aspects of the behaviour (i.e., the pointing) remained more or less the same, the prospect of a positive consequence altered the function and thus changed the results of the experiment dramatically (cf. Byrant, 1974). Obviously, for a full functional analysis one has to consider the context which preceded, accompanied, and followed her previous experience with the biscuits in question (i.e., had she tried them before? did she like them?) and her present state of food deprivation (i.e., was she hungry?).

Some developmental psychologists recognise the limitations of a purely structural account and are becoming interested in functional accounts (Meadows, 1992), especially since the utility of functional accounts is fairly obvious. At present, however, there is some confusion because the terms 'structure' and 'function' themselves are defined very differently depending on the theoretical leaning of the speaker. Traditionally it seemed that '. . . [s]tructural research tends to be described in the cognitive . . . vocabulary, and functional research in the behaviorist vocabulary'. (Catania, 1973, p. 435)

Not surprisingly this difference in vocabularies and associated epistemologies (Morris, 1980) has not been helpful but has served only to further obfuscate the core issues. Vasta (1992), for example, stated that in cognitive psychology, '. . . structure tends to be identified with mental structure and function with psychological process' (p. 90). Leslie (1996), on the other hand, stated that behaviourally speaking structurally-defined behaviours consist of '. . . movements that fall within certain physical limits' (p. 46), and functionally-defined behaviours are '. . . all the behaviours that could produce a particular environmental change, and thus have a particular function for the organism' (p. 46). Both cognitive as well as behavioural definitions recognise that a structural account does not tell us about the circumstances under which the behaviour occurs, and that this question can only be answered by a functional account. The main difference between the two definitions lies in the fact that when cognitive psychologists speak of structure they mean 'structure of the mind', while when behavioural psychologists speak of structure they mean structure of behaviour. When cognitive psychologists speak of function they mean 'an inner psychological process'. Behavioural psychologists use the term 'function' in two complementary ways. On the one hand, they talk about the *function that a certain behaviour has* for the organism, that is, they view behaviour as a process that brings about consequences for the person. These consequences may be temporally proximate or temporally distal to the behaviour in question. On the other hand, they see that *behaviour is a function* of the antecedents or consequences that are operating. In empirical investigations, antecedents or consequences are then analysed as independent variables while the behaviour of the whole person[2] is viewed as the dependent variable. The importance of this type of functional analysis will become evident later. For the meantime let us return to the argument regarding traditional developmental theories.

---

[2]   A useful definition of behaviour is to consider behaviour as anything a dead person can not do, such as observable, private (thoughts and feelings) and verbal behaviours.

Constraints of traditional developmental psychology

To date, traditional developmental theories have given us a narrative as to what children are likely to do at approximately what age, yet, their search for explanations of these observations has often been based on a common mistake which involves 'mentalism' (Newman, 1992; Nye, 1992, Schlinger, 1992) or reification, (the practice of making 'an abstract idea or concept real or concrete' (*Collins English Dictionary*, 1991)). What starts off as an observation of a child behaving in certain, structural ways becomes reified into a mental entity or structure of the mind, for example a concept or schema. In the search for an explanation of the observed behaviour, traditional theorists then look to these mental entities or cognitive processes and state that the behaviour in question was caused by them. As Schlinger (1995) put it, theories used to explain the development of observed behaviours are '. . . all too often . . . arrived at through logical error or circular reasoning. First, the behavioral class is given a name. Second, the name is treated as if it referred to a (concrete) material object (i.e., it is reified), so that the name itself becomes the object of study. Finally, the name for the behavioral class becomes the explanation of the observed behavior'. (p. 18) Take for example, Piaget's conservation experiments mentioned earlier. Piaget found that children pointed towards one of two lots of objects when asked which one was more or bigger. This class of behaviours (pointing) can be labelled conserving behaviours. Piaget treated this descriptive label, however, as if it referred to a concrete entity, called conservation. He explained the behaviour of the child by stating that the child had developed a 'concept of conservation'. These kinds of interpretations deduce a mental or cognitive cause for the observed behaviour, in other words, the cause for the observed behaviours is hypothetically placed inside the person whose behaviour is to be analysed.

The main problem with this kind of circular reasoning or 'mentalism' (see Baum, 1994, for an excellent discussion of mentalism) is that it leads to the assumption that an explanation or underlying cause for the behaviour is identified, while in fact, nothing is added to the analysis. Instead, this kind of reasoning may distract from the search for the real underlying causes and instead lead prematurely to a form of biological determinism. The real cause of behaviour can only be found if the independent variables responsible for the observed behaviours are identified. Similar to the approach taken by other natural sciences, an experimental analysis would change one variable at a time until the particular independent variables responsible for a change in behaviour (i.e., the dependent variable) are identified (Poling, Methot & LeSage, 1995; Richelle, 1993; Sidman, 1960). Psychologists who follow this rigorous approach can then confidently state that they have found the underlying cause for the behaviour (Iwata, Dorsey, Slifer, Bauman & Richman, 1982). Bijou (1992) elaborates Johnston's earlier statement when he wrote that, '. . . the subject matter of psychology is the interaction between a biological individual and circumstances . . . all concepts – descriptive, analytical, and theoretical – are traceable to the subject matter'. (p. 175)

Take, for example, our earlier observations of Tara's searching behaviour when his toy fell behind the flowerpot out of his sight. He crawled around the pot and retrieved the toy. Rather than inferring a concept of object permanence, a functional explanation of searching behaviours identifies the variables responsible for this kind of behaviour. The key variables can be found in the child's past experiences and in present circumstances (Thyer, 1992). A thorough analysis would probably find that the child has a long history of 'hide and seek' or 'peek-a-boo' games during which searching behaviours are taught, that is reinforced in the sense of making them more likely to recur under similar circumstances. These games are commonly played with children in Western societies. Furthermore, we would find that, at the time of the observation, the child was in a context which provided the appropriate independent variables to support the occurrence of the dependent variable, searching behaviour.

Not only is observable behaviour influenced by past experiences and present circumstances but so also are not so readily observable changes, that is, changes that occur inside the skin of the developing person. Rather than analysing them separately these changes are best considered part and parcel of the overall behaviour of the whole person. Skinner (1953) called changes that happen inside the skin 'private events', because they are events that are private and observable only by one person. The important point here is, that they do not *cause* observable behaviour. Instead, they themselves constitute part of the whole organism that has changed. Consequently, they are viewed as further dependent variables (cf. Hayes & Brownstein, 1987). For example, the way a child feels and what she thinks is influenced by the circumstances in which she finds herself. As Reese (1978) put it, behaviour is '. . . anything that people do, including what they say and what they think and feel'. (p. 2)

Another good example of the limitations of mentalistic thinking is the approach usually taken to attachment and separation behaviours. Bowlby (1973) pioneered work in this area and his research has lead to a vast amount of interest. He observed a range of behaviours especially in very young children such as crying, whining, reaching out, babbling, and other '. . . gestures and signals that promote and maintain proximity to care-takers' (Crain, 1992, p. 38), and labelled these 'attachment behaviours'. He concluded that attachment behaviours were caused by attachment; a reification that leads to a circular interpretation of the phenomenon.

Bowlby's work was followed by Ainsworth (1973) whose most famous experiment was the so-called 'strange situation'. She observed children in a range of situations where they were briefly separated from their mothers. She recorded the responses made by the children, while the mother was out of the room, when a stranger entered the room, and on the return of the mother. She found a range of different responses made by the children and grouped these into three distinct patterns labelling them 'secure', 'insecure-avoident' and 'insecure-ambivalent'. She then went on to use these labels to explain the observed behaviours. A child was said to behave in these ways because her attachment was secure, insecure-avoident or insecure-ambivalent (Crain, 1992). Again, this type of analysis falls prey to the mistakes of circular reasoning.

Traditional texts recommend this procedure as a measure of the quality of attachment (Nugent, 1996). However, because Ainsworth and colleagues gauged attachment by purely structural parameters there is a real danger that this method of assessment will misjudge parents and label them in negative ways. Imagine parents who have taught their child adequate separation behaviours early on, for example, not to cry when they are briefly separated (Dillenburger & Keenan, 1993). In many cases this is exactly what happens when parents leave to go to work. When the parent leaves, the child does not cry and probably continues playing contentedly. Is this behaviour of the child a sign of poor attachment? A functional analysis of attachment behaviours demonstrates that

. . . infant protest can be shaped, maintained, and increased by patterns of contingent . . . responding, and that these protests can be decreased or eliminated by a [parent] responding independently (non-contingent) of her [or his] infant's protests and contingently upon other, more constructive, infant behaviours (e.g. vocalisations, play, smiles). (Gewirtz & Peláez-Nogueras, 1992, p. 1414)

We suggest, therefore, that rather than labelling a child-parent relationship with terms like 'insecure-ambivalent attachment', some attachment behaviours such as not crying or fussing at separation could be a result of skilful and thoughtful parenting by people who consider the acquisition of such behaviours as beneficial to their child's ability to adjust to new situations. To prevent premature or mistaken labelling of child-parent relationships, the assessment of attachment behaviours has to start with an analysis of the conditions (independent variables) that brought about these behaviours (dependent variables).

A major achievement of traditional developmental psychology is that we are now in a position to predict the incidence of many regularly occurring behaviours quite accurately. Unfortunately much of the cataloguing of these behaviours was done in a climate of outdated theoretical positions. The result of this legacy is that development is often cast as an inevitable sequence of stages that is age related. As Baer (1973) put it, '. . . it is undeniable that a great deal of behaviour regularly occurs in its turn' (p. 186). However, besides the problems with mentalism, traditional stage theories have other inherent

problems. For one, they are usually culturally determined. The prevailing culture obviously influences any theorist not only in regard to the actual research
questions but also in terms of theory formulation. It is therefore important to
re-assess the relevance of stage theories continuously in the light of the specific
culture in which they are to be applied. A good example of this is the fact that
in one of Piaget's experiments high mountains are a feature of the test. This was
obviously part of the familiar environment of his Swiss child subjects but may
lead to totally different results with, say, Dutch children who may never have
seen a mountain in their lives. While these differences may be small and
relatively insignificant within a European context, imagine the impact when
testing children from totally different ethnic or cultural backgrounds. The
consequences of this all to easily leads to ethnic discrimination (see Lynn, 1996).

Another problem with stage theories of human development that include
mentalistic concepts is their inability to offer concrete guidance in dealing with
unwanted or aberrant behaviours. Take for example the phrase 'terrible twos'.
While this phrase probably originated from the observation of some two-year-
old children who behaved in ways which could be described as 'terrible' (presumably they were lying on the floor, kicking, shouting, crying, saying things
like 'I want, I want' or 'no, no'), it is now used to explain some of these behaviours in young children. Adults, when they see these behaviours often say, 'I
see he is going through the stage of *terrible twos*. Just leave him, there is
nothing you can do. He will grow out of it.' If analysed properly and scientifically the cause of these behaviours can be established by looking at the past
experiences of the child and the independent variables that make up the
context of the observation. We are most likely to find that when the child first
displayed these types of behaviours, or approximations thereof, (possibly
imitating them from an older sibling or play mate), the carer responded in ways
which reinforced them and therefore, by definition, increased their frequency.
If this had not been the case we would not see these types of behaviours too
often. Phrases such as, 'he will grow out of it', or 'this is a stage he is going
through' (Stoppard, 1990), tell us nothing about the process that will lead him
either to grow out of it or to develop from one stage to another. An explanation of this process cannot be found in the descriptive label of the behaviours.
It can only be found in a thorough functional analysis of the past and current
independent variables.

Our earlier observation of baby Tara will illustrate this point. On that
Sunday morning Tara proceeded to climb up onto the settee, clambered over
to the yucca plant and reached for one of the leaves, pulling it tightly. We
remained where we were and just called *No, Tara!*; he looked at us and let the
yucca leaf go and then climbed down from the settee, legs first. Traditionally
these two behaviours would probably have been analysed separately. His response to our saying *No, Tara!* would have been looked at either as part of his

moral or his social development; his climbing down from the settee would have been viewed as a result of either his physical or his cognitive development and appropriate stages of development would be cited.

However, these were two behaviours for which we personally did not need any new theory. We knew exactly how these behaviours had developed, because over the past few weeks we had taught Tara to respond appropriately to *No, Tara!* and over the past three days we had taught him how to climb down from the settee, legs first, instead of head first. We had used behavioural principles, such as shaping, differential reinforcement and stimulus control to teach him these behaviours (Grant & Evans, 1994; Martin & Pear, 1996; Poling, Schlinger, Starin & Blakely, 1990). An explanation for these obser- vations that does not refer to the behavioural principles of which his behaviour was a function is therefore seriously misleading. The rationale for a scientific epistemology can be stated simply: Whatever is done to produce the behaviour in question must be at the root of the formulation of an explanation for that behaviour. In so far as a scientist can produce changes in behaviour, the search for an explanatory principles will be advanced. As Gewirtz and Peláez- Nogueras (1992) stated '. . . [a] functional analysis of . . . behaviour must focus on the many variables likely to be directly responsible for behaviour change patters denoting development'. (p. 1419)

The idea that knowledge of behavioural principles can be used to explain behavioural developments is not far fetched. In fact, that is exactly what behav- iour analysts who are interested in behavioural development have been doing over the past four decades. Sidney Bijou and Donald Baer spearheaded the application of behaviour analysis to child development (Bijou & Baer, 1961; 1965; 1967; 1978; Baer, 1970; 1973), and continue to do so to the present day (Bijou, 1992; 1993; Rosales-Ruiz & Baer, 1996); Baer and colleagues paying particular attention to the ability to develop behaviours through imitation and modelling (Baer, Peterson, & Sherman 1967); others, such as Jacob Gewirtz and colleagues concentrating on the analysis of attachment and separation (Gewirtz, 1956; 1991; Gewirtz & Boyd, 1977; Gewirtz & Kurtines, 1991; Gewirtz & Pelaez-Nogueras, 1991; 1992). Bruce Thyer (1992) is looking at a behavioural life span approach and Henry Schlinger (1992; 1995) is giving lucid introductions to the behaviour analytic view of areas traditionally analysed separately, such as memory, motor development, perceptual development, cogni- tive development, language development, and social and emotional development.

Interestingly the recent upsurge in publications of behaviour analytic thinking on human development and the accompanying increase in numbers of people joining the special interest group for behavioural development of the International Association of Behavior Analysis has been ignored in British publications, as is evidenced in a recent edition of a major text book on devel- opmental psychology (Schaffer, 1996). Schaffer asks where all the behaviourists have gone. He suggests that '. . . many developmentalists from a behavioural tradition have become information processing researchers' (p. 303). Given what was said above, this is obviously a misleading conclusion and a gross misrepresentation of the facts. This type of behaviour is not uncommon in diverging areas of science and it has been well documented by authors within the discipline of behaviour analysis (Morris, 1985; Todd & Morris, 1983, 1992).

Behaviour analysis

A behaviour analytic concept of human behaviour offers a new basis for understanding developmental phenomena. Development is no longer viewed as an innate phenomenon which leads to an inevitable sequence of behaviours. 'In behavioural analysis, the term *development* is an abstraction for progressive, orderly changes in the organisation of environment-behaviour relations' (Gewirtz & Peláez-Nogueras, 1992, p. 1419).

An example of behaviour analytic developmental research will clarify what this means. Wendell Jeffrey (1958, in Baer, 1970), in his study of mediational processes in children, for example, looked at four-year-olds and their ability to tell left from right. He used two cards which depicted essentially the same stick-figure; however, in one of the pictures the figure was pointing to the right, in the other one it was pointing to the left. Jeffrey was interested to see if children could learn to call the one pointing to the right 'Jill' and the one pointing the left 'Jack' simply by reinforcing the correct response. While it seems obvious that, say, seven-year-olds would have easily learned to distinguish between the two pictures, four-year-old subjects were still unable to distinguish reliably after eighty trials. Rather than concluding that four-year-olds are not at a stage yet where they know left from right and looking for older children that were able to do this, Jeffrey was interested in the exact variable responsible for achieving the task. He therefore modified the task slightly and continued his work with the four-year-olds. Instead of naming the cards he asked the children to make a motor response, in other words, to touch one of two push-bottoms which were mounted on top of the table on either side of the child. When the stick-figure on the card pointed to the right, the children were to touch the push-bottom on their right, when the other card was shown they were to touch the push-bottom on their left. The results were interesting. While these children had not been able to make the correct verbal responses in the first experiment, they were able to make correct motor responses. Jeffrey continued by returning to the initial experiment which required verbal responses. Interestingly, most of the children were now able to learn verbal left-right discrimination easily.

In order to establish a behaviour analytic concept of developmental changes we should, rather than concentrate on hypothetical internal events, concentrate on changes in the environmental contingencies and analyse how they affect human behaviour (Dillenburger & Keenan, 1994a; Guerin, 1993). Clearly there are some situations in our lives which especially promote behavioural development; usually these are times of change, for example getting a new job, moving house. These kinds of changes afford new environments and new sets of contingencies therefore necessitate new interactions, in other words new behaviours (Dillenburger, 1996; Dillenburger & Keenan, 1994b). Times of change may not always be as clear cut as the ones mentioned above. They may be a visit, a drive in the car, the first smile, the first word, or the first step. With new environments new behaviours are necessary and with new behaviours new environments open up. This is a two-way, never-ending process. For this analysis Rosales-Ruiz and Baer (1996) have coined the term 'developmental cusps'. 'A cusp is an interaction, or complex of interactions, that enables access to new reinforcers, new contingencies and new communities of reinforcement contingencies – and thus to new behaviours. And to new cusps, not all of which need by seen by all of us as positive or desirable'. (p. 175)

According to this definition the ability to walk clearly marks a cusp in the course of human development. Walking affords a vast range of new environments and experiences and thus behaviours. Traditionally the ability to walk is analysed as physical development and it is observed that most children will take their first steps at around 12 months. Usually there is no explicit explanation offered in textbooks as to how this behaviour develops. On the contrary, it is said that '. . . the development of walking requires no special teaching. It follows a fixed time-ordered sequence that is typical for all physically capable members of our species' (Zimbardo, 1988, p. 68). In search for an explanation of the behaviour in question this assertion is clearly unsatisfactory, especially since the same textbook contradicts the above statement by saying that '. . . in cultures where there is more stimulation, children begin to walk sooner' (Zimbardo, 1988, p. 68).

A scientific explanation can, however, be found if we can identify exactly those variables that are in operation when the child is stimulated in these cultures (Keenan, 1993). For obvious reasons the necessary experiment is difficult since it would require a physically capable human child that has not developed the ability to walk and an environment in which a range of independent variables can be experimentally controlled. To set up such an experiment artificially would be ethically unacceptable and totally undesirable for the child in question. Yet there are cases in which this situation occurs in natural environments. O'Hagan and Dillenburger (1995) report such a case. One of their Master of Social Work students was placed in a refuge for battered women where she was given key responsibility for working with a newly admitted 19-month-old baby boy and his mother. Although able-bodied, the baby did not show the expected physical development. While he was able to sit, he was not able to walk. Rather than seeking an explanation of his inability to walk in hypothetical internal entities, the student, together with the mother, identified and arranged appropriate reinforcement contingencies. Soon the baby took his first steps (for details on how to conduct such research see Sulzer-Azaroff & Mayer, 1991; Sulzer-Azaroff & Reese, 1982). Thus the student was able to identify exactly the variables responsible for the development of walking in this child. Said another way, she was able to identify the 'underlying causes' why this boy had not developed walking behaviour previously, or the functions of walking behaviour.

Theoretical knowledge gained in a thorough analysis of one case is only useful if it transcends the boundaries of the case in question (Lamal, 1991). As Schlinger (1995) put it '. . . theory is essentially a summary . . . of numerous facts which, themselves, consist of repeatable functional relations between objective variables. Thus, theory, as the term is used by scientists, is not a guess or conjecture but an extension of these summary forms to novel instances of the subject matter' (p. 13). Dillenburger, Godina and Burton (1997) make use of theory in this sense in relation to walking behaviour. They describe the case of an 84-year-old woman. Sudden blindness had forced the women to leave her own home and come to live in a sheltered residential home for older people. Since admission she had not walked out of her room unaided. Thus, while structurally speaking her behaviour obviously differed from that of the 19-month-old boy described earlier, functionally speaking both were unable to walk on their own. A traditional assessment of the two cases would have been based on different theories. While the little boy would have been assessed, according to Bowlby or Ainsworth, for example, as insecurely attached, the assessment of the 84-year-old woman would probably have been based on Erikson's theory of psycho-social life-span development. Erikson (1963) asserts that in later adulthood people have to solve the conflict between ego-integrity vs despair. Consequently staff in the residential unit described the women as depressed and despairing. The solution of the Eriksonian conflict in this case was classed 'inadequate'.

From a behaviour analytic view of development, however, this kind of assertion is unsatisfactory and unethical in that it labels the woman negatively, and leads to staff responding to her in restrictive ways (Hayes, Hayes, Moore & Ghezzi, 1994; Kimmel, 1996). As Baldwin and Baldwin (1986) put it '. . . the two main reasons for applying behaviour principles to everyday life are increased understanding and practical benefits' (p. 1). Dillenburger *et al.* describe how, based in behaviour analytic knowledge, the worker, together with the client, identified and arranged appropriate reinforcement contingencies and how the women was soon able to walk around the residential unit unaided. Interestingly, traditional assessment of the case would now have to conclude that the conflict between ego-integrity vs despair was adequately resolved.

Baron, Myerson and Hale (1988) generalise this functional approach to development in later life when they state that '. . . [t]he power of conditioning variables provides a basis for questioning the pessimistic view that changes in the elderly are exclusively a biological matter. From a conditioning standpoint, the environments to which older adults are exposed (or to which they expose themselves) are not especially conducive to the acquisition and maintenance of competent behaviors' (p. 164). In the case described above, the environment in the residential home as well as the physical condition of blindness had not been conductive to establish competent walking for the client. However, carefully arranged contingencies soon lead to the development of the desired behaviours.

Interestingly most traditional developmental theorists would not class this research as developmental. This is the case because most developmental researchers are concerned only with child development. From a behaviour analytic perspective of development it is not the age of the client, but the function of the behaviour that counts (Dillenburger & Keenan, 1994b). This analysis leads us to a new way of conceptualising human development. First of all, it concentrates our attention on the environmental influences (i.e., antecedents and consequences) of behaviour. Secondly, it offers a life-span approach to development. Thirdly, it is applicable cross–culturally and cross–racially and is thus anti-discriminatory and anti-racist. Fourthly, it is open to individual differences while at the same time being sensitive to the detection of abnormalities.

Conclusion

We have argued that traditional developmental theories have concentrated in the main on the structure of behaviour and they have used descriptive labels inappropriately in an attempt to explain human development. This approach has largely been adopted by succeeding generations of child and developmental psychologists as well as by child care workers, social workers, health visitors and teachers. Behaviour analysts have obvious difficulties with this approach (Hudson & McDonald, 1991; Pinkston, Levitt, Green, Linsk & Rzepnicki, 1982). A child is said to behave in a certain way because she/he is at a certain stage. Today we need a more scientific approach. Regardless of how important a structural description of behaviour may be, an explanation for behaviour can never be found simply in a description of it. An explanation of behaviour can however, be found in an functional analysis of the contingencies responsible for it.

As a final caveat, we have to be careful not to limit our definition of development solely to progress or betterment (Morss, 1993). Development has to be understood as the changing interaction of an organism with his/her environment. This will lead to a more flexible and open approach to human development. As Morss (1993) put it, '. . . systematic prescriptions of the life course can only compromise human freedom. . . . To treat certain patterns of human change as natural or as manifesting progress – irrespective of concrete context – is to oppress' (p. 19).

Future developments

Based on a natural science approach, behaviour analysis has the potential to become a unified theory of developmental psychology. Already behaviour analysis addresses a number of interesting developmental phenomena and in time more and more ground will be covered. Potentially behaviour analysis could offer a basis for a unified approach to psychology as a whole, since it already addresses most of the issues raised traditionally in psychology such as personality (Lundin, 1969), memory (Catania, 1992), self control and thinking (Skinner, 1953), morality (Malott & Whaley, 1983), individual differences (Lee, 1988), perception (Schlinger, 1995), language (Catania, 1992), abnormal psychology and disability (O'Reilly, 1994), emotion and anxiety (Skinner, 1953), social issues (Guerin, 1994), attachment (Gewirtz & Kurtines, 1991). While most of the traditional theories in these areas are based on mentalistic interpretations, paradoxically when it comes to practical implications they offer a clearly defined and often rather prescriptive list of behaviours that need to be incorporated into people's repertoires to achieve improvements in personalities, memory, motivation or emotions, individual differences, health, stress or coping, mental health or disability, social issues, or attachment (Nugent, 1996). In other words, they offer a task analysis of the behaviours necessary for these 'summary labels' (Grant & Evans, 1994) to be achieved. Since this is exactly what behaviour analysts have been doing over the years there is hope that some day behaviour analysis can be recognised for what is really is, an approach that encompasses Kunkel and Lamal's (1991) recognition that '. . . it is generally agreed that theories that account for a wide range of phenomena are more useful than theories of a more limited scope' (p. 245).

References

Ainsworth, M. D. S. (1973). The development of infant-mother attachment. In B. M. Caldwell & H. N. Ricciuti (Eds) *Review of child development research* (Vol. 3) Chicago: University of Chicago Press.

Baer, D. M. (1970). An age-irrelevant concept of development. *Journal of Developmental Psychology, Merrill-Palmer Quarterly, 16,* 238–245.

Baer, D. M. (1973). The Control of the developmental process: Why wait? In J. R. Nesselroade, & H. W. Reese. *Lifespan developmental psychology* (pp. 185–193). London and New York: Academic Press.

Baer, D. M., Peterson, R. F., & Sherman, J. A. (1967). Developing imitation by reinforcing behavioral similarity to a model. *Journal of the Experimental Analysis of Behavior,* 10, 405–416.

Baldwin, J. D. & Baldwin, J. I. (1986). *Behavior principles in everyday life.* (2nd Ed.). Englewood Cliffs, NJ.: Prentice Hall.

Baron, A., Myerson, J., & Hale, S. (1988). An integrated analysis of the structure and function of behavior: Ageing and the cost of divided attention. In G. Davey & C. Cullen *Human operant conditioning and behavior modification* (p. 139–166). Chichester: John Wiley.

Baum, W. (1994). *Understanding behaviorism.* USA: HarperCollins. Academic.

Bijou, S. W. (1992). Early childhood and parent education. In R. P. West & L. A. Hamerlynck (Eds). *Designs for excellence in education: The legacy of B. F. Skinner.* Longmount: Sopris West.

Bijou, S. W. (1993). *Behavior analysis of child development.* Reno: Context Press.

Bijou S. W. & Baer D. M. (1961). *Child development. A systematic and empirical theory.* Vol. 1. Englewood Cliffs, NJ: Prentice Hall.

Bijou S. W. & Baer D. M. (1965). *Child development: Universal stage of infancy.* Vol. 2. Englewood Cliffs, NJ: Prentice Hall.

Bijou S. W. & Baer D. M. (1967). (Eds) *Child development: Readings in experimental analysis.* New York: Appleton-Century-Crofts.

Bijou S. W. & Baer D. M. (1978). *Behavior analysis of child development.* Englewood Cliffs, N.J.: Prentice Hall.

Bowlby, J. (1973). *Attachment and loss: Vol. 2. Separation, anxiety and anger.* London: Hogarth.

Byrant, P. E. (1974). *Perception and understanding in young children. An experimental approach.* London: Methuen.

Catania, C. (1973). The psychologies of structure, function and development. *American Psychologist,* May, 434–443.

Catania, C. (1992). *Learning.* Englewood Cliffs: Prentice-Hall.

Collins English Dictionary (3rd Edition) (1991). Glasgow: HarperCollins.

Crain, W. (1992). *Theories of development. Concepts and applications.* Englewood Cliffs, NJ: PrenticeHall.

Dillenburger, K. (1996) Helping children in care deal with trauma. *Child Care in Practice. Northern Ireland Journal of Multi-disciplinary Child Care Practice,* 4, 40–45.

Dillenburger, K., Godina, L., & Burton, M. (1997). Behavioral social work training: A pilot study. *Research in Social Work Practice, 1,* 70–78.

Dillenburger, K. & Keenan, M. (1993). Mummy don't leave me. The management of brief separation. *Practice,* 1, 66–69.

Dillenburger, K. & Keenan, M. (1994a). Smacking children: Dangers of misguided and outdated applications of psychological principles. *The Irish Psychologist,* 6, 56–58.

Dillenburger, K. & Keenan, M. (1994b). Bereavement: A behavioural process. *Irish Journal of Psychology, 15*, 324–339.

Erikson, E. (1963). *Childhood and society*. (2nd ed.). New York: Norton.

Freud, S. (1976). Three essays on the theory of sexuality. In J. Strachey (Ed. and Trans.), *The standard edition of the complete psychological works of Sigmund Freud*. (Orig. 1905).

Gewirtz, J. L. (1956). A program of research on the dimensions and antecedents of emotional dependence. *Child Development, 27*, 205–221.

Gewirtz, J. L. (1991). Social influence on child and parent via stimulation and operant-learning mechanisms. In M. Lewis & S. Feinman (Eds) *Social influences and socialization in infancy* (pp. 137–163). New York and London: Plenum.

Gewirtz, J. L. & Boyd, E. F. (1977). Experiments on mother-infant interaction underlying mutual attachment acquisition: The infant conditions the mother. In T. Alloway, P. Pliner & L. Krames (Eds). *Attachment behavior. Advances in the study of communication and affect* (pp. 109–143). New York and London: Plenum.

Gewirtz, J. L. & Kurtines, W. M. (Eds.) (1991). *Intersections with attachment*. Hillsdale, NJ: Lawrence Erlbaum.

Gewirtz, J. L. & Peláez-Nogueras, M. (1991). Proximal mechanisms underlying the acquisition of moral behavior patterns. In W. M. Kurtines & J. L. Gewirtz. *Handbook of moral behavior and development* (pp. 153–182). Hove and London: Lawrence Erlbaum.

Gewirtz, J. L. & Peláez-Nogueras, M. (1992). B. F. Skinner's legacy to human infant behavior and development. *American Psychologist, 47*, 1411–1422.

Grant, L. & Evans, A. (1994). *Principles of behavior analysis*. New York: HarperCollins.

Guerin, B. (1993). *The analysis of social behavior*. Reno: Context Press.

Hayes, S. C. & Brownstein, A. (1987). Mentalism, private events, and scientific explanation: A defence of B. F. Skinner's view. In S. Modgil & C. Modgil (Eds), *B. F. Skinner: Consensus and controversy*. New York: Falmer Press.

Hayes, L. J., Hayes, G. J., Moore, S. C., & Ghezzi, P. M. (Eds) (1994). *Ethical issues in developmental disabilities*. Reno: Context Press.

Howard, M. L. & Keenan, M. (1993). Outline for a functional analysis of imitation in animals. *The Psychological Record, 43*, 185–204.

Hudson, B. L. & McDonald, G. M. (1991). *Behavioural social work: An introduction*. Basingstoke: Macmillan Education.

Iwata, B. A., Dorsey, M. F., Slifer, K. J., Bauman, K. E., & Richman, G. S. (1982). Toward a functional analysis of self-injury. *Analysis and Intervention in Developmental Disabilities, 2*, 3–20. (reprinted (1992) *Journal of Applied Behavior Analysis, 27*, 197–209.)

Johnston, M. (1989). Did I begin? *New Scientist, 9 Dec.*, 36–42.

Keenan, M. (1993). For evil to persist all it takes is for good men to do nothing: Dealing with misrepresentations of a caring profession. Multi-media presentation at the *Annual Conference of the Psychological Society of Ireland*, Sligo, Ireland. Abstract in *The Irish Psychologist, 11*, 34.

Keenan, M. (1997). W-ing: Teaching about private events in the classroom. *Behavior and Social Issues, 2*, 75–84.

Kimmel, A. (1996) *Ethical issues in behavioral research*. Oxford: Blackwell.

Kohlberg, L. (1964). Development of moral character and moral ideology. In M. L. Hoffman & L. W. Hoffman (Eds), *Review of child development research* (Vol. 1). New York: Russell Sage Foundation.

Kunkel, J. H. & Lamal, P. A. (1991). The road ahead. In P. A. Lamal. *Behavioral analysis of societies and cultural practices* (pp. 243–247). New York: Hemisphere Publishing Corporation.

Lamal, P. A. (Ed.) (1991). *Behavioral analysis of societies and cultural practices.* New York: Hemisphere Publishing Corporation,

Lee, V. (1988). *Beyond behaviorism.* New Jersey: Lawrence Erlbaum.

Leslie, J. C. (1996). *Principles of behavioral analysis.* Amsterdam: Harwood Academic Publishers.

Lundin, R. W. (1969). *Personality. An experimental approach.* New York: Macmillan.

Lynn, R. (1996). 'Women dumber': Academic is unrepentant. *Irish Independent, 10 May*, 7.

Malott, R. W. & Whaley, D. L. (1983). *Psychology.* Holmes Beach, Florida: Learning Publications.

Martin, G. & Pear, J. (1996). *Behavior modification: What it is and how to do it* (5th ed.). New Jersey: Prentice Hall.

Meadows, S. (1992). *Understanding child development.* London: Routledge.

Morris, E. K. (1980). Contextualism: The world view of behavior analysis. *Journal of Experimental Child Psychology, 46*, 289–323.

Morris, E. K. (1985). Public information, dissemination, and behavior analysis. *The Behavior Analyst*, 8, 95–110.

Morss, J. R. (1993). Keeping ourselves regular. On the necessity of an anti-developmental psychology. *University of Cambridge, Centre for Family Studies*, pp. 1–25.

Mussen, P. H. (1992). Foreword. In R. Vasta (Ed). Six theories of child development. *Revised formulations and current issues* (pp. xi–xii). London: Jessica Kingsley.

Newman, B. (1992) *The reluctant alliance: Humanism and behaviorism.* Buffalo NY: Prometheus.

Nugent, O. (1996). Issue of bonding and attachment. *Child Care in Practice. Northern Ireland Journal of Multi-disciplinary Child Care Practice, 4*, 24–28.

Nye, R. D. (1992) *The legacy of B.F. Skinner: Concepts and perspectives, controversies and misunderstandings.* Pacific Grove: Brooks/Cole.

O'Hagan, K. & Dillenburger, K. (1995). *The abuse of women within childcare work.* Buckingham: Open University Press.

O'Reilly, M. (1994). Assessing challenging behaviors of persons with severe mental disabilities. *European Journal of Mental Disability, 1*, 13–23.

Piaget, J. (1977). *The development of thought: Equilibrium of cognitive structures.* New York: Viking Press.

Piaget, J. & Inhelder, B. (1967). *The child's conception of space.* New York: Norton.

Pinkston, E. M., Levitt, J. L., Green, G. R., Linsk, N. L., & Rzepnicki, T. L. (1982). *Effective Social Work Practice.* London, Washington: Jossey-Bass Publishers.

Poling, A., Schlinger, H., Starin, S., & Blakely, E. (1990). *Psychology: A behavioral overview.* New York: Plenum.

Poling, A., Methot, L.L., & LeSage, M.G. (1995) *Fundamentals of behavior analytic research.* New York: Plenum.

Pryor, K. (1985). *Don't shoot the dog! The new art of teaching and training.* New York: Bantam Books.

Reese, E. P. (1978). *Human operant behavior. Analysis and application* (2nd ed.). Iowa: WM. C. Brown Company Publishers.

Richelle, M. N. (1993). *B.F. Skinner: A reappraisal.* Hove: Lawrence Erlbaum.

Rosales-Ruiz, J. & Baer, D. M. (1996). A behavior-analytic view of development. In S. W. Bijou & E. Ribes (Eds) *New directions in behavior development* (pp. 155–180). Reno: Context Press.

Schaffer, D. R. (1996). *Developmental psychology. Childhood and adolescence* (4th ed.) Pacific Grove: Brooks/Cole Publishing Company.

Schlinger, H. D. (1992). Theory in behavior analysis. An application to child development. *American Psychologist, 11*, 1396–1410.

Schlinger, H. jr. (1995). *A behavior analytic view of child development*. New York: Plenum.

Sidman, M. (1960). *Tactics of scientific research: Evaluating experimental data in psychology*. New York: Basic Books.

Skinner, B. F. (1953). *Science and human behavior*. New York: Macmillan.

Stoppard, M. (1990). *New baby care book. A practical guide to the first three years*. London: Dorling Kindersley.

Sulzer-Azaroff, B. & Mayer, G. R. (1991) *Behavior analysis for lasting change*. San Francisco: Holt, Rinehart & Winston.

Sulzer-Azaroff, B. & Reese, E. (1982). *Applying behavior analysis: A program for developing professional competence*. New York: Holt, Rinehart & Winston.

Thyer, B. A. (1992). A behavioral perspective on human development. In M. Bloom (Ed.) *Changing lives: Studies in human development and professional helping* (pp. 410–18). Columbia, SC: University of South Carolina Press.

Todd, J. T. & Morris, E. K. (1983). Misconception and miseducation: Presentations of radical behaviorism in psychology textbooks. *The Behavior Analyst, 6*, 153–60.

Todd, J. T. & Morris, E. K. (1992). Case histories and the great power of study misrepresentation. *American Psychologist, 47*, 1441–1453.

Vasta, R. (Ed). (1992). *Six theories of child development. Revised formulations and current issues*. London: Jessica Kingsley.

Zimbardo, P. G. (1988). *Psychology and life* (12th Ed.). Boston: Scott, Foresman and Company.

2

Private events: A neglected and misunderstood construct in radical behaviourism

Ian Taylor and Mark F. O'Reilly

Abstract

Although privacy is an essential thesis for understanding many of the underlying constructs of radical behaviourism (e.g., the nature of scientific understanding) and how radical behaviourism relates to other contemporary theoretical and philosophical approaches in psychology (e.g., cognitivism, mentalism, literal dualism), it has received relatively little empirical attention. This may be due to the inherent methodological difficulties in evaluating functional relations involving private behaviour. Operationism and private events are discussed in terms of the theoretical writings of B. F. Skinner. It is argued that if radical behaviourists are to redress the misconception that they exclude private events from their analyses, they must develop a systematic program of research facilitating the empirical investigation of private events.

Introduction

When behaviour analysis began to inform practice in applied settings with human participants, a behavioural model with its origin in the animal laboratory became the accepted theoretical base for intervention development. Many within the clinical and educational domains accepted the animal model because it provided not only an explanatory system, but also a means to change behaviour (Lowe, 1983). Although many applied behavioural interventions continue to be based on work originating in the animal laboratory, evidence is now accumulating that questions the assumption that interventions based on principles of conditioning derived solely from the study of animal learning are sufficient to account for all complex human behaviour (Barnes, 1993; Catania, Matthews, &

Shimoff, 1982; Hayes, 1989; Jones, Williams, & Lowe, 1993; Lowe, 1983; Lowe, Horne, & Higson, 1987; Taylor & O'Reilly, 1997; Vaughan, 1989).

One strand of evidence supporting the assumption that the animal model is an insufficient theoretical base for human intervention development is the extensive experimental work on schedules of reinforcement. This body of literature indicates that human patterns of responding are intrinsically different from those of other animals (see Baron & Galizio, 1983; Hayes & Hayes, 1992a; Lowe, 1983 for reviews). For example, on fixed-interval (FI) schedules, animal performance is characterised by a pause after reinforcement followed by an accelerated rate of responding which terminates at the next reinforcement (Ferster & Skinner, 1957). While the literature indicates two kinds of performance – 'scalloping' and 'break-run' (cf. Cumming & Schoenfeld, 1958; Staddon, 1972) – research indicates that even where cumulative records suggest a rapid transition from post-reinforcement pause to a constant response rate (i.e., break-run performance), a detailed analysis of response rate and interresponse time duration reveals a gradual acceleration in responding following the post-reinforcement pause (Branch & Gollob, 1974; Lowe & Harzem, 1977). Overall response rate and running rate (i.e., response rate calculated by excluding the post-reinforcement pause) are declining functions of fixed-interval duration while both the post-reinforcement pause and succeeding interresponse times increase as a function of schedule value (Lowe & Harzem, 1977; Skinner, 1938).

In contrast, several investigators have found that on fixed-interval (FI) schedules, human subjects do not produce the pause-respond patterns that are ubiquitous across the rest of the animal kingdom (Hayes & Hayes, 1992a). Instead they demonstrate either: (*a*) a steady high response rate throughout each interval (Leander, Lippman, & Meyer, 1968; Lippman & Meyer, 1967; Weiner, 1965); or (*b*) a very low response rate consisting of one or two responses in each interval, at the time when the next reinforcement is due (Baron, Kaufman & Stauber, 1969; Leander *et al.*, 1968; Lippman & Meyer, 1967; Weiner, 1964, 1965, 1969). Whether a subject demonstrates a high or low rate of responding, neither response pattern resembles the performance of animals on FI schedules. Given these findings, it could be concluded that if the principles of behaviour derived from animal research cannot adequately describe the behaviour of humans in relatively controlled experimental settings, they surely are an inadequate basis upon which to construct a technology of human intervention in complex applied settings.

Another strand of evidence suggesting the limitations of the animal model for human intervention development is that the ability to predict and control human behaviour in complex applied settings with interventions derived solely from the animal model remains elusive (Jones, *et al.*, 1993; Lowe, 1983; Whitman, 1990). This is exemplified by the continuing difficulties of generalisation and maintenance of newly acquired skills outside the training setting for people with intellectual disabilities (Horner, Dunlap & Koegel, 1988; Stokes & Baer, 1977). Research indicates that many people with intellectual disabilities when taught a new skill often fail to use the skill outside the training setting (Cullen, 1981; Gifford, Rusch, Martin & White, 1984; Wacker & Berg, 1983; Whitman, 1990). The applied implication of the continuing generalisation and maintenance difficulties is that skills which only appear in the training situation fail to provide the necessary foundation for integration of people with intellectual disabilities into the community. Effective education ultimately should change the way people live their lives with hardwon changes in a training setting being functional across the range of situations that may be encountered in the community (Horner, *et al.*, 1988).

These two strands of evidence suggest that the animal model is inadequate to account for all human behaviour. Although the reliance upon the animal model has provided applied behaviour analysis with a model which has advanced therapeutic intervention in clinical and educational settings considerably, it is a model which ignores important determinants of human behaviour (Lowe, 1983). What is required is the development of more sophisticated models which capture the complexity of human behaviour. We do not need to abandon all that has been learned from the animal model but we do need to expand the model to include those processes which are uniquely human.

Skinner (1972) has argued that 'we cannot discover what is "essentially" human until we have investigated nonhuman subjects' (pp. 201–202). Lowe (1983) suggests a corollary which equally seems appropriate: 'we cannot discover what is essentially human until we have also investigated humans' (p. 84). Focused as it was on observable behaviour and external environmental stimuli, the application of the animal model to humans was taken by some (though not by Skinner himself; see Skinner, 1953; 1969; 1974) to exclude all consideration of private or unobservable events. Others, while theoretically acknowledging the role of private events in human behaviour, failed to demonstrate this theoretical commitment when analysing the function of behaviour. This is shown by a dearth in the early experimental and applied behavioural literature of research examining the role of private phenomena.

One emerging theme from the experimental research involving human participants has been the need to consider private events for a complete behaviour analysis of human behaviour. For example, much of the recent operant schedule research has examined the role of covert self-rules on human responding (e.g., Bentall & Lowe, 1985, 1987; Hayes, 1989; Hayes & Hayes, 1992a; Lowe, 1979). This operant schedule research has once more focused attention on the issue of private events, which despite Skinner's theoretical lead (1945, 1953), had been ignored by many radical behaviourists in their research practices.

In this chapter we present a summary of private events from a radical behavioural perspective. Extensive reference is made to Skinner's work. This is not because he alone represents radical behaviourism (indeed many radical behaviourists–even Skinnerians–would not find themselves in total agreement with Skinner), but because his conceptualisation of private events is regarded as most representative of the traditional radical behaviourism position.

Private events from a Skinnerian perspective

Two classes of private phenomena are identified in the radical behaviourism literature: (*a*) internal sensations and (*b*) covert behaviour (Moore, 1995). An example of an internal sensation is the private phenomenon of hunger. When we are hungry, we typically experience hunger pangs. These are not readily observable to other individuals and are therefore considered to be private. Other internal sensations would include pain following the blow from an object, and bodily functions. An example of covert behaviour would be the statement of a covert self–rule the first time we drive a motor car (e.g., 'Put the car into gear.'). We usually state such rules in the early stages of learning until behaviour becomes contingency shaped (Skinner, 1974). Other covert behaviour would include problem solving, imagery, thinking, etc.

Skinner (1953) referred to an individual coming into contact with these private phenomena as a private event. The media for such contact are the interoceptive and the proprioceptive feedback systems. The interoceptive system carries stimulation from organs, glands and blood vessels. The proprioceptive system carries stimulation from the muscles, joints, tendons and skeletal frame. Just as we make contact with our public behaviour via our exteroceptive system (the system concerned with seeing, hearing, tasting and feeling) we make contact with private phenomena via our interoceptive and proprioceptive systems (Moore, 1980; 1995; Skinner, 1953; 1974). For example, pain is ordinarily a result of certain kinds of stimulation (e.g., a blow with an object) which results in the bodily condition felt as pain. We sense the internal stimulation by means of our interoceptive system. Following differential reinforcement (see below) we may label or report the internal sensation of pain. It is the occurrence of the private phenomenon (i.e., pain), the sensing of the private phenomenon by the interoceptive feedback system (i.e., the 'coming into contact with'), and the subsequent response (e.g., labelling or verbal reporting of the private phenomenon) that constitute the private event.

Scientific legitimacy of private events

The problem which private events present for behaviour analysis is the difficulty of studying them objectively. The apparent difficulties of studying private events objectively has resulted in a number of those within behaviour analysis arguing that behaviour analysis cannot become a genuine empirical science until it abandons the idea that private events are part of its subject matter

(Bergmann, 1956; Branch & Malagodi, 1980; Brigham, 1980; Spence, 1948; Watson, 1913). This position is known as 'methodological behaviourism'.

Methodological behaviourism is usually defined as the attempt to explain behaviour solely in terms of publicly observable variables. Perhaps the most familiar statement of methodological behaviourism is from Bergmann (1956):

It must in principle be possible to predict future behavior, including verbal behavior, from a sufficiency of information about [publicly observable] present (and past) behavioral, psychological, and environmental variables (p. 270).

In contrast to the position adopted by methodological behaviourism, Skinner consistently argued that a science of behaviour, like other physical sciences, must deal with events which are not directly observable (see Day, 1976, for a historical and conceptual analysis of the differences between methodological and radical behaviourism). He viewed methodological behaviourism as being fatally flawed in that it put private experience – an important phenomenon of human life – totally beyond the reach of scientific investigation:

Methodological behaviourists, like logical positivists, argued that science must confine itself to events that can be observed by two or more people; truth must be by agreement. There is a private world of feeling and states of mind, but it is out of reach of a second person and hence of science. That was not a very satisfactory position of course. How people feel is often as important as what they do (Skinner, 1989, p. 3).

Within the radical behaviourism framework, behaviour is defined as all observable human action, not all publicly observable human action as espoused by methodological behaviourists (Hayes & Brownstein, 1986; cf. Heidbreder, 1933, and her discussion of the flaws of classical behaviourism). Unlike methodological behaviourism, there is no commitment to publicly observable behaviour per se (i.e., phenomena that can be inter-subjectively verified) as the defining characteristic of scientific observations. For example, when an individual monitors his or her own overt behaviour (e.g., frequency of cigarettes smoked in a day), the individual often is the sole observer. For the radical behaviourist, the fact that there is not another individual there to observe and verify the overt behaviour does not make such overt behaviour unsuitable for a scientific analysis. On the contrary, it just means that it is not inter-subjectively verifiable.

Similarly, private events are viewed to be behavioural events and therefore part of the radical behaviourists' subject matter. Although private events are not publicly observable – just like the example of an individual self-monitoring his or her own smoking behaviour – they are directly observable to the individual involved. The radical behaviourist accepts that one can arrive at an accurate prediction of an individual's behaviour that involves private stimulation (if these can be accessed) equally as well as when stimulation is overt:

[Radical behaviourism] . . . does not insist upon truth by agreement and can therefore consider events taking place in the private world within the skin. It does not call these events unobservable, and does not dismiss them as subjective (Skinner, 1974, p. 16).

How then can private events be considered scientifically legitimate if they cannot be inter-subjectively verified? Skinner rejected the conventional approach to science (i.e., inter-subjective verification) and argued for the need of a contingency analysis. He adopted the pragmatic criterion of truth-by-successful working (in behaviour analysis, the name for successful working is prediction and control; see Hayes & Brownstein, 1986), in opposition to the criterion of truth-by-agreement (Pepper, 1942):

The ultimate criterion for the goodness of a concept is not whether two people are brought into agreement but whether the scientist who uses the concept can operate successfully upon the material – all by himself if need be. What matters to Robinson Crusoe is not whether he is agreeing with himself but whether he is getting anywhere with his control over nature (Skinner, 1945, p. 293).

Skinner argued that scientific or objective observations are termed 'scientific' because of the contingencies surrounding the observation. He argued that the purpose of the scientific methodology is to insure that scientific observations are tacts, controlled by events in the subject matter of the science, and not by states of deprivation, audience factors or other such sources of control (Moore, 1981). Since public agreement provides no such assurances of this, and since private observations can be tacts given the proper prior history (see below), private events are no more or less scientific than public events based on their privacy per se. As such, observations could be private and objective (scientifically legitimate) or public and subjective (scientifically illegitimate), depending upon the contingencies controlling the observations.

Hayes and Hayes (1992b) offer a useful example to illustrate this point. A class is shown the following words on a chalkboard for a few seconds:

> Paris in
> the
> the spring

The class is asked to write down what they read. Virtually all will write 'Paris in the spring'. Inter-observer agreement would be very high, and if that were the metric for objectivity we would be confident the words indeed were 'Paris in the spring'. But these observations would be subjective in the sense that they are controlled by individual histories – 'Paris in the spring' is familiar and 'the the' unfamiliar.

In Skinner's view, the observation of the class is scientifically illegitimate, even though inter-observer agreement is high. Skinner rejected methodological behaviourism and the requirement of publicly observable events as the subject matter because he did not believe that public agreement provided assurance of proper contingency control. In contrast, he argued that if the contingencies of a behavioural event (private or public) can be reliably determined, then they are scientifically legitimate (Skinner, 1945). As the example above shows, it is possible to find instances where whole groups of observers are similarly influenced by motivational states and other subjective conditions. Thus agreement is not the key to workability and truth (and therefore scientific legitimacy), the key is proper contingency control (Hayes & Hayes, 1992b).

Private events and mentalism

Private events play a central role in a complete behaviour analysis of human behaviour (Skinner (1953). It is the treatment of private events which distinguishes radical behaviourism from other disciplines (Schneider & Morris, 1987), therefore, knowing how radical behaviourism accommodates private events is important not only to our understanding of radical behaviourism but behaviour analysis in general (Keenan, 1997). Without a scientific analysis of private events such as that offered by radical behaviourism, the way is left open for alternative and less effective accounts of behaviour. The most significant of these are mentalistic accounts which influence much of the contemporary psychological literature.

Mentalistic accounts refer to feelings and inner states as causes of behaviour (Day, 1980). Common examples of mentalism are explanations of behaviour that appeal to the initiating causes of feelings, mental states, cognitive processes, subjective interpretations, subjective perceptions, attitudes, thoughts, ideas, drives, needs, memories, images, representations, sensations, reasons, purposes, beliefs, wants, desires, attributions, the ego/superego/id, moods, brain states, expectations etc. These various examples of mentalism typically claim that (a) there are private or inner phenomena; (b) these phenomena are part of a dimensional system that differs from the one in which behaviour takes place; and (c) the causal explanation of behaviour consists of accounting for behaviour in terms of the autonomous causal efficacy of these phenomena at the expense of any concern with the relation between the behaving organism and its external environment (Moore, 1990).

Given this analysis, radical behaviourist objections to mentalism can be placed into two broad categories, metaphysical and metatheoretical (Hayes & Brownstein, 1986). The metaphysical objections are directed primarily at the concept of 'literal dualism'. The metatheoretical objections are concerned with the incompleteness of explanations such as those contained in mental physiology accounts.

Literal dualism

Literal dualism can be defined as the belief that there are two kinds of 'stuff' in the world, one type that exists in time and space (physical) and another which is non-spatiotemporal (mental) (see Hayes & Brownstein, 1986). The skin often correlates with the boundary between public and private events. This roughly maps onto the common usage of the terms physical and mental. As a result, the assumption that public events are physical and private events are mental proliferates much of the psychological literature. Unfortunately, this dualistic usage of mental and physical implies a bifurcation of nature into two mutually exclusive ontological realms perpetuating the notion of literal dualism (Moore, 1980, 1984; Zuriff, 1985). For the radical behaviourist, the fact that a mind or a mental dimension is distinguished from the body or a physical dimension is an error. Radical behaviourists recognise the distinction between public and private, but consider both to be within the physical domain (i.e., the distinction between public and private is not the same as the dualistic distinction between physical and mental). For example, Skinner (1945) considered a toothache to be just as physical as a typewriter, though the former is clearly private and the latter public. The world is regarded as homogeneously physical and material. Organisms interact with respect to features of that world in the process called behaviour with all aspects of these processes being physical and material.

Skinner states that he is a radical behaviourist in the sense that there is no place in his formulation for anything that is mental. This does not mean that what have been called 'higher mental processes' (e.g., thinking, problem-solving) cannot be investigated by a science of behaviour, or that they can be investigated only through measuring what are presumed to be their physical manifestations. On the contrary, Skinner (1964) explicitly stated that 'no entity or process which has any useful explanatory force is to be rejected on the grounds that it is subjective or mental. The data which make it important must, however, be studied and formulated in effective ways' (p. 96). Radical behaviourists, therefore, do not object to the assumption that 'higher mental activities' take place, but they do object to the conclusion that they take place in the mysterious psychic world of the mind rather than the physical world of behavioural events.

Mental physiology

In recognition of the problems of literal dualism (Eccles, 1973; Fodor, 1968; Natsoulas, 1984; see also Hayes & Brownstein, 1986), a variety of tactics have been used (particularly within cognitive psychology) to try to bring scientific legitimacy to dualistic accounts of private events. One such tactic is to create a pseudophysiological analysis of mentalism (Hayes & Brownstein, 1986). This is typically attempted by substituting the word 'brain' for the word 'mind' and providing a physiological explanation of behaviour. In this way the scientist can appear to be interested in physical events while continuing to use the terms in a mentalistic way. Although the study of the brain and the nervous system is relevant to a behaviour analysis, it is no less mentalistic to substitute the word 'brain' for 'mind' and then to engage in the same kind of analysis as before:

Usually [the mind is said to be] the thinking agent. It is the mind which is said to examine sensory data and make inferences about the outside world, to store and retrieve records, to filter incoming information, to put bits of information in pigeonholes, to make decisions, and to will to act. . . . The brain is . . . the agent which processes incoming data and stores them in the form of data structures. Both the mind and the brain are not far from the notion of a homunculus – an inner person who behaves in precisely the ways necessary to explain the behaviour of the outer person in which he dwells (Skinner, 1974, p. 117).

Given that public and private events are behavioural events means that the physiology of the individual is necessarily involved. Thus there will always be a close connection between behaviour and physiology in the analysis of any behavioural event. Such a statement does not, however, imply that behaviour is identical or reducible to physiology (see Baer, 1996; Donahoe, 1996; Reese, 1996 for recent discussions on this matter). An exclusively physiological explanation of a behavioural event (private or public) does not explain why the behaviour took place. For example, to say that a pigeon pecks a key because of certain anatomical structures or because of certain physiological activities in its brain does not constitute an explanation of the response; Skinner (1953) labelled such accounts as naive physiologising. To explain private behaviour (or any behaviour for that matter) in purely physiological terms is therefore an incomplete explanation. A natural science of behaviour ultimately needs to provide a comprehensive statement relating an organism's behaviour to stimuli that impinge upon it.

Private events and a natural science of behaviour

From the radical behaviourist perspective, there are four classes of factors that occasion explanations consistent with a natural science of behaviour. First, there is the reinforcing consequence that the to-be-explained response has achieved in the past. Second, there is the antecedent condition that makes the to-be-explained response more likely, by virtue of its relation to the reinforcing consequence. Third, there is the contingent relation among the antecedent condition, the response, and the reinforcer. Fourth, there are the characteristics of the living organism itself, which are brought to the situation in which the behavioural event occurs. These include the general physiological characteristics of the organism: (*a*) a genetic endowment that accommodates innate, operant, and respondent behaviour; (*b*) sensory systems that are responsive to stimulation in various forms; and (*c*) a nervous system that provides continuity between a stimulus and response.

Usually, explanations are offered in terms of the first three factors, because those are the factors that offer the most practical means of prediction and control (see below for the importance of prediction and control in the epistemology of the radical behaviourist). By their very nature, factors in the fourth class (physiological) are unlikely to be manipulated within a behavioural event, therefore most explanations of a behavioural event are in terms of organism-environment interactions, i.e., contingencies (Moore, 1990).

The importance of providing an account of private events consistent with a contingency analysis cannot be underestimated. Explanations that do not engage contingencies are inadequate, and interfere with those that do. As a consequence, the environmental conditions of which behaviour is a function remain unanalysed, the contribution of private stimuli and responses go unrecognised, and the explanatory integrity of a naturalistic science of behaviour is compromised (Moore, 1995). Additionally, if private events are not dealt with in the same manner as other behavioural phenomena then dualistic accounts similar to those presented above come to predominate. Such an effect can only retard both an analysis of the conditions that do cause behaviour and the role of private events (Skinner, 1953). A comprehensive account of private events consistent with a natural science of behaviour must therefore: (*a*) operationalise private events in a manner consistent with other behavioural phenomena (i.e., in terms of a contingency analysis); (*b*) specify how private events develop a discriminative function over subsequent behaviour; and (*c*) explain the role of private events in a scientific or causal analysis.

Operationism and private events

Private events are a class of behavioural events in which the stimulus, the response, or both are obscured from view (i.e., occur inside the skin, Skinner, 1953).

Private stimuli

In Skinner's analysis, private stimulation is primarily concerned with the digestive, respiratory and circulatory systems. Additionally, Skinner concerned himself with 'the position and movement of the body in space and . . . the position and movement of parts of the body with respect to other parts' (Skinner, 1953, p. 258). Other internal sources of stimulation addressed by Skinner include irritation or inflammation of tissues, as in the cases of an itch and pain arising from a decayed tooth. Skinner argued that such private stimuli may enter into controlling relations (as do public stimuli), particularly in a discriminative or elicitive capacity (Skinner, 1953, 1957, 1974), but they are not regarded as having any 'causal' status (Skinner, 1957, p. 437; 1969, p. 257). Causal properties are ascribed to stimuli arising from the surrounding environment only.

Private responses

Skinner distinguished private responses from public responses primarily on the basis of their magnitude (Skinner, 1953, p. 282; 1957, p. 141; 1969, p. 242; 1974,

p. 27). He argued that private responses are executed with the same musculature as public responses but on such a small scale as to be invisible to an external observer–or even to the person in whom the event is occurring (Skinner 1974). Skinner held that private responses operate in the same manner as public responses, and are subject to the same laws. He said 'there are no important distinctions made between the two levels or forms of activity' (Skinner, 1957, p. 437).

Unclassified events

Private events which are not readily classified as responses or stimuli include those which apparently are not executed by the muscular apparatus (e.g., thinking, imagery, feeling). For example, in an emotional or feeling episode one may react to various conditions of the body and its movement, but the nature of such reactions is not specified (Skinner, 1969). Equally, one can think and the nature of such a reaction is not specified. Presumably these reactions or responses do not involve muscular action:

The range of verbal behaviour is roughly suggested in descending order of energy, by shouting, loud talking, quiet talking, whispering, muttering 'under one's breath', subaudible speech with detectable muscular action, subaudible speech of unclear dimensions, and perhaps even the 'unconscious thinking' sometimes inferred in instances of problem solving (Skinner, 1957, p. 438).

Although Skinner argues that '[t]here is no point at which it is profitable to draw a line distinguishing thinking from acting on this continuum' (1938, p. 6), the point at which it would seem reasonable to do so is the point where muscular action is no longer involved. While Skinner is reluctant to specify the dimensions of these events, the only plausible naturalistic dimensions of a pre-muscular response are neurological (Parrott, 1983)

For the most part, events of unclear dimensions such as thinking are regarded as response events. For example, Skinner discusses such events in the context of rapid self-editing of ongoing speech. In such instances, 'changes are made on the spur of the moment and so rapidly that we cannot reasonably attribute them to an actual review of covert forms' (Skinner, 1957, p. 371). It appears, instead, that an individual is able to react to and reject responses before they have occurred at a muscular level (p. 435) or before they have reached their final form (p. 371) on the basis of a prior neural response. Hence from Skinner's perspective, neural activity corresponding to a particular muscular event is believed to precede the muscular event in time, is a link in a behavioural chain and is itself a response to external stimuli.

Operationism

Despite their covert nature, the radical behaviourist does not consider private events to be qualitatively different from publicly observable behavioural events.

Private stimuli and private responses primarily serve the same functions as their public counterparts (with the exception of private stimuli which, unlike public stimuli, for philosophical reasons cannot have causal status–see below). They are viewed as being physical and material; their only distinctive feature being limited accessibility to an observer (Skinner, 1974). The observer in this context includes both the person in whom the event is occurring as well as an external observer. Regarding the external observer, limited accessibility is not intended to include circumstances under which an event is not observed simply because an observer is not present when it occurs. It refers to an impossibility of unaided observation resulting from the fact that the event is taking place inside the skin of another person (Skinner, 1953; 1974).

Regarding the person within whom the private event is occurring, limited accessibility in these events is a consequence of two circumstances. The first of these has to do with the physical structure of the human organism and its evolutionary history. Skinner (1974) claims that observation of events taking place inside one's own body is limited by the fact that certain areas of the body are not innervated to allow reactions to events taking place in those areas. For example, one may react to conditions of the body produced by some malfunction or injury to the spleen but the spleen itself is not innervated sufficiently to allow the organism to identify the location of these conditions. This situation occurred because the conditions under which the human species evolved biologically did not afford greater chances of survival to organisms capable of observing events taking place inside the skin.

The second set of circumstances which limit the accessibility humans have to events occurring within their skin is the social origin of self-knowledge. Skinner (1974) explains:

We might expect that because a person is in such intimate contact with his own body he should be able to describe its conditions and processes particularly well, but the very privacy which seems to confer a special privilege on the individuals makes it difficult for the community to teach him to make distinctions. For example, it can show him colored objects, ask him to respond with color words, and commend or correct him when his responses correspond or fail to correspond with the colors of the objects. . . . The community cannot, however, follow the same practice in teaching him to describe the states of his own body because it lacks the information it needs to commend or correct him (pp. 22–23).

Despite these difficulties, the community can and does teach its members to identify and react to events within their own skins, primarily on the basis of correlated public events (see below). The fact remains, however, such self-knowledge is limited even for events taking place in appropriately innervated areas, and is lacking altogether with respect to inadequately innervated areas. For these reasons, private events are characterised as having limited accessibility even to the person in whom the event is taking place (see Parrott, 1983, for an extended discussion on these matters).

Given that the only difference between private behavioural events and public behavioural events is that of accessibility, radical behaviourists argue that a similar analytical framework is required for both (i.e., a contingency analysis). For the radical behaviourist it is unacceptable to account for public events in terms of one conceptual framework leading to one type of analysis and for private events in terms of an alternative conceptual framework leading to a different type of analysis (Moore, 1980). To do so is inherently dualistic.

The fundamental unit of analysis of any behavioural event (including private events) for the radical behaviourist is the three-term contingency, that is, the interrelations among (*a*) the antecedent discriminative stimulus that sets the occasion upon which (b) a response will produce (*c*) a reinforcing consequence. To illustrate a contingency analysis of private events, consider the earlier example of pain. An individual may feel pain following a blow with an object. The individual will sense the internal stimulation of pain by means of his/her interoceptive system. The individual may subsequently report the internal sensation of pain following differential reinforcement from the verbal community to do so. The verbal report 'I am in pain' may be considered as the middle term in the contingency (i.e., the response). The antecedent discriminative stimulus, or what the verbal report is about, is the private internal sensation of pain. The reinforcing consequence, as in most cases, is the social attention provided by the verbal community for reporting the pain.[1]

As can be seen from this example, when radical behaviourists ask for an operational definition, they are not endorsing logical positivism as conventionally interpreted (Moore, 1980; Skinner, 1945). They are asking for an assessment of the discriminative stimuli that lead an individual to behave in a particular manner (Moore, 1981). When 'private' events are involved, operationism means specifying how internal events exert stimulus control over subsequent behaviour including verbal behaviour (e.g., a verbal report of a private phenomenon).

This view of operationism may be contrasted with conventional interpretations which argue that the meaning of a psychological term can only be established in terms of it relation to some publicly observable, inter-subjectively verifiable event (Moore, 1980). Conventional operationism holds that because phenomena are private and subjective, one must study instead their manifestations, because they are public, objective, and measurable. A close examination of this argument indicates that it is a dualistic account. It argues that one world is an empirical, physical world, consisting of objective phenomena which are inter-subjectively verifiable and therefore acceptable for direct study. The other world is subjective and mental, not capable of inter-subjective verification, and therefore can only be studied indirectly by means of outward manifestations.

---

[1] A detailed account of the operationism of private events is not possible in this chapter. The interested reader is referred to Skinner (1945). Moore (1984) and Schnaitter (1978) also provide detailed accounts of the operational issues of private responses and private stimuli.

The radical behaviourist rejects such a formulation because it perpetuates dualistic accounts of human behaviour:

Another proposed solution to the problem of privacy argues that there are public and private events and that the latter have no place in science. . . . Far from avoiding the traditional distinction between mind and matter . . . this view actually encourages it. . . . (Skinner, 1953, pp. 281–282).

How private events develop discriminative control

A difficulty arises when one attempts to invoke private events in behavioural explanations without some plausible specification of the process by which the private phenomena (i.e., internal sensations or covert behaviour) acquire their functional role. To do so without such a specification is to offer only a spurious explanation of behaviour. Once again, consider the verbal response 'I am in pain'. The critical issue is how painful interoceptive stimulation comes to acquire discriminative control over this verbal response. These interoceptive stimuli are only available to the person feeling the pain. Yet it is someone from the verbal community who must be attentive to the verbal response 'pain' for the response to develop to the internal stimulation. A complete science of behaviour needs to explain (*a*) the process by which a vocabulary describing (i.e., verbal report) internal bodily states and conditions is acquired and maintained and (*b*) the process by which covert phenomena come to exert discriminative control over the verbal report.

As operant behaviour, verbal reports of private events develop through differential reinforcement supplied by the verbal community. The difficulty for the verbal community is that important aspects of the contingencies involved are private. Skinner acknowledged such difficulties:

There is apparently no way of basing a response entirely upon the private part of complex stimuli. A differential reinforcement cannot be made upon the property of privacy. *This fact is of extraordinary importance in evaluating psychological terms* (Skinner, 1945, p. 275; emphasis in the original).

Despite the inherent difficulties, Skinner concluded that a contingency analysis of behaviour where some of the stimuli are private is still tenable (the very existence of the language of private events implies its selection by natural contingencies). He argued that the necessary differential reinforcement is originally administered on the basis of public features and may even include publicly observable behaviour. However, after the behaviour is established, stimulus control is transferred to the private stimuli.[2]

Skinner (1945, pp. 273–274) suggested a number of ways in which a response comes under the control of private phenomena. The first three deal

---

[2]   See Wittgenstein (1953) and Skinner (1945), for discussions of the difficulties created by positing a language of private events not based on the public practice of the verbal community.

with internal sensations, the fourth is primarily concerned with covert behaviour. Firstly, the verbal community may administer differential reinforcement based on 'public accompaniment' to a presumed private stimulus. For example if an individual is forcibly struck by an object (public accompaniment), this will result in a private condition felt as pain. The verbal community may reinforce the use of the word pain by instructing the individual to report 'pain'. Alternatively, the verbal community may administer differential reinforcement based on a 'collateral response' to a presumed private stimulus. For example, an individual may hold the part of the body (collateral response) that is damaged. The verbal community may then reinforce the use of the term pain by encouraging the individual to report pain. Thirdly, the private stimulus may come to exert control by virtue of stimulus generalisation from public to private stimuli. For example, suppose an individual has learned to use the term 'fluttering' when a butterfly brushes against the skin. In the future, an individual may speak of 'butterflies in the stomach' on the basis of its intermittent temporal qualities and the association of similar properties with a butterfly brushing against the skin in the past. Finally, the private stimulus may come to exert control by virtue of the stimulus control shared between public and private stimuli as a response occurs. For example, when a behaviour is being performed some of the control may be exerted by the public stimuli. It is these stimuli that the verbal community uses in the first instance to establish the response. However, control may also be acquired by any private stimuli that are present as well. In these ways, the verbal community overcomes the problem of privacy, and speakers gain the ability to describe events with which they alone are in direct contact.

This analysis leads to an important question, namely, why should public behaviour recede to the covert form? One possibility is that the public form is punished. For example speaking out loud in a community setting while performing a particular task may be socially unacceptable. Another reason why the verbal behaviour might be made at reduced levels relates to a lack of environmental support for the overt form. Thus in the absence of the full set of stimuli necessary to occasion the overt form, the response is made at the covert level. A third possibility is that the behaviour is faster and less troublesome in the covert form (e.g., reading quietly is quicker than reading aloud). The verbal behaviour might re-emerge in an overt form when a person is alone, and begins to talk to oneself out loud as he or she tries to solve a difficult problem (Skinner, 1957, pp. 434 ff.).

The role of private events in a causal analysis

To best understand the role of private events in a causal analysis, we need to consider the goals of radical behaviourism. For many radical behaviourists, the major aim of science is understanding (Holland, & Skinner, 1961; Killeen, 1987; Moore, 1980; Schnaitter, 1978). In the behaviour analytic literature, understanding has been operationally defined as prediction and control (Hayes & Brownstein, 1986). Skinner in particular has forcibly argued that a science of behaviour must at least potentially allow both prediction and control simultaneously. There are two good reasons to evaluate understanding or the truth of scientific propositions in terms of prediction and control: (1) These evaluations are straightforward, science has clear-cut methodologies for determining whether prediction and control really occurred in any given instance–both traditional statistical and individual-case are well developed methodologies (Malott & Malott, 1991), and (2) the use of the criteria of prediction and control provides a good basis for the development of effective technologies (Killeen, 1987).

Skinner acknowledged that some kinds of variables in principle can only allow prediction and not control. Other kinds of variables can allow both in principle, though for practical reasons control may presently be impossible (Hayes & Brownstein, 1986). Skinner called this second set of variables 'environmental variables' or 'external variables'. It is Skinner's insistence on both prediction and control that prevents the organism itself, or behaviour itself (including private behavioural events), from being an initiating cause. In particular, his insistence upon the need for control, forces us to emphasise external variables that are functionally related to the behaviour. This is so because it is impossible to manipulate variables other than real, physical variables external to the behavioural system.

Unfortunately, we cannot always do the experiments needed to demonstrate control of a dependent variable by a manipulated independent variable (this is particularly true in complex applied settings; especially historical ones and with analyses of private events). We may chose to reject the strict criterion of prediction and control rather than reject those areas of study (Killeen, 1987; Malott & Malott, 1991; Schnaitter, 1978). Scientists probably decrease their errors of commission by insisting on the evaluation of all cause-effect relations in terms of prediction of experimentally controlled results. The price, however, may be too high in terms of the cost of errors of omission of important cause-effect relations in our understanding of the world (Malott & Malott, 1991). We may conclude that to define truth and understanding solely in terms of prediction and control is carrying operationalism too far. This was indeed the case for Skinner. Skinner's radical behaviourism arose largely in opposition to the extreme positivistic influence of methodological behaviourism with its limitations on legitimate scientific inquiry (Lowe, 1983).

Skinner (1969) argued that interpretation along with prediction and control are essential for understanding. For three reasons, behaviour analysts will inhabit a much more understandable world, if they take a cautious step outside the constraints of prediction and control (see Malott & Malott, 1991): (1) Even when we can't predict and control, most individuals are still interested in post hoc analyses of why things happened as they did; (2) some of the most important theories in the history of science were not based on the prediction of experimentally controlled results (e.g., Darwin's theory of evolution by natural selection. Additionally, Skinner's theoretical work of Verbal Behaviour is not based on the prediction of experimentally controlled results); and (3) we may be better able to understand overt behaviour if we infer covert behaviours as being functionally related to overt behaviour, even if we cannot always control and predict those private behaviours (Killeen, 1987).

There are major difficulties of incorporating inferences into scientific endeavour but our confidence in an inferential explanation will increase to the extent that the explanation is in terms of basic scientific principles that have been or can be directly verified by their utility in the prediction of experimentally controlled results (Schnaitter, 1978). In Skinner's words, 'As in other sciences, we often lack the information necessary for prediction and control and must be satisfied with interpretation, but our interpretations will have the support of the prediction and control which has been possible under other conditions' (Skinner, 1974, p. 176).

Discovering variables–such as private events–that in principle cannot perform the full functions (prediction and control) required of a scientific analysis is, therefore, not objectionable to the radical behaviourist. Such analyses are important in the context of a complete understanding of behavioural systems (Hayes, 1986). Behavioural analyses that implicate private events are, however, incomplete if they fail to extend the analysis to environmental variables that can be manipulated. Such analyses are only a description of behaviour-behaviour relations; a description of the phenomena to be explained. They must not be mistaken for an explanation of these very phenomena. If behaviour-behaviour relations are orderly, they themselves can allow prediction of the same behavioural phenomena. No amount of description of behavioural events, however, will allow their direct control. To think otherwise is to make the structuralist error (Skinner, 1974). For example, the private phenomenon of anxiety may be used to explain agitated behaviour exhibited by an individual. But we are still left without an explanation of what caused the anxiety. Similarly, in a complex sequence of behaviour such as problem solving, some elements may be covert, others may be overt. The private nature of the covert behaviour does not imply that it causes the overt behaviour. The covert behaviour may exert some control over the overt behaviour, but this behaviour-behaviour relation is not the causal relation with respect to the subsequent overt behaviour. The 'cause' of the overt behaviour is to be found in an analysis of the contingencies of reinforcement that are responsible for both the overt and covert behaviour. Private events therefore do not explain behaviour, they are additional behavioural events to be explained:

[T]he private event is at best no more than a link in a causal chain, and it is usually not even that. We may think before we act in the sense that we may behave covertly before we behave overtly, but our action is not an 'expression' of the covert response or the consequence of it. The two are simply attributable to the same variables' (Skinner, 1953, p. 279).

Private events are simply important aspects in an overall causal chain (Skinner, 1984), but for philosophical reasons (i.e., the need for prediction and control) the search is never ended until sources of environmental control are established. Thus we must be clear that studying private events is not an effort to study initiating causes.[3] We are studying the nature of behavioural systems (Hayes & Brownstein, 1986).

This may seem paradoxical, because private events such as self-rules control behaviour, by definition. Just as in a chain of behaviour, however, one response may be said to control another, but only in the context of initiating causes that establish both responses and the relation between them. The word cause is reserved for events that allow prediction and control in principle to be met. Thus the causes of the private events lie outside the private events themselves. This does not mean that private events are epiphenomena. Behaviour-behaviour relations are real. They require analysis, and thus they must be identified and measured. Out of these analyses may come a greater understanding of how private events are established, and how they come to participate in the control of responding.

In summary, prediction and control may be shallow scientific goals if used without interpretation. Behaviour analysts therefore need to describe all links in a causal chain (of which some will be inferred), not just the first (environmental discriminative conditions) and the last (response), if we are to understand complex behavioural processes (Malott & Malott, 1991). For two obvious reasons we should deal with all components of the causal chain. First, to support the ultimate scientific goal of understanding the entire process under analysis, we need to describe all links in a causal chain, not just the first and last. This is in keeping with Skinner's argument that we should concern ourselves with private events 'for the sake of completeness of our analysis' (Skinner, 1953, p. 258). Second, technologically, we might better design various training programs if we specify all the variables which control behaviour. For example, it may be worthwhile to consider covert behaviour in teaching mental arithmetic, in predicting the results of 'mental' or covert arithmetic, and in teaching mnemonic

---

[3]   Linda Hayes argues that Skinner's position is inconsistent regarding the causal status of private stimuli. Despite the fact that private stimuli may have elicitive, discriminative, and reinforcing effectiveness, they are not regarded as having causal status. Only public stimuli may serve this capacity. By this restriction, we must assume that causality refers to something other than elicitation, discrimination, and reinforcement operations. However, in all other contexts, the stimuli involved in these operations are regarded as the causes of behaviour. Hayes argues that Skinner's conceptualisation of private events as something which occurs inside the skin rather than in implicit fields as proposed by Kantor leads to this inconsistency (Hayes, 1994; Malott & Malott, 1991).

techniques. True, we must ultimately start and end with external events; but that does not necessarily negate the role of the private events. Perhaps private events are useful only if we can explain them in terms of public events, but that does not mean that those private events are useless; nor does it mean that we should discard our inferences to private events just because they must ultimately be tied to public events.

Conclusion: An accommodation of the term 'radical' in their research practices by radical behaviourists

Skinner's most important contribution is his system of science which allows for a consistent, systematic, comprehensive, natural science of behaviour. Central to Skinner's analysis is the issue of objectivity. We can summarise the issue of objectivity from the standpoint of radical behaviourism as follows. First, the emphasis upon experimental control in the analysis of behaviour is not based on a concern for 'objectively investigating the real world of psychological laws' as much as an interest in effective means of identifying controlling variables and contingencies. Second, the traditional linkage between objectivity and the exclusive study of public behaviour does not apply to radical behaviourism, since the latter considers occurring private events as directly observable (at least for the individual concerned) and to be included in a complete scientific formulation of behaviour (Leigland, 1989).

Given this analysis of Skinner in particular and radical behaviourism in general, there remains the question of why the misconception that radical behaviourism does not include private events in its subject matter is apparently so widespread (Wyatt, 1990). Part of the explanation may be found in the activities of radical behaviourists themselves. Despite the clear theoretical lead given by Skinner, radical behaviourists have been generally reluctant to investigate the role of private events in human behaviour. If we take the example of covert self-instruction, whereas Vygotsky's (1962) ideas inspired a huge amount of valuable Soviet research on the ways in which covert speech is established and interacts with other behaviour, Skinner's writings concerning self-rules (1945, 1953, 1969, 1974), which in many respects closely resemble those of Vygotsky's, have not until relatively recently been empirically investigated to anything like the same degree. In short, it seems that some radical behaviourists are willing to consider the issue of private events, in large part to avoid being accused of neglecting them (Skinner, 1974). But to avoid being identified as cognitivists they are unwilling to elaborate upon the nature and operation of such events let alone get involved in their empirical investigation.

To redress the misconception that radical behaviourism does not include private events in its subject matter, radical behaviourists need to examine their own behaviour (i.e., their research practices). What is called for is a systematic program of research to develop methodologies which facilitate the empirical investigation of private events. Only then will radical behaviourists be able to build upon the theoretical foundation (as outlined in this chapter) laid by Skinner and fully incorporate private events into their analyses.

References

Baer, D. M. (1996). On the invulnerability of behavior-analytic theory to biological research. *The Behavior Analyst*, 19, 83–84.

Barnes, D. (1993). *Stimulus equivalence and relational frame theory*. Paper presented at the Experimental Analysis of Behaviour Group Annual Conference, University College, London.

Baron, A., Kaufman, A., & Stauber, K. A. (1969). Effects of instructions and reinforcement-feedback on human operant behavior maintained by fixed-interval reinforcement. *Journal of the Experimental Analysis of Behavior*, 12, 701–712.

Baron, A. & Galizio, M. (1983). Instructional control of human operant behavior. *Psychological Record*, 33, 495–520.

Bentall, R. P., & Lowe, C. F. (1987). The role of verbal behavior in human learning III: Instructional effects in children. *Journal of the Experimental Analysis of Behavior*, 47, 177–190.

Bentall, R. P., Lowe, C. F., & Beasty, A. (1985). The role of verbal behavior in human learning II: Developmental differences. *Journal of the Experimental Analysis of Behavior*, 43, 165–181.

Bergmann, G. (1956). The contribution of John B. Watson. *Psychological Review*, 63, 265–276.

Branch, M. N. & Gollub, L. R. (1974). A detailed analysis of the effects of d-amphetamine on behavior under fixed-interval schedules. *Journal of the Experimental Analysis of Behavior*, 21, 519–539.

Branch, M. N. & Malagodi, E. F. (1980). Where have all the behaviorists gone? *The Behavior Analyst*, 3, 31–38.

Brigham, T. A. (1980). Self-control revisited: Or why doesn't anyone actually read Skinner anymore? *The Behavior Analyst*, 3, 25–33.

Catania, A. C., Matthews, B. A., & Shimoff, E. (1982). Instructed versus shaped human verbal behavior interaction with nonverbal responding. *Journal of the Experimental Analysis of Behavior*, 38, 233–248.

Cullen, C. (1981). The flight to the laboratory. *The Behavior Analyst*, 4, 81–83.

Cumming, W. W. & Schoenfeld, W. N. (1958). Behavior under the extended exposure to a high-value fixed-interval reinforcement schedule. *Journal of the Experimental Analysis of Behavior*, 1, 245–263.

Day, W. F. (1976). The case for behaviorism. In M. H. Marx & F. E. Goodson (Eds), *Theories in contemporary psychology*. New York: Macmillan.

Day, W. F. (1980). Historical antecedents of modern behaviorism. In R. W. Rieber & K. Salzinger (Eds), *Psychology: Theoretical-historical perspectives* (pp. 203–262). New York: Academic Press.

Donahoe, J. W. (1996). On the relation between behavior analysis and biology. *The Behavior Analyst*, 19, 71–3.

Eccles, J. C. (1973). *The understanding of the brain*. New York: McGraw-Hill.

Ferster, C. B., & Skinner, B. F. (1957). *Schedules of reinforcement*. New York: Appleton-Century-Crofts.

Fodor, J. A. (1968). *Psychological explanation.* New York: Random House.

Gifford, J. L., Rusch, F. R., Martin, J. E., & White, D. M. (1984). Autonomy and adaptability: A proposed technology for the study of work behaviour. In N. R. Ellis & N. R. Bray (Eds), *International review of research in mental retardation* (Vol. 12, pp. 285–318). New York: Academic Press.

Hayes, L. J. (1994). Thinking. In S. C. Hayes, L. J. Hayes, M. Sato, & K. Ono (Eds), *Behavior analysis of language and cognition.* Reno, NV: Context Press.

Hayes, S. C. (1986). The case of the silent dog–verbal reports and the analysis of rules: A review of Ericsson and Simon's 'Protocol Analysis: Verbal Reports as Data'. *Journal of the Experimental Analysis of Behavior, 45,* 351–363.

Hayes, S. C. (1989). *Rule-governed behavior, cognition, contingencies and instructional control.* New York: Plenum.

Hayes, S. C. & Brownstein, A. J. (1986). Mentalism, behavior-behavior relations, and a behavior-analytic view of the purposes of science. *The Behavior Analyst, 9,* 175–190.

Hayes, S. C. & Hayes, L. J. (1992a). Verbal relations and the evolution of behavior analysis. *American Psychologist, 47,* 1383–1395.

Hayes, S. C. & Hayes, L. J. (1992b). Some clinical implications of contextualistic behaviorism: The example of cognition. *Behavior Therapy, 23,* 225–249.

Heidbreder, E. (1933). *Seven psychologies.* New York: Century Company.

Holland, J. G. & Skinner, B. F. (1961). *The analysis of behavior.* New York: McGraw-Hill.

Horner, R. H., Dunlap, G., & Koegel R. L. (1988). *Generalisation and maintenance: Life-style changes in applied settings.* Baltimore: Brookes.

Jones, R. S. P., Williams, H., & Lowe, C. F. (1993). Verbal self-regulation. In I. Flemming & B. Stenfert Kroese (Eds), *People with learning disabilities and challenging behaviour: Advances in research, service delivery and interventions.* Manchester: Manchester University Press.

Keenan, M. (1997). See Chapter 3, 'W'-ing: Teaching exercises for radical behaviourists.

Killeen, P. R. (1987). Radical behaviorism under the microscope: Clarity gained, depth of field lost. In S. Modgil & C. Modgil (Eds), *B. F. Skinner: Consensus and controversy* (pp. 236–238). Barcomb, UK: Falmer Press.

Leander, J. D., Lippman, L. G., & Meyer, M. E. (1968). Fixed-interval performance as related to subjects' verbalizations of the reinforcement contingency. *Psychological Record, 18,* 469–474.

Leigland, S, (1989). On the relation between radical behaviorism and the science of verbal behavior. *The Analysis of Verbal Behavior, 7,* 25–41.

Lippman, L. G., & Meyer, M. E. (1967). Fixed-interval performance as related to instructions and to subjects' verbalization of contingencies. *Psychonomic Science, 8,* 135–136.

Lowe, C. F. (1979). Determinants of human operant behaviour. In M. D. Zeiler & P. Harzem (Eds), *Advances in analysis of behaviour, Vol. 1: Reinforcement and the organisation of behaviour* (pp. 159–192). Chichester: Wiley.

Lowe, C. F. (1983). Radical behaviourism and human psychology. In G. Davey (Ed.), *Animal models and human behaviour: Conceptual, evolutionary and neurobiological perspectives* (pp. 71–93). Chichester: Wiley.

Lowe, C. F., Beasty, A., & Bentall, R. P. (1983). The role of verbal behavior in human learning: Infant performance on fixed-interval schedules. *Journal of the Experimental Analysis of Behavior, 39,* 157–164.

Lowe, C. F. & Harzem, P. (1977). Species differences in temporal control of behavior. *Journal of the Experimental Analysis of Behavior, 28,* 189–201.

Lowe, C. F., Horne, P. J., & Higson, P. J. (1987). Operant conditioning: The hiatus between theory and practice in clinical psychology. In H. J. Eysenck & I. Martin (Eds), *Theoretical foundations of behaviour therapy* (pp. 162–188). London: Plenum.

Malott, R. W. & Malott, M. E. (1991). Private events and rule-governed behavior. In L. J. Hayes & P. N. Chase (Eds), *Dialogues on verbal behavior* (pp. 237–254). Reno: Context Press.

Moore, J. (1980). On behaviorism and private events. *The Psychological Record, 30*, 459–475.

Moore, J. (1981). On mentalism, methodological behaviorism, and radical behaviorism. *Behaviorism, 9*, 55–77.

Moore, J. (1984). On privacy, causes, and contingencies. *The Behavior Analyst, 7*, 3–16.

Moore, J. (1990). On mentalism, privacy, and behaviorism. *Journal of Mind and Behavior, 11*, 19–36.

Moore, J. (1995). Radical behaviorism and the subjective-objective distinction. *The Behavior Analyst, 18*, 33–49.

Natsoulas, T. (1984). Gustav Bergmann's psychophysiological parallelism. *Behaviorism, 12*, 41–69.

Parrott, L. J. (1983). Systemic foundations for the concept of 'private events': A critique. In N. W. Smith, P. T. Mountjoy & D. H. Reuben (Eds), *Reassessment of psychology: The interbehavioral alternative* (pp. 251–268). Washington: University Press of America.

Pepper, S. C. (1942). *World hypotheses: A study in evidence*. Berkeley: University of California Press.

Place, U. T. (1993). A radical behaviorist methodology for the empirical investigation of private events. *Behavior and Philosophy, 21*, 25–36.

Reese, H. W. (1996). How is physiology relevant to behavior analysis. *The Behavior Analyst, 19*, 61–70.

Schnaitter, R. (1978). Private causes. *Behaviorism, 6*, 1–12.

Schneider, S. M. & Morris, E. K. (1987). A history of the term radical behaviorism: From Watson to Skinner. *The Behavior Analyst, 10*, 27–39.

Skinner, B. F. (1938). *The behavior of organisms*. New York: Appleton-Century-Crofts.

Skinner, B. F. (1945). The operational analysis of psychological terms. *Psychological Review, 52*, 270–277 .

Skinner, B. F. (1953). *Science and human behavior*. New York: Macmillan.

Skinner, B. F. (1957). *Verbal behaviour*. New York: Appleton-Century-Crofts.

Skinner, B. F. (1964). Behaviorism at fifty. In T. W. Wann (Ed.), *Behaviorism and phenomenology* (pp. 79–106). Chicago: University of Chicago Press.

Skinner, B. F. (1969). *Contingencies of reinforcement: A theoretical analysis*. New York: Appleton-Century-Crofts.

Skinner, B. F. (1972). *Cumulative record. New York*: Appleton-Century-Crofts

Skinner, B. F. (1974). *About behaviorism*. New York: Knopf.

Skinner, B. F. (1984). Coming to terms with private events. *Behavioral and Brain Sciences, 7*, 572–581.

Skinner, B. F. (1989). The origins of cognitive thought. *American Psychologist, 44*, 13–18.

Spence, K. W. (1948). The postulates and methods of 'behaviorism.' *Psychological Review, 55*, 67–78.

Staddon, J. E. R. (1972). Temporal control and the theory of reinforcement schedules. In R. H. Gilbert & J. R. Millenson (Eds), *Reinforcement: Behavioral analyses* (pp. 209–262). New York: Academic Press.

Stokes, T. F., & Baer, D. M. (1977). An implicit technology of generalization. *Journal of Applied Behavior Analysis, 10,* 349–368.

Taylor, I. & O'Reilly, M. F. (1997). Toward a functional analysis of private verbal self-regulation. *Journal of Applied Behavior Analysis, 30,* 43–58.

Vaughan, M. (1989). Rule-governed behavior in behavior analysis: A theoretical and experimental history. In S. C. Hayes (Ed.), *Rule-governed behaviour, cognition, contingencies and instructional control* (pp. 97–118). New York: Plenum.

Vygotsky, L. (1962). *Thought and language.* New York: Wiley.

Wacker, D. & Berg, W. N. (1983). Effects of picture prompts on the acquisition of complex vocational tasks by mentally retarded adolescents. *Journal of Applied Behavior Analysis, 16,* 417–443.

Watson, J. B. (1913). Psychology as the behaviorist views it. *Psychological Review, 20,* 158–177.

Weiner, H. (1964). Conditioning history and human fixed-interval performance. *Journal of the Experimental Analysis of Behavior, 7,* 383–385.

Weiner, H. (1965). Conditioning history and maladaptive human operant behavior. *Psychological Reports, 17,* 935–942.

Weiner, H. (1969). Controlling human fixed-interval performance. *Journal of the Experimental Analysis of Behavior, 12,* 349–373.

Whitman, T. L. (1990). Self-regulation and mental retardation. *American Journal of Mental Retardation, 94,* 347–362.

Wittgenstein, L. (1953). *Philosophical investigations.* New York: Macmillan.

Wyatt, W. J. (1990). Radical behaviorism misinterpreted: A reply to Mahoney. *American Psychologist, 45,* 1181–1183.

Zuriff, G. E. (1985). *Behaviorism: A conceptual reconstruction.* New York: Columbia University Press.

3

'W'-ing:
Teaching exercises for radical behaviourists

Michael Keenan[1]

Abstract

The widespread misrepresentation of radical behaviourism may be a reflection of the difficulties of teaching its views on private events. Consequently, this paper begins with a discussion of the behavioural stream and it contains exercises in self-observation that are intended to be used in classroom situations. Students who are actively encouraged to participate in self-observation under the guidance of a behavioural perspective may be more discerning of the seriousness of misrepresentation when it appears in their course of study.

Introduction

Though vast in quantity, the great majority of behavioural findings tell us little of worth about ourselves. In a sense, having denied the importance of subjective data, their findings appear limited, alien, even 'soul-less'. (Spinelli, 1989, p. 175)

In recent years there have been attempts by members of the behavioural community to redress the type of serious misrepresentation quoted above (Catania, 1991; Lee, 1989; Lonigan, 1990; Morris, 1985, 1990; Wyatt, 1990). The primary objective of this chapter is to contribute to the general debate about what should

[1] I dedicate this paper to Karola, Kalinka, Tara and the twins. A special thanks to Paul Smeets for providing me valuable thinking space in Holland. Thanks also to Leo Baker, Dermot Barnes, Giulio Lancioni and Harrie Boelens for their comments on parts of an initial draft. An abridged version of this chapter 'Teaching about private events in the classroom' appeared in *Behavior and Social Issues*, *Vol. 6*, No. 2 (1996) pp. 75–84. Reprinted with the permission of the Cambridge Center for Behavioral Studies. Quotations from *The tao of physics* are reprinted with the permission of Shambala Publications, Inc.

be done by offering suggestions for teaching exercises that address specific features of the philosophy of radical behaviourism.

The rationale for these exercises hinges on some of the problems incurred in the dissemination of conclusions reached by fellow scientists. Skinner (1989) touched on this issue when he said that '. . . everything scientists now do must at least once have been contingency shaped in someone, but most of the time scientists begin by following rules. Science is a vast verbal environment or culture' (p. 44). In that same chapter he discussed the differential effects of contingency-shaped and rule-governed behaviour. The points he made are relevant here because they contain general guidelines that may help in the design of effective methods for teaching:

Those who have been directly exposed to contingencies behave more subtly and effectively than those who have merely been told, taught, or advised to behave or who follow rules. There is a difference because rules never fully describe the contingencies they were designed to replace. There is also a difference in the states of the body felt. (Skinner, 1989, p. 44)

Radical behaviourists distinguish their discipline from methodological behaviourism in terms of how they view private events (Hayes & Brownstein, 1987; Moore, 1980, 1981; Schneider & Morris, 1987; Skinner, 1953, 1974). This being the case it would seem reasonable to suppose that the behavioural community should produce teaching exercises concerned with the study of private events that take into account the observations outlined by Skinner. If teachers were provided with, for example, precise instructions for producing the type of differential behavioural effects described above, then the ways in which radical behaviourists resolve some of the difficult issues that arise in the study of private events would be open to inspection by students. Students who are exposed to well structured exercises along these lines may be then less likely to view radical behaviourists as 'contingency accountants'[2] who are insensitive to the richness of human experience.

A second related objective of the exercises contained here is to stimulate others to contribute to the development of a wide range of teaching gambits for teachers of radical behaviourism. The development of such material would ensure that our teaching of scientific verbal behaviour is brought under strong discriminative control. Before describing the exercises, the next section of the paper contains a general overview of some of the issues that they were designed to address.

Radical Behaviourism and the Behavioural Stream

On being a person

Skinner (1989) noted that the word 'Experience' originally meant '. . . something a person had "gone through" (from the Latin *expiriri*) . . .' (p. 13).

---

[2]   I thank Giulio Lancioni for suggesting this term to me.

Nowadays we say that this 'something' refers to the network of contingencies that a person is exposed to over a period of time. When a person 'travels through' this context their body changes and these changes are somehow integrated with changes that have already taken place. 'Being a person', then, can be seen as the evolution of a dynamic process comprising physical and behavioural changes (Lee, 1988; Smith 1985). The nature and extent of these changes is dependent on the interplay between 'the dynamic limitations inherent in the adaptiveness of the [human] biological system and the dynamic limitations [in organism–environment interactions that are] imposed across time by the structure of the prevailing contingencies' (Keenan & Toal, 1991, p. 113). This mercurial-like quality of being a person is nicely captured by the idea of a behavioural stream that continually changes,[3] and is changed by, its physical and social embankment/environment (Schoenfeld & Farmer, 1970; Appendix 1 suggests imagery that can be used in the classroom to help convey the idea of a behavioural stream).[4]

Given that behavioural phenomena typically involve combinations of enduring and transient changes and temporal patterns thereof (cf. Epstein, 1984, 1985), the primary concern of behaviour analysts is the delineation of the types of relations that exist between various categories of change and the corresponding current and historical context from which these relations emerge (Hayes & Brownstein, 1986; Lee 1981; Michael, 1982). Bearing in mind that any observed behavioural phenomenon is inexorably linked with changes that have previously taken place, when a behaviour is observed to recur at later times a relation can be formulated between the occurrence of these behaviours in such a way that the dynamic character of their relatedness is emphasised. Skinner (1966), for example, suggested that a 'natural datum in a science of behaviour is the probability that a given bit of behaviour will occur at a given time. An experimental analysis deals with that probability in terms of frequency or rate of responding' (p. 213). Commenting on Skinner's use of time as an independent variable, Hineline (1990) further noted: 'Rate, although comprised

---

[3]   The suggestion that an organism can be viewed as a continuous stream of change can also be found in biology: 'My emergence as a unique individual with my own identity began in the ovaries and testes of my parents when they themselves were embryos in the grandparental womb. The events occurring then were in themselves linked via a continuous thread back through successive ancestral germ lines to the emergence of humanity itself. Just as anthropologists cannot define an exact and absolute point during evolutionary time when our ancient ancestors became human, so I cannot define any single developmental transition at which I became an individual with a clear identity. The evolution of humans and the development of my identity are both continuous processes.' (Johnston, 1989, p. 41)

[4]   Surprising parallels can be drawn between the notion of an organism as a stream and phenomena which arise in the study of water. For example, continual movement can give rise to a form which appears static: '. . . when a wave appears behind a stone in a stream, a form is all the time being created out of movement, with new substance constantly flowing through it. This is an archetypal principal of all living creation – an organic form, in spite of continuous chemical change, remains intact.' (Schwenk, 1990, p. 33)

of tangible, observable events, is an abstraction. You can look right through a rate; that is, it can be going on right now, even though none of the events that comprise the rate is occurring at this moment'. (p. 305)

The development of conceptual tools for the analysis of complex streams of behaviour has been aided by the study of schedules[5] of reinforcement. Most importantly, perhaps, the realisation that schedules of reinforcement could guide the behavioural stream into recognisable patterns helped contribute to the notion that *prediction* and *control* of behaviour across time are essential corner stones of behavioural epistemology (Hayes & Brownstein, 1986). Essentially this means that if behaviour can be moved around in a predictable manner (i.e., if aspects of it can be controlled), then the variables that are manipulated (which are necessarily *outside* of the target behaviour) are considered to be functionally related to the target behaviour. In other words, the practical steps that are taken by the scientist in his/her attempt to control and thus predict behaviour provide the terms of reference for 'explaining' the behavioural profile that is subsequently observed.

On being a scientist

This last statement can be reformulated so as to reveal an important and distinguishing concern of radical behaviourism, the behaviour of the scientist. When reference is made to the behaviour of the scientist the following can be said: the behaviour of the behavioural scientist when acting upon the environment provides the context for the emission of the term 'explanation' when the consequence of that scientific behaviour leads to the prediction and control of a target behaviour.

This formulation switches the target behaviour of interest from the subject being studied to the scientist him/herself. Said another way, the perspective controlled by this new statement functions as a way of transforming the observer (the scientist) into the observed. The reason for formulating the sentence in this way is the following. In view of the fact that at any point in time the actions of a scientist (or any other person) constitute the end-product of his/her interactions with the environment (i.e., constitute the leading edge of his/her behavioural stream), it is encumbent upon a thorough behavioural analysis to elucidate the manner in which this training sustains the epistemological assumptions that are brought to bear in a scientific analysis. Indeed this task has been at the heart of much of Skinner's writings (e.g., Skinner, 1945, 1977, 1985). The significance of giving attention to the behaviour of the

---

[5] A schedule is defined here in the manner outlined by Keenan and Toal (1991): '. . . a schedule is more properly conceived as providing an opportunity for examining the dynamic behavioral system that "crystallizes out" when a biological system is exposed to environmental constraints . . .'. (p. 113)

scientist has also been commented upon in a recent paper by Hayes, Hayes, & Reese (1988):

. . . scientists cannot stand apart from the world under analysis; they are, rather, a part of that world. . . . Behavior analysts acknowledge the fact that science is, among other things, the action of scientists – action meaningful only by reference to its context. (p. 103)

As an example of the implications of this position consider a key term in the conceptual armament of a scientist, namely the term 'objectivity'. Objectivity in scientific investigation is traditionally viewed as 'the extent to which findings are independent of the investigator as regards the ways they are obtained, evaluated and interpreted' (Eysenck, Arnold, & Meili, 1975, p. 735). Figure 1 shows how this definition might be represented pictorially. In the figure two observers (scientists) are shown looking down on a somewhat condensed linear version of the behavioural stream of a human and of a rat. Each stream depicts 'snapshots' in the life of each organism from birth through to death. (The streams are shown converging because all organisms share similar destinies.)

From the way that this diagram is constructed, an obvious question presents itself. That is, in his/her search for an explanation of a particular phenomenon can a scientist really stand outside of nature in the manner depicted? Clearly this can not be the case and therefore the claim to be able to develop something called an objective perspective that is independent of the effects propagated by previous interactions with the physical and social environment is in need of reappraisal. Furthermore, not only is such a view at odds with the image of a person that has been portrayed so far, but it has also come under criticism from recent developments in other sciences like atomic physics. Capra (1975), for example, has said that:

A careful analysis of the process of observation in atomic physics has shown that the subatomic particles have no meaning as isolated entities, but can only be understood as interconnections between the preparation of an experiment and the subsequent measurement. . . . The human observer constitutes the final link in the chain of observational processes, and the properties of any atomic object can only be understood in terms of the object's interaction with the observer. This means that the classical idea of an objective description of nature is no longer valid. The Cartesian partition between the I and the world, between the observer and the observed, cannot be made when dealing with atomic matter. (pp. 68–9)

Within the context of nuclear physics, Capra's statement can be considered as an exposé of the working assumptions of those scientists who represented the mainstream opinion of their discipline. Adherence to the idea of an objective reality may possibly have blinded these scientists to the fact that their conclusions/observations were heavily influenced by current and historical factors. (Note that although Capra's conclusion is entirely commensurate with the position of radical behaviourism (cf. Williams, 1986), this is not generally recognised to be the case (Briggs & Peat, 1984; Capra, 1975; Spinelli, 1989)).

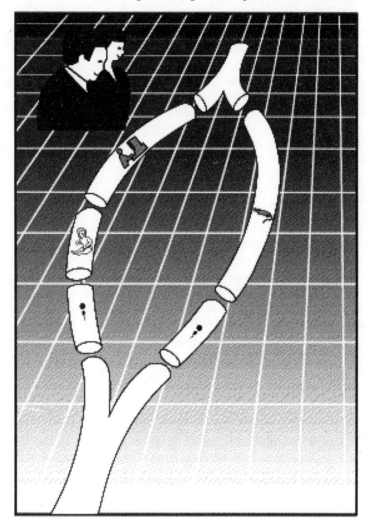

Figure 1:   A possible representation of a traditional perspective on 'objectivity'. Two observers are shown looking down on a highly condensed version of the behavioural streams of a human and of a rat.

Within psychology, radical behaviourism has been engaged in a similar type of exposé. This is not the place, however, for a detailed explication of a behavioural approach to the term objectivity (see Leigland, 1989a). Suffice to say, the point being made here is that questions concerned with the meaning of psychological terms like this have been the mainstay of radical behaviourism. In Skinner's (1988) words radical behaviourism is '. . . a thoroughgoing analysis of traditional mentalistic terms' (p. 151). A strategy he adopted to help deal with the problems caused by the mentalism[6] rampant in traditional explanations of human behaviour was to include in his analysis the effect of a specific type of historical factor, the fact that scientists were formally children. When viewing things from this perspective he raised a fundamental question concerning the development of a child's understanding of psychological terms: 'How is it possible to learn to refer to or describe (and I would say know) things or events within our bodies [e.g., having an objective perspective, having a feeling of anticipation, being self-aware] to which our teachers do not have access? How can they tell us that we are right or wrong when we describe them?' (p. 162)

Explaining

The general significance of these questions for the analysis of scientific behaviour can be appreciated if we return to the problem of how behavioural scientists come to use the term 'explanation'. The issue addressed here comes under the topic of 'operationism' and can be illustrated briefly. For example, it is clearly the case that historical precedents have ensured that the term 'explanation' has been passed on to us by our ancestors instead of an arbitrary sound like, say, 'wibbly-wobbly'. Acknowledging the possibility that scientists today could be looking for 'wibbly-wobblies' instead of explanations directs attention to the fact that the meaning of a word is to be found from an analysis of the contingencies controlling its use (Creel, 1987; Day, 1969; Moore, 1975, 1985; Smith, 1986).

When this view is applied to the use of the word explanation by behaviour analysts, the following can be said: as the neophyte passes through the context created by his/her scientific forebears their verbal behaviour of emitting a word like 'explanation' is refined to the extent that it comes to be used in a stereotypic fashion. The contingencies currently governing the behavioural community's analysis of the appropriateness or meaning of a word have themselves evolved from a system of contingencies which helped to mould Skinner's verbal behaviour with respect to the notion of operationism. Creel (1987) has paraphrased Skinner thus:

Operationism insists that the concepts, claims and procedures of science be interpretable in terms of physical properties and operations. It seeks 'an effective experimental approach' to each subject matter. This approach is encouraging because its primary concern is demonstrable prediction and control, not communication or disputation. It

---

[6] Moore (1981) noted that mentalism is characterised by several explicit or implicit features: '(a) the bifurcation of human experience into a behavioral dimension and a prebehavioral dimension, (b) the use of psychological terms to refer to organocentric entities from the prebehavioral dimension, and (c) the use of organocentric entities as causally effective antecedents in explaining behavior.' (p. 62)

places little value on argument or logical dialectics. Its aim is not to win the agreement of others; it is to increase our control over nature. (pp. 110–111)

A key factor responsible for Skinner's formulation of operationism was his early empirical work with schedules of reinforcement. The opportunity afforded by schedules for the study of purposeful/intentional behaviour brought him to an important conclusion. That is, when regularities in the performance of organisms appeared, these regularities were independent of an observer's speculation about what was going on inside the organism in terms of either physiological changes or in terms of cognitive processes. Thus, even if one was to initially adopt a non-behavioural approach in accounting for perfor-mance of an organism on a schedule, one would eventually have to concede that the organism would not have changed in the way that it did without exposure to the scheduled contingencies. Consequently, the development of a behavioural explanation of performance on a schedule is viewed as synonymous with the development of an empirically derived database of behavioural facts that is under the discriminative control of the behavioural dynamics controlled by the structure of the prevailing contingencies.

Earlier it was noted that the objective of behaviour analysis was to relate aspects of the changing organism to the context in which it is observed. The perspective which evolves from this endeavour can be extended to the dyad comprising the scientist and his/her subject matter. In the language of the behavioural stream, at the interface between the scientist and his/her subject is a dynamic process which regulates the ensuing course of their respective behavioural streams. In any study, for example, it can be said that the behav-iour of the subject entrains the behaviour of the scientist. When only passive observation (i.e., actions associated with the monitoring of behavioural change) is involved, the nature of the ensuing observer-observed synchronisation is different from that which develops when active observation (i.e., actions involved in monitoring and controlling the direction of behavioural change) leads to an evolving process of reciprocal determination between the behaviour of the scientist and the changes produced in the behaviour of the subject.

The verbal behaviour of the scientist is necessarily included in this perspective. Consequently, the implications which are derived from it extend into the realm of epistemology. Consider again, for example, the issues that arise when a non-behavioural scientist seeks an explanation of performance on a schedule of reinforcement. Given that the inferring of inner causal processes by such a scientist arises as a function of the contingencies operating on the observed organism, and that performance of this organism is, as we have already noted, independent of these inferences, the verbal behaviour of equating expla-nation exclusively with the operation of inner processes is more informative of the behavioural processes of the scientist than it is about the behaviour of the organism under investigation (Barnes, 1989; Leigland, 1989b; Morris, Higgins, & Bickel, 1982).

This behavioural perspective on the meaning of the term explanation contains the essence of Skinner's view of operationism. That is to say, it is consistent with his view that an operational definition entails an empirical description of the conditions under which a term is used, i.e., the functional relations governing its emission as a verbal response. This approach is markedly different from that taken by logicians, linguists, or cognitive scientists when they attempt to give a formal analysis of language or behaviour (Marr, 1983; Terrell & Johnston, 1989). To the extent that they engage in logical analyses that do not explicitly incorporate reference to the context supporting the phenomenon they observe, the consequences of their analysis must necessarily differ from a behavioural analysis. In spite of this difference, however, the epistemological assumptions which characterise the respective behavioural streams of these scientists can be accommodated within a behavioural perspective. Consider, for example, the possibility that one was able to identify the contingencies responsible for the development of the epistemological assumptions of, say, cognitive science. One would then be able to bring a person to the perspective in which human behaviour is viewed as a result of information processes similar to those which are said to occur inside a computer; such a person is shown sitting in front of a computer in Figure 1. This possibility is not as far fetched as it first sounds because any university course in cognitive science manipulates the appropriate contingencies to bring about exactly this effect.

Adult children

In one sense the discussion has now come full circle. The scientist, as a person, as a behavioural stream, is seen to change in ways which are functionally related to the current and historical context through which he/she passes. The act of engaging in a functional analysis can be said to have 'folded in upon itself' consequently producing far reaching questions concerned with the 'doing' of science. Before exploring some of these questions it might be useful to recap at this point. An effective means of doing so is to caricature the interests of the mature scientist as having evolved from the games of a young child. The games that scientists once played when they were younger were transformed as new sets of contingencies came into operation. At one time, for example, it was fashionable for psychologists to play the 'objective game'. 'Adult children' who played this game were called Methodological Behaviourists and they incorporated the rules of another game called Logical Positivism. Leigland (1989a) has noted that some of the rules involved in playing this game include:

(1) the definition of the (empirically-based) subject matter as publicly-observable behavior (related to historical ties with logical positivism); (2) the focus upon the study

of behavior as a means of investigating internal, causal mechanisms of a conceptual nature which form the basis of scientific explanation; (3) a commitment to the practice of operational definitions in the traditional sense . . .; and (4) a position which has been described in terms of reductionism and mechanism. . . . (p. 26)

When Skinner appeared on the scene he explored the possibility that the objective, purposeful or intentional behaviour of other scientists could be accounted for by the same type of functional analysis that he used to account for the behaviour of a 'lower' organism on a schedule of reinforcement. That is, he speculated about the contingencies controlling the game played by the other children. Such speculation by Skinner was inexorable given his recognition of the controllability of behaviour and it is commensurate with one of his primary aims as a radical behaviourist, that is, developing more effective means of identifying the variables of which behaviour is a function. Being able to control the behaviour of interest without being side-tracked by mentalism was, he considered, a fundamental step in this direction. This concern with pragmatism is a central feature of Skinner's philosophy of science and it serves as a pivotal 'truth criterion' for discriminating between possible alternative explanations of behavioural phenomena (Smith, 1986; Zuriff, 1985).

As already indicated above a recurrent theme in the position taken by radical behaviourism is that the person observed at any point in time is an 'end-product' of a process of change resulting from interactions with the environment, or as Skinner (1974) has said, the person observed is a focal point of a number of influences:

A person is not an originating agent; he is a locus, a point at which many genetic and environmental conditions come together in a joint effect. (p. 168)

This being the case, a scientific analysis of the observable behaviour of another person is inevitably faced with the problem of reformulating the traditional role usually ascribed to private events. The crux of Skinner's arguments in dealing with this issue can be paraphrased by noting that since the functioning of the person observed is an integral segment in the continuation of that particular behavioural stream, the initiating role usually ascribed to private events can be no longer considered tenable. Skinner argued further that no special ontological status should be conferred on private events simply on the grounds that they are private. In effect, the view he took was that changes localised in the biological substratum of an organism that are not open to inspection (and hence are considered private) stand in relation to observable behaviour in such a way that a contextually framed coordinated system evolves as one continuous process[7] (Hayes & Brownstein, 1986; Morris, 1980, 1992).

---

[7]   A water-related image is useful for encapsulating the contextualistic perspective that is advanced here. For example, a vortex is 'a form which has separated itself off from the general flow of water; a self-contained region in the mass of water, enclosed within itself yet bound up within the whole.' (Schwenk, 1990, p. 44)

The implications that unfold from this perspective can be better appreciated if you imagine for a moment that a scientist has been given the opportunity to observe a 'translucent person.' Imagine further that this opportunity permits an unlimited extension of the range of private events that can now be observed. Such a scenario would permit a scientific observer of a behavioural stream to demarcate a host of functional relations that arise between specific categories of change that are localised within the boundaries of the skin. He/she could also formulate laws which connect these intradermal relations to those extradermal relations that extend from the skin to the external environment (Lee, 1988). In effect, it would be possible to derive an integrated system of functional relations which covers all aspects of the functioning of the whole person. The contextual boundaries within which all of the various functional relations were formulated would serve as reference points for a map or directory of the types of changes that happened to our translucent person during the period of observation (cf. Hayes, Hayes, & Reese, 1988). This map could then be referred to in the event of an explanation being required for specific behaviours at any point in time.

Let's consider now the implications to be derived from another scenario wherein our translucent person swops places with the observer; the observer has now become translucent whilst the person observed is opaque. In terms of furthering our understanding of the behaviour of the scientist, this situation helps to highlight the fact that a scientist's act of, for example, positing hypothetical internal entities as explanations for the observable behaviour of another person is merely an aspect of their observing behaviour under stimulus control. This point is all the more poignant when one considers that the functioning of the translucent scientist is seen to be a complex system of co-ordination within and between (what would previously have been categorised as) private behaviours and public behaviours.

When the scientific behaviour of a number of people is subjected to this perspective their behaviour of 'meeting the criteria imposed by the strictures of intersubjective agreement' can be considered as one facet of *group* observing behaviour that is under stimulus control. The observable behaviours of the opaque person that constitute the stimuli in this instance are contextually bound, intersubjectively verifiable, relational elements, and they have gained control because of the effects of historical contingencies that operated during the observers' training.

Investigative rules that arise as a direct function of the problems faced by the limited accessibility of private events of the observed (opaque) person are a major constituent of group observing behaviour (cf. Johnston & Pennypacker, 1980). These rules, in conjunction with other rules derived from the powerful reinforcing effects of demonstrable prediction and control of observable behaviour contribute to the scientific rubric of the time (Lee, 1985). In summary, when scientific practices focus on the observable behaviour of another person epistemological guidelines evolve such that the relationship between the observer(s) and the observed is enshrined in a particular type of synchronisation that is a function of identifiable constraining factors.

Introduction to the exercises

In light of what has been said so far, the suggestion that prediction and control can be construed as constraining factors may seem a little odd to say the least. However, the issue being raised here is not whether prediction and control per se are constraining factors, but whether an overriding concern for truth by public agreement has usurped their usefulness as guidelines for exploring private behaviour.[8] Although the public behaviour of a person observed can be controlled and thus predicted without referencing associated private behaviour, this does not in any way condemn private behaviour as unworthy of investigation (cf. Hayes & Hayes, 1992). On the contrary, given that the private events of the observer participate in the synchronisation between the observer and the observed, it is imperative that methods are developed for investigating this private behaviour that is brought to bear on the context called scientific observation.[9] That is to say, a thorough analysis recognises that when a scientist is giving attention solely to the observable behaviour of another person, he/she is, by definition, not giving attention to the perspective of 'the other one' (Skinner 1974, p. 171) from where the origins and ramifications of the conclusions or epistemological assumptions involved in that observation are considered as investigatable. When the perspective of 'the other one' is engaged it functions as a necessary check for ensuring that the scientist is mindful that not only is the person observed the focal point of a number of influences, but so also is the observer.[10]

Support for this line of argument comes from a parallel situation that is familiar to all teachers of radical behaviourism. When teachers are faced with the challenge of teaching students to recognise the mentalism that is sometimes inherent in their analyses of behaviour, they are in fact teaching them to monitor the operation of their own private events. It is sometimes necessary, for example, for a teacher to point out to students that they can not see inside

---

[8] Note: 'When privacy is invaded with scientific instruments, the form of stimulation is changed; the scales read by the scientist are not the private events themselves.' (Skinner, 1964, p. 82)

[9] The terms 'observation' or 'attention' could be considered as tacts for the relative degree of discriminative control that is evident at the interface between the current context of a stimulus collage and the changes wrought on an organism by an historical context that is brought to bear on that stimulus collage.

[10] Working with the images used earlier, it can be said that the perspective that emanates from the conceptual foundations of intersubjective agreement is but one strand in the fabric of achievable ends of the behavioural stream of a translucent person (cf. Hayes & Hayes, 1992).

the observed person to determine what it is that he/she is feeling or thinking before he/she behaves; even if one could see inside, all that would be observed is part of the overall profile that constitutes the leading edge of a behavioural stream. Consequently, when explanations for an observed person's behaviour are located inside that person, students can be informed that they are in fact really only observing their own private changes in the context supporting the observation[11] (cf. Hineline, 1990). Teaching a student the perspective of behaviour analysis, then, is a complex issue which involves the construction of experiences for the student such that he/she becomes self-aware with respect to the impact that their mentalistic training has on their own analysing and categorising behaviour. In some respects, teaching a student to discriminate between a behavioural perspective and a mentalistic perspective is tantamount to conducting 'educational therapy' whereby intrusive private events that masquerade as explanations (and which might interfere with effective action) are brought under control. From the perspective of the student, the transition to their new mode of functioning can often be a difficult journey because of the sustained attack on established beliefs by behavioural literature. At the same time, however, new avenues for self-awareness may be opened in which case the opening quotation by Spinelli (1989) will be seen as woefully misinformed.

Returning to the issue raised earlier, the above analysis highlights one way in which the unsuspecting observer can be transformed by the perspective of 'the other one'; in this instance, the perspective of 'the other one' is actualised in the actions of the teacher. As a consequence of adopting this perspective (i.e., of being exposed to these contingencies) the student may be made aware of the limitations of his/her previous conclusions. That is, the contingencies which are responsible for the transition from one perspective to another provide the conditions for the use of the term awareness. Details of the observations that constitute this awareness are not open to inspection by others. Yet, interestingly, it is through the judicious manipulation of appropriate contingencies that the skilled teacher, like the parent, embraces the problem of privacy[12] with the result that the process of self-observation is initiated. With this in mind, the behavioural student is now in a position to pursue an understanding of how his/her private events are a function of contextual influences. He/she can begin

[11] Perhaps the attributional processes at work here are a form of 'projection' that might be accounted for by an analysis of the equivalence relations that operate when animated stimuli form a social context. Steps have already been taken to forge links between stimulus equivalence and another area of social learning, social categorisation, although the static stimuli employed were contained within the boundaries of a computer screen (Kohlenberg, Hayes, & Hayes, 1991; Watt, Keenan, Barnes, & Cairns, 1991).

[12] Wann (1964) has paraphrased Skinner's general approach to the problem of privacy. 'The "boundary" for public-private is not the skin, but the line between the verbal community's being able to reinforce behavior differentially and its not being able to do so, or able to only with great difficulty.' (p. 107)

simply by noting that there are contingencies operating to control their current perspective of the phenomenon to be investigated. The question then arises as to what contingencies can be manipulated to reveal what effects? Essentially this question involves a role play of the perspective of 'the other one'.

There are many difficulties involved in developing a rigorous behavioural approach to self-observation and its counterpart, self-experimentation, as this quotation by a phenomenologist testifies:

The phenomenologist begins his observation of phenomena by suspending his biases, by putting his implicit assumptions in brackets. If your immediate comment is that it is impossible to observe anything without bias, all that I can say is that I heartily agree. There is no observation without bias, but there can be a deliberate attempt to identify bias and temporarily suspend it or at least to shift observation systematically from one bias to another. (MacLeod, 1964, p. 52)

While this statement contains much of what has already been said it makes no reference to the role of context in supporting observations. That being said, though, the statement serves as a useful reminder of the fact that apart from Skinner's writings (see also Neuringer, 1981; Ulrich, 1975) very little in the way of behavioural exercises exist for students who may be interested in exploring private events. It would be a strange state of affairs if this should continue to be the case, for, as already mentioned above, scientists interested in the effects that the environment has on behaviour cannot remain aloof from the implications that their findings have for them on a personal level. On a more pragmatic note, if teaching about radical behaviourism's perspective on private events is confined to a *description* of Skinner's arguments, then, in accordance with the differential effects of contingency-shaped and rule-governed behaviour, we should not be surprised if many students continue to view his interpretations as mere rhetoric. Since these students will already have been trained to self-observe by the verbal community they may instead opt for other approaches, like phenomenology, with which they might more easily identify.

The exercises which follow are in response to this vacuum that exists for teaching exercises concerned with a behavioural approach to self-observation. To set the scene for them consider these quotations from Skinner:

The environment, whether public or private, appears to remain undistinguished until the organism is forced to make a distinction. (1953, p. 260)

. . . self-observation is also the product of discriminative contingencies, and if a discrimination cannot be forced by the community, it may never arise. Strangely enough, it is the community which teaches the individual to 'know himself'. (1953, p. 260–261)

The kind of self-knowledge represented by discriminative verbal behavior – the knowledge which is 'expressed' when we talk about our own behavior – is strictly limited by the contingencies which the verbal community can arrange. (1953, p. 261)

It is true that psychologists sometimes use themselves as subjects successfully, but it is only when they manipulate external variables precisely as they would in studying the behavior of someone else. The scientist's 'observation' of a private event is a response to that event, or perhaps even a response to a response to it. (1953, p. 280)

We should not be surprised that the more we know about the behavior of others, the better we understand ourselves. It was a practical interest in the behavior of 'the other one' which led to this new kind of self-knowledge. The experimental analysis of behavior, together with a special self-descriptive vocabulary derived from it, has made it possible to apply to oneself much of what has been learned about the behavior of others, including other species (1974, p. 171).

We may take feeling to be simply responding to stimuli, but reporting is the product of the verbal contingencies arranged by a community. There is a similar difference between behaving and reporting that one is behaving or reporting the causes of one's behavior. In arranging conditions under which a person describes the public or private world in which he lives, a community generates that very special form of behavior called knowing. . . . Self-knowledge is of social origin. It is only when a person's private world becomes important to others that it is made important to him. It then enters into the control of the behavior called knowing. But self-knowledge has a special value to the individual himself. A person who has been 'made aware of himself' by the questions he has been asked is in a better position to predict and control his own behavior. (1974, p. 31)

Contained within these excerpts are guidelines for the construction of contingencies that promote self-observation and self-awareness. The classroom exercises that are offered here in response to these guidelines are by no means considered as definitive. Instead, the reader is encouraged to refer to these excerpts again after he/she has participated in the exercises so that a critical appraisal of the exercises may be promoted along with suggestions for improvements.

Exercise 1

Textual control of awareness

It may take several readings of these introductory paragraphs before they develop sufficient discriminative control over your behaviour. One way to help facilitate this process is for you to leave time for contemplation after reading each paragraph.

Paragraph 1

Imagine a scientist (B) observing another person (A). When A is engaged in behaviour such as observing his/her world 'inside' (i.e., introspecting) or observing the world 'outside', B's scientific behaviour can express itself in the conclusion that A's behaviours are a function of his/her current and historical context. But B's observing and categorising behaviour of A can also be seen as a focal point of his/her current and historical context, as viewed by another person 'C'; in other words, B is both the observer and the observed. The same applies to C as viewed by 'D', and to D as viewed by E, and so on ad infinitum.

Paragraph 2

Imagine now what would happen if you set out to implement the linear progression in the above scenario. One way you could do this would be to get together all of the people on the earth and align them in one long chain. However, if you did this you would soon run into an obvious problem; that is, there is only a finite number of people on the earth. Once you had reached the last person in the chain you would be forced to conclude that the practical demonstration of an infinite progression is impossible in a finite world. This argument is all the more cogent when you consider that each one of us, from a certain perspective is already that last person in the chain. You may, of course, argue that the problem of an infinite progression could be addressed by arranging the people into a circle. However, this way of thinking is different from above in that it presupposes that the first person will eventually be observing the last person in the chain.

What lesson is to be drawn from your reading of these two paragraphs? The intention behind writing them was simply to construct two pieces of text that produced different but related feelings. The first paragraph was designed to give you the feeling that infinity 'exists', whereas in the second paragraph that feeling was made to disappear. (Whether you agree or disagree with each of the arguments in the paragraphs is immaterial. I am only concerned that you respond differently to each of them.) That text can have powerful control over one's feelings and imagining behaviour is common knowledge, but insofar as this chapter is concerned with experiments in self-observation, the analysis of the differential effects that were produced by these two paragraphs provides important guidelines for how one should proceed.

A useful starting point is to consider how the respective views portrayed in the paragraphs shed light on the meaning of the term 'infinite progression'. The incompatibility of these views in effect demonstrates that this term is only a label for a particular type of imagining behaviour. To be more precise, your understanding of this term can be seen as an indication of the extent to which you have been taught to consider it as an appropriate label for a specific type of private event that occurred as a consequence of you reading Paragraph 1.

Clearly this analysis of your understanding behaviour is framed from the perspective of someone observing you. That is, another person would characterise the consequences of your reading behaviour (i.e., the feeling that infinity exists) as a specific type of change in you that was somehow related to the nature of the text. (Notice how this realisation marks a shift in emphasis from 'inside' to 'outside' when it comes to specifying the source of control over private events.) The advantage of adopting this perspective is that a crucial point now arises when you consider the way you would be functioning if you could arrive at a similar conclusion about your own behaviour. In effect, the 'you' who interacted with and was self-absorbed by the first paragraph (call this ME 1) would be replaced by a different way of functioning (call this ME 2). Functioning from this new perspective usually occasions the use of the term 'self-awareness'. Metaphorically speaking, you would have managed to step outside of your own behaviour. (This doesn't mean that there are two of you, you and your self. Rather, any suggestion of a duality is merely a characteristic feature of our style of talking when reference is made to the transition from one mode of functioning to another.)

Perhaps an interesting way for you to further your understanding of what is meant here would be for you to try and become fully self-aware with respect to changes produced within the context of this current paragraph. Giving attention to the nature of this process provides you with an opportunity to reflect upon the efficacy of the analysis offered above. Before beginning this process, however, consider the fact that when I drew your attention to the practicalities involved in working with the human chain in Paragraph 2 you were drawn away from the depth of feeling one normally associates with the term 'infinite progression'. In fact the imagining behaviour of 'progressing' was replaced by the behaviour of 'experimenting' i.e., in its simplest form, making something happen. (Actually, the experiment itself was also only an imaginary activity and it didn't have to be carried out for the shift in perspective to have been accomplished.) Inasmuch as this current paragraph has so far produced a different feeling relative to the feelings produced by all the paragraphs above, you have already been seduced into another 'transition'. This time, however, it is likely that you will readily formulate an explanation as to why you have your current feelings. This is in marked contrast to your behaviour in the context of Paragraphs 1 and 2 where 'it may never have occurred to you to do this'.

The process of relating changes in one's behaviour to changes in the environment functions as a way of transforming the observer into the observed and thereby increasing awareness of oneself. As another example, consider now how you may have functioned intuitively as the observer when you first picked up this book and began reading this chapter. By the time you got to this sentence you had read the previous pages. You may even have formulated some phrase or other to summarise your reaction to what I have said so far. Perhaps the longer you stay in this paragraph the more likely you are to recognise that you made a transition some time ago but had forgotten how it affected you. Whatever you feel now, it may be difficult for you to verbalise the nature of the change that has taken place, but you may now be aware that certain contingencies are responsible for this feeling.

In terms of personal experimentation, you are in a position to experiment further and attain another perspective which again transcends your current perspective of you the observer (i.e., the you who is currently reading this sentence) into you the observed. See if you can do it now before continuing with the text below!

There are a number of reasons why you may be reading this paragraph just now. If we work with your behaviour of reading it for the first time, then it is possible to discern three main reasons for this behaviour. Firstly, you may have 'ignored' the request at the end of the previous paragraph and simply continued reading. This possibility would reflect the power of your environmental history in ensuring that the behaviour of reading an article until the end is reached continues as per usual. A second possible reason for reaching this paragraph is that you have been successful in following the previous request. If this possibility applies, then you may find it interesting to contemplate the power of that simple request in terms of the context in which it is embedded. Finally, you may be reading this paragraph because you were not able to accomplish what was requested of you, or else you feel frustrated at not understanding what it is I am driving at. In either case I would ask you now to just wait until your current feeling passes; do not continue with your reading of the chapter; **STOP!**

In behavioural epistemology, the pragmatic step of controlling a behavioural phenomenon plays a crucial role in the delineation of what is regarded as an explanation. If, as part of a particular experiment, you can arrange circumstances such that an organism is likely to engage in a specific behaviour, then from a behaviour analytic perspective the search for an explanation of the organism's behaviour has stopped. The contingencies that allow for the prediction and control of behaviour provide the explanation for that behaviour. The relevance of this to personal experimentation has already been alluded to in the text above. That is, part of the explanation for any changes which occurred in you as you read each of the paragraphs above can be found in the manner in which the text was structured. Furthermore, the reading of this paper can in itself be considered as an exercise in personal experimentation.[13] In lay terms you made a decision to read this paper knowing in advance, consciously or unconsciously, that it would change you in some way. Given this perspective, it is important to understand the rationale behind the design of the text so that the understanding of how to 'control' can be relinquished by the writer and 'given' to the reader in order for further experimentation to be conducted. An example of further experimentation is given below, but first here is a summary of the steps that were taken in designing the text above:

1 Paragraphs 1 and 2 were presented for you to read.

2 Your attention was then drawn to the way that you were changed by each of these paragraphs; producing awareness of how you had changed.

3 Your attention was then drawn to the discriminative control responsible for the change in your feelings; producing awareness of why you had changed.

4 Steps 1, 2, & 3 were provided as a way of developing a short experimental history which might encourage the emergence of a different calibre of awareness,[14] i.e., the behaviour of 'recognising a transition'. Once established, this awareness accompanies future transitions,[14] i.e., it becomes incorporated into the behaviour of monitoring the nature of subsequent transitions.

5 Further opportunities were created that allowed you to practise changing your awareness.

[13] Neuringer's (1991) Two–Labs strategy for the study of covert phenomena is relevant here: 'Self-experimenter W observes a covert phenomenon as [a] dependent or independent variable, publishes the findings, and self-experimenter Z attempts to replicate. The goal of self-experimental covert research is descriptions of intersubjectively reliable functional relationships' (p. 45). Everyone who reads this paper is participating in the same 'experiment'. The relative changes that are produced may vary across subjects, but if the contingencies are properly designed then the relative changes that are produced in each person should occur at roughly the same location. At the same time, each person may be aware of his/her relative changes but their descriptions of these changes are not the changes themselves.

[14] The recurrence of this behaviour (i.e., 'recognising a transition') constitutes the act of self-remembering that was considered by Gurdjieff and Ouspensky (see Nicholl, 1984) to be an essential step in the development of higher states of consciousness. Increasing the probability of this behaviour has also been considered by some (e.g., Krishnamurti, 1986, 1988) to be a primary objective of personal explorations of private behavioural changes; this is so even when there are no manifest changes in the environment outside of the body, as in some forms of meditation for example.

One problem with the method, and the medium, used above to produce changes in you and to 'reflect them back onto you' is that the changes were probably too subtle and therefore difficult for you to monitor; notwithstanding the powerful effects of your environmental history in determining your acceptance of an unconventional writing style for an academic paper. To circumvent some of these problems the exercise below was developed as a way of producing more significant behavioural changes for you to monitor.

The objective of the exercise is similar to the discussion above in that it raises pertinent issues in the study of private events. The design of the exercise relies heavily on differential effects associated with contingency-shaped and rule-governed behaviour. By providing an opportunity for a contrast to emerge between an imagined reality[15] and a currently experienced reality[16] you can learn how to recognise characteristics of your own private behaviour. Making opportunities for that type of contrast to appear is one of the simplest ways of self experimentation. In one sense, then, the exercise functions as a 'mirror' for one's private behaviour so that, for example, in this instance the behaviour of predicting can be seen for what it is, i.e., an activity arising out of the dynamic interplay of current and historical contexts; or said another way, the behaviour of predicting is an extension of the past into the present. The principal message of the exercise can be extracted from the following maxim: it is important to recognise the limitations of your conclusions; the biggest problem you will have, however, is first of all to recognise when you are 'in a conclusion'.

The whole exercise is more easily understood with the help of the schematic diagram of the behavioural stream shown in Figure 2. The diagram is composed of two related parts with the larger human figure (in fact there are two versions of the same person, one opaque and one 'translucent') in the foreground representing a more abstract version of the scene depicted in the film strip on the left-hand side. Points A, B, C, and D represent 'snapshots' in time. A person who is observed at each of these times has arrived there by virtue of his/her preceding interaction with the environment. Suppose, for example, a person is initially observed at point A; this point we will call the 'present'. Further experiences/interactions with the environment lead the person to point B. At point B, A becomes a 'past'; B, which was formally a 'future', becomes a present and C becomes a 'future'. At point C, B becomes a past; C, which was formally a future, becomes a present and D becomes a future, etc. How this diagram can be used to help us analyse the behaviour of 'anticipating the future' is rather simple. The consequences of the way one covertly and overtly behaves while moving from A to B results in similar or dissimilar behaviour when moving from B to C, etc. As a person interacts with the environment,

---

[15]   The phenomenological perspective which functions as predicting behaviour.
[16]   The phenomenological perspective/foundations from which the predicting behaviour emerges.

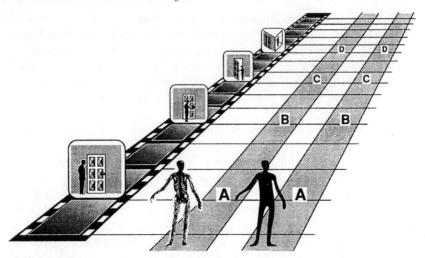

Figure 2:   Snapshots in time of the behavioural stream of an imaginary person engaged in Exercise 2. See text for details.

then, it is evident that the act of anticipating can only arise as a function of previous experiences. Furthermore, this behaviour is observed to occur in the present because the past is over with and because the future has not yet happened.

As a more concrete example of this analysis, the film strip on the left-hand side of the diagram represents a few of the possible stages contained in the exercise below. In the strip a person is shown initially standing in front of a closed door (point A). He then puts his hand on the door handle (point B), opens it and enters through it (point C), and he is finally shown standing on the other side of the door (point D). In the exercise a person at point A is asked to imagine what it is like on the other side of the door of the room that they are currently in. In effect, he/she is asked to imagine what it would feel like to be at point D. The interesting aspect of this request is that a person will almost always acknowledge that of course he/she knows what it feels like to be on the other side of the door! But how can they when that world does not yet exist for them? One can not experience the contingencies associated with point D unless one is at point D. Consequently, the imaginative behaviour which occurs at point A must necessarily differ from the full blown experience of being at point D. In what sense, then, do they 'know' what it is like to be on the other side of the door? The answer to this question represents another major objective of the exercise. That is, the exercise was in part designed to teach the idea that 'know' in this context is a word used to label a feeling of familiarity (i.e., a recurring private behaviour) which arises because of the combined effects of instructions and previously experienced contingencies. As has already been mentioned, the act of taking note of changes in one's private behaviour and relating these changes to the environmental context is a key step in behaving with self-awareness. Finally, given that one can be taught to differentiate between the two classes of behaviour discussed here (i.e., imagining behaviour and 'actual' behaviour[17]), it is an easy step to generalise from the exercise and teach the functional significance of current and historical contexts in the production of other behaviour apart from anticipatory behaviour.

[17] In the public arena measurement is a particular type of observational behaviour brought under discriminative control and through it scientists have categories with which to work. But scientific behaviour also includes comparison, i.e., relating one measurement to another. Scientific behaviour in general, then, can be seen as relational observation that is under discriminative control. In the case of private events, the categories one works with are necessarily defined as relative changes. Relative changes can be monitored no matter how ineffable or 'fuzzy' the edges of the behavioural categories. When there is sufficient relative change to produce a 'noticing response' then a scientific observation can be said to have taken place.

Exercise 2

The Private Events of Past and Future

This exercise should be conducted in a room that has its windows covered. Select a few volunteers and then read the following instructions slowly to each of them.

Initial relaxation and orientation
The first thing that I want you to do is to close your eyes for about one minute and just relax.

Before you open your eyes I want you to concentrate on the feeling of your presence in this room. I want you to get a summary in your mind's eye of what it means to be you at this particular moment in time.

Enhancement of contextual control
Now that you have an image of your presence I want you to add to it by opening your eyes.

I want you to feel the impact of all of the physical objects that come into contact with your field of view. Concentrate on my presence; on the walls surrounding you; on the lighting in the room; on the presence of others . . . . I want you to concentrate if you can on the feeling you have of actually being IN a room. That is, there is a world outside of here which for the moment is not accessible to you.

Stimulation of covert behaviour (imagination)
We are now ready to proceed with the next step in this experiment. I want you to *imagine* what it feels like to be outside of this room. Try to create in your mind's eye the feeling you would get if you were outside of this room. Imagine that *feeling* you would get if you were on the other side of the door.

Priming imagining behaviour so that it persists until contact is made with a changed environment
Now that you have hold of that I want you to do something very simple. In a moment I will be asking you to actually leave the room and stand outside the door. Before you go, however, I would like you to pay close attention to my next instruction.

When you reach the other side of the door I want you to notice the contrast between your imagination of what it would feel like to be there and what it actually feels like. Also, as this new experience continues to grow I want you to notice how the intensity of your present experience gradually recedes until it is 'just a memory'. In other words, there will come a point when you notice your current experience is just a memory, like the memory you have now of what it feels like to be *outside* of this room.

. . . . REPEAT THE SECTION ABOVE IF NECESSARY . . . .

Priming a potential new imagining behaviour so that it persists until contact is made with a second change in the environment
When you reach this point I want you to prepare yourself for the next stage of the experiment. I want you summarize in your mind's eye the feeling you have as you stand there. Having done that I want you to imagine what it will feel like to be on the other side of the door.

When you are ready I want you to open the door and enter. As you enter I want you to notice the contrast between what it actually feels like and what you thought it would feel like.

Summary of instructions
Are you clear as to what you are to do? Just to summarise: firstly, I want you to pay attention to the 'decrease' in the intensity of your current experience and the initial 'increase' in the intensity of your new experience. Then, after you have adapted to the new experience I want you to return. As you return I want you to notice the initial 'increase' in the intensity of the next new experience and the 'decrease' in intensity of the feeling you got from being outside of the room.

Priming self-consciousness
One final point. As you return, you may notice a special relationship between yourself and me. If you do feel this I would like you to consider the possibility that I know of something that is going on inside your head. *End of instructions*

Send your volunteers out of the room one at a time and wait a few minutes after he/she returns before sending the next one. Do not allow a discussion to develop until everyone has gone through the exercise. It is advisable to work with a limited number of people (about three or four) in a session. When all volunteers have returned you can begin a class discussion. Below is a list of possible topics you could cover:

1. Did anyone feel slightly 'paranoid' or separate from the group as they returned to the room? (This only happens sometimes, more so with shy individuals.)

2. Did everyone appreciate the contrast between their imagination of an experience and the actual experience itself?

3. Imagination of an IN or an OUT experience was only possible given the previous environmental history with these or similar experiences.

4. Emphasise the power of the environment to produce the changes which were experienced; without the NEW interaction with the environment there would have been no NEW experience of that environment.

5. How many times a day do similar transitions between experiences occur without the attention that was given to them to-day? What would be the benefit of giving more attention to the ways in which we change in particular contexts?[18]

6. Talk to the class members who didn't participate in the experiment and draw attention to the power of verbal behaviour to move humans across space and time. Talk about the volunteers as if they were no longer in the room. (It can also help if you talk to the class about a volunteer while he/she is talking.) This helps to focus your listeners' attention to the demands made on the scientist in his/her attempt to be objective.

7. Draw attention to the variability in verbal reports from the volunteers in the experiment.

8. Verbal reports are not effective in producing changes comparable to those produced by direct contact with the environment. To start a discussion on this and on the general notions of contingency-shaped and rule-governed behaviour ask your volunteers to communicate to the class the changes which occurred within them during the experiment. Draw attention to the fact that unless the rules of the procedures are followed there can be no 'understanding' of the effect of the contingencies.

9. If you are working with an advanced class, discuss the problems posed by the study of private events.

10. Terminate the session by discussing the diagram of the behavioural stream and show how it can be used to develop the concept of the three-term contingency.

There may be issues that are raised in discussion with your class that can be incorporated into sessions with other classes. A goal to keep in mind is that you should gather as much information as possible so that with future classes you can improve your chances of teasing students into believing that you can read their minds.

---

[18] Insofar as this exercise helps to draw attention to contingencies responsible for 'futuring' and 'pasting' behaviour it serves as a useful introduction to other writings concerned with similar issues. Consider, for example, the following two quotations: 'The essence of meditation is nowness. Whatever one tries to practice, is not aimed at achieving a higher state or at following some theory or ideal, but simply, without any object or ambition, trying to see what is here and now. One has to become aware of the present moment. . . .' (Trungpa, 1969, quoted in Brandon, 1990, p. 63)

'Living in the here and now is behaviour derived from the Zen experience. Guilt and anxiety are children of the past and future. To the extent that a person dwells upon the should-have-been or might-be of life at the expense of living life in the reality of the present, he suffers.' (Keefe, 1975, quoted in Brandon, 1990, p. 63)

Exercise 3

'W'-ing

Methodological behaviorists, like logical positivists, argued that science must confine itself to events that can be observed by two or more people; truth must be truth by agreement. There is a private world of feelings and states of mind, but it is out of reach of a second person and hence of science. That was not a very satisfactory position, of course. How people feel is often as important as what they do (Skinner, 1989, p. 3)

This statement by Skinner would undoubtedly come as a surprise to students who have been led to view behaviourism as 'black-box' psychology. Their teachers who are responsible for propounding this view may be admonished for doing so. However, as is well known, punishment by itself does not result in the establishment of new behaviours; other contingencies must be implemented so that the desired behaviour ensues. If we work with the premise that 'the rat is always right', then the teachers, who themselves were former students, are responding as a consequence of the combined effects of personal environmental histories and the instructional contingencies to which they were exposed in the classroom. Any misrepresentation by them may, perhaps, be a result of the existing imbalance between the plethora of methodologically sophisticated procedures designed for studying public behaviours and the paucity of pro-cedures concerned with private events. The three exercises described here were conceived as possible ways of redressing this imbalance. They provide scope for discussions of behavioural interpretations of the relationship between public and private behaviours by arranging contingencies within the classroom so that students can see at first hand the effects of those contingencies.

Earlier it was noted that many of the conclusions reached by scientists are initially contingency-shaped. The problem of teaching, then, is a problem of disseminating these conclusions in light of the fact that there are differential effects associated with contingency-shaped and rule-governed behaviour. Accordingly, there may be occasions when one must be careful not to fall into the trap of expecting students to dutifully remember these conclusions without them ever tasting the hunt that inspired them. In this final exercise we explore issues concerned with the labelling of private events (see Skinner 1953, chapter 17). The word 'explore' is chosen deliberately because the exercise is designed to provoke questions in students rather than to supply them with answers.

Priming an appreciation of the contrast between 'external' stimulus control and 'internal' stimulus control

In this exercise I want to explore the idea of 'separateness'. To start with, I would like you to consider the simple notion that your presence is part of my environment and that my presence is part of your environment.

As you each see me now, you can discern the edges of my being. You can see where my body begins and where it ends. To some extent, I appreciate your perspective of me because I perceive something similar when I look at each of you. However, when I close my eyes and look into the darkness I can no longer see any edges; mind you, I can feel the semblance of edges that form parts of my body. From here, though, I don't fully appreciate the edges which you see in me.

Now I would like you close your eyes and to look for your own edges in the way that I have just done.

So close your eyes.

Stimulation of covert behaviour

For the rest of the time I would like you to keep your eyes closed until I tell you to open them.

In this section I will be asking you to concentrate on various parts of your body. Let's start with your feet.

I want you to concentrate on the feeling in your feet. Without moving your feet, I want you to concentrate on the tightness of your shoes around them. Now, if you can, I want you to trace in mind's eye the outline of the shoe around your foot.

Next, I want you to concentrate on your ankles.

Now the calves of your legs.

And now your knees.

Moving up a little higher, I want you to concentrate on your hips as they press against the seat of your chair.

I want you to feel the expanse of your back.

And now your shoulders.

I now want you to concentrate on your arms, and then your hands. Some of you have your hands on the desk, while some of you are supporting your head with your hands. I want you to feel the point of contact whichever way you hands are positioned.

Now, still keeping your eyes closed and without moving, I want you to concentrate on the feeling you have of a person beside you. Notice how it feels as if you are actively doing something. You can actually feel a change taking place on that side of your body. I'll give you a second or two until you have accurately localised this activity.

Tacting a feeling

I now want to do something very simple. I want to give this feeling an arbitrary name. I want to call it 'W'. At this very moment, then, I can quite freely conclude that you are all 'W'-ing.

If I were to ask you if you knew what it means to 'W', you would be able to answer affirmatively. So, again, to 'W' is to persist in that which you are doing just now.

Using the tact as a basis for stimulating further covert activity

Now that you are able to 'W' you can appreciate, perhaps, a small increase in awareness of yourself. Consider for a moment an interesting possibility that might follow from this. Wouldn't it be fascinating if our society could teach us to identify and label a host of experiences like this?

Making a link between newly-stimulated covert activity and previously-stimulated covert activity

The funny thing is, it has already done so. I have just demonstrated this to you: foot, ankle, calves, . . . Can you feel them again?

Using recently learned behaviour as a basis for stimulating 'questioning behaviour' and 'imagining behaviour'

There is an interesting problem here. I cannot feel what you are feeling, yet I taught you how to label a feeling that only you have access to. How was I able to do this? Indeed, how was I able to design the exercise in the first place?

Shaping 'understanding behaviour'

Keep your eyes closed.

When your eyes were open at the start of the exercise you were aware of our separateness. Now you are sensitive to the energy of my words as if they somehow reached inside of you and moved you around. You may also have noticed that those times in which you were moved around in a familiar way were the times when you would probably feel inclined to use the word 'understanding' to characterise this familiarity. In other words, 'understand' is a word you use to describe something you do, much the same way that you would use 'W'.[19]

Imagine for a moment the difficulty you would have in explaining to someone the nature of 'W'-ing. After you leave this class, for example, imagine telling your friends that you 'W'-ed today. It would be like using words to describe to an Eskimo what a banana tastes like. The understanding of 'W'-ing comes from the doing of it.

---

[19] See Morris, 1990 and Schnaitter, 1987.

The skin does not separate you from the world, it unites you to it: An appreciation.

To close this session I want to return for a moment to the idea of separateness. I have here a few quotations from a book by Fritjof Capra called *The Tao of Physics* (Capra, 1975). In this book Capra relates the conclusions of some modern nuclear physicists with some conclusions reached by Eastern philosophers and mystics.

To help prepare you for these quotations, I would like you, still with your eyes closed, to focus on the space which separates our physical bodies.

Physicists now tell us that if the molecules which constitute this space are divided into atoms and these atoms are further divided, and so on, we reach a point when there is no separately existing matter.

Here is the first quotation:

When we divide some gross (or composite) matter, we can reduce it to atoms. But as the atom will also be subject to further division, all forms of material existence, whether gross or fine, are nothing but the shadow of particularisation and we cannot describe any degree of (absolute or independent) reality to them. (p. 292)

Here's another:

In ordinary life we are not aware of this unity of all things but divide the world into separate objects and events. This division is, of course, useful and necessary to cope with our everyday environment, but it is not a fundamental feature of reality. It is an abstraction devised by our discriminating and categorizing intellect. To believe that our abstract concepts of separate 'thing' and 'events' are realities of nature is an illusion (p. 277)

And another:

It is an artificial attitude that makes sections in the stream of change, and calls them things . . . When we shall know the truth of things, we shall realise how absurd it is for us to worship isolated products of the incessant series of transformations as though they were real or eternal. Life is no thing or state of a thing, but a continuous movement or change (p. 278)

May I remind you here that 'w'-ing was not a static event but a process of change that was localised within you.

Another quotation:

The Buddhist does not believe in an independent or separately existing world into whose dynamic forces he could insert himself. The external world and his inner world are for him only two sides of the same fabric, in which the threads of all forces and of all events, of all forms of consciousness and of their objects, are moving into an inseparable net of endless, mutually conditioned relations (p. 143).

Stimulation of post-session investigative behaviour.

I will leave you now with an interesting question. How separate are we really, and to what extent do we help to determine the nature of each other's consciousness?[20]

You may open your eyes now.

[20] See Blackman, 1991.

Conclusion

Although the public behaviour of a person can be controlled and thus predicted without referencing associated private behaviour, this does not in any way condemn private behaviour as unworthy of investigation (cf. Hayes & Hayes, 1992). On the contrary, it may be the case that an overriding concern for truth by public agreement has usurped the usefulness of prediction and control as important guidelines for exploring the private behaviour of the observer. Alternatively, it may be simply that there is still much to be done to address the difficulties in developing suitable teaching gambits to complement the existing philosophy of radical behaviourism.

Much of what Skinner said in the analysis of private events could be viewed as a commentary on the legacy of our childhood. The challenge to the teacher is to make Skinner's arguments persuasive. One way to do that is to take control of private events in the manner outlined here. To do so means continuing, in a sense, with the practices previously employed by our parents. The seriousness with which we adhere to the notion that self-knowledge is of social origin can be judged best by how we teach it. Said another way, the suggestion that the 'verbal community can solve the problem of privacy to the extent that it can establish a best fit in its shaping of verbal terms for private events' (Chiesa, 1994, p. 189) will find more support if it moves beyond the level of description to practical examples. Perhaps the experiences of behaviour analysts working in clinical settings will prove essential for the development of such practicals (Cordova & Koerner, 1993; Follette, Bach & Follette, 1993; Hayes & Wilson, 1993; Kohlenberg, Tsai, & Dougher, 1993).

Skinner (1990) said that one of his great aims in life was 'to discover what it means to be a knower' (p. 103). Many students come to psychology on similar quests. It is hoped that exercises like the ones described here may function as establishing operations (Michael, 1993) that provoke self-experimentation by students (cf. Neuringer, 1984). After all, looking at it from a student's point of view, if they can be shown that an every-day activity like walking through a door presents a veritable gold mine of opportunities for exploration, they might be more intrigued by what our discipline has to offer. In conclusion, it is important to remember that the art of teaching behaviour analysis involves more than the design of contingencies to enable students to remember the facts of behaviour. It also involves an appreciation that the students we teach will be the ones who develop our discipline further:

You don't draw people into science by saying that science is the basis of technical innovation – which it is – because that's too remote when you are at school. But if you can say, these are the big questions we are asking and we are making progress, and you can help us to answer some of the questions, then you are making science come alive. (Efstathiou, 1993, p. 33)

Appendix 1

Koyaanisqatsi and the Behavioural Stream

The film Koyaanisqatsi (directed by Godfrey Reggio) contains some fascinating time-lapse photography of life in a city. Because behaviour is shown to occur at a high rate, students are confronted with overall patterns that make it difficult to engage in mentalistic analyses. By way of an introduction to this section of the film the following passage can be read to students:

Imagine for a moment that you have been given a special privilege. On a day of your choosing you are invited to sit on top of a hill overlooking a small village. The village is normal in appearance, with cottages, a school, a church, a few shops, and a pub.

Imagine now that you are on the hill beneath the shade of a tree resplendent in a profusion of tiny blossoms. You close your eyes and concentrate on the rhythm of your breathing. The more you concentrate on this rhythm the more you find your breathing slowing down. The movement of every scented inhalation is accompanied by an infusion of relaxation that fills your body from the top of your head to the tip of your toes. With the sound of every exhalation you discover forgotten traces of tension in your body and you watch dispassionately as they flake gently away from you. You begin to feel warm and secure and you notice your skin sensitive to the caresses of the air circulating around you.

When you feel ready to open your eyes you do so and you focus your attention expectantly on the village. Removed in time and in space from the people in the village you prepare yourself to watch life flow past at an incredible rate.

The sky changes and beneath flickering cycles of night and day the village is shrouded in the pulse of the changing seasons. From within each household synchro-nised streams of life emerge, continuously shaping and being shaped by their physical and social embankments. Children passing through adult children etch a myriad of patterns across the plane of your perspective. Eventually the changes arising throughout the entirety of each villager's life appear before you in one frozen image as a mesh of giant interconnected snowflakes, each with their repetitions of form.

Gazing at the majesty of this scene you find yourself filled with a sense of wonder-ment. Untold secrets are now at your disposal and you need only go down into the village to collect them. You close your eyes once more and quieten yourself in readiness.

With calmness and clarity of mind attained you again open your eyes and scan the intricacies of the frozen movement. Your awareness of its impending dissolution prompts you to carefully harness your attention so that you can focus effectively on particular features. You don the protective clothing of disciplined and systematic thinking and make your way down into the village.

Once the film is finished you can inform the students that behaviour analysts are engaged in the development of a holistic perspective which views human behaviour as inseparable from the context in which it is observed. This perspective is critical of traditional assumptions implicit in the mentalism of mainstream academic psychology. Tell the students that a useful exercise for them would be to consider how the 36 million minutes of each of their lives on earth would appear from the hill. Like one of the villagers, they also would be seen as the focal point of changes that follow the contours of the environment through which they pass. It follows from this that if this is the case for them, then it is necessarily so for other people who behave in ways that are classified as scientific; that is, it must not be forgotten that a scientist is also a child who has been taught to relate to the world in specific ways? This realisation begs a question as to what becomes of the term 'explanation'?

At this point you can refer to a segment which shows the throbbing of the traffic in a city. Point out the fact that each of the people sitting in the cars is a unique individual, 'free' to make decisions about when to start and stop the car. Note that any reference to what the drivers are thinking does not supply an explanation for their behaviour. Instead it leaves unanswered the question as to why the driver is thinking in this way. You can refer to the current context in terms of how the city is designed (buildings and traffic lights) and the sequence in which the lights change colours as contributing to decisions that are made by each driver. Point out that if the buildings were organised differently, and/or if the light sequences were reorganised you would end up watching a different pattern of driving behaviour. This means that the explanation for the new and old patterns that are observed is to be found in the way in which the environment is organised. Be sure to mention that you are not dismissing the personal experience of the drivers, that is they are not black boxes. You are merely looking at the way in which current context determines that experience. At this point you can refer to the role played by historical factors in the development of your explanation (This analysis is contextualistic in character; see Morris, 1980, 1992; Hayes, 1987, 1988; Hayes & Hayes, 1992; Hayes, Hayes & Reese, 1988). That is, buildings had to be build (end-products of architects' and town planners' behaviours), cars had to be built, drivers had to be trained to respond to traffic lights. These historical factors evolved into the situation that was observed. At this point you can show another clip of the film on the car assembly line and work through a similar analysis for the explanation of the behavioural pattern being observed. At this point you could fast forward a video of an animal on a schedule.[21] This easily reveals patterns that can be discussed while at the same time keeping mentalistic analyses at arm's length. Once you have worked through the video material you can introduce the diagrams on the behavioural stream and work through the basic argument again.

[21] Members of the behavioral community should take note that there is no commercially produced video material for classroom use of animal performances on the basic schedules of reinforcement. Teachers who do not have access to animal facilities, or who may also not have training in specific areas of Applied Behaviour Analysis, have a difficult task of persuading students to be interested in the ways that behaviour can be controlled by contingencies when demonstrations are not abundantly available for classroom use.

References

Barnes, D. (1989). Behavior-behavior analysis, human schedule performance, and radical behaviorism. *The Psychological Record, 39*, 339–350.

Blackman, D. E. (1991). B. F. Skinner & G. H. Mead: On biological science and social science. *Journal of the Experimental Analysis of Behavior, 55*, 251–265.

Brandon, D. (1990). *Zen in the art of helping*. London: Arkana.

Briggs, J. P. & Peat, F. D. (1984). *The looking glass universe*. London: Fontana.

Capra, F. (1975). *The tao of physics*. Berkley: Shambala

Catania, A. C. (1991). The gifts of culture and of eloquence: An open letter to Michael J. Mahoney in reply to his article, 'Scientific psychology and radical behaviorism'. *The Behavior Analyst, 14*, 61–72.

Chiesa, M. (1994). *Radical behaviorism: The philosophy and the science*. Boston: Authors Cooperative.

Cordova, J. V. & Koerner, K. (1993). Persuasion criteria in research and practice: Gathering more meaningful psychotherapy data. *The Behavior Analyst, 16*, 317–330.

Creel, R. E. (1987). Skinner on science. In S. Modgil & C. Modgil (Eds), *B. F. Skinner: Consensus and controversy*. New York: Falmer Press.

Day, W. F. (1969). On certain similarities between the philosophical investigations of Ludwig Wittgenstein and the operationism of B. F. Skinner. *Journal of the Experimental Analysis of Behavior, 12*, 489–506.

Efstathiou, G. (1993). *New Scientist*, 26 June.

Epstein, R. (1984). Simulation research in the analysis of behavior. *Behaviorism, 12*, 41–59.

Epstein, R. (1985). Animal cognition as the praxist views it. *Neuroscience and Biobehavioral Reviews, 9*, 623–630.

Eysenck, H. J., Arnold, W. J., & Meili, R. (1975). *Encyclopaedia of psychology: Volume 2, L–Z*. London: Fontana.

Follette, W. C., Bach, P. A., & Follette, V. M. (1993). A behavior-analytic view of psychological health. *The Behavior Analyst, 16*, 303–316.

Hayes, S. C. (1987). A contextual approach to therapeutic change. In N. Jacobsen (Ed.), *Psychotherapists in clinical practice: Cognitive and behavioral perspectives*. New York: Guildford.

Hayes, S. C. (1988). Contextualism and the next wave of behavioral psychology. *Behavior Analysis, 23*, 7–22.

Hayes, S. C. & Brownstein, A. J. (1986). Mentalism, behavior-behavior relations and a behavior-analytic view of the purposes of science. *The Behavior Analyst, 9*, 174–190.

Hayes, S. C. & Brownstein, A. (1987). Mentalism, private events, and scientific explanation: A defence of B. F. Skinner's view. In S. Modgil & C. Modgil (Eds), *B. F. Skinner: Consensus and controversy*. New York: Falmer Press.

Hayes, S. C. & Hayes, L. J. (1992). Some clinical implications of contextualistic behaviorism: The example of cognition. *Behavior Therapy, 23*, 225–249.

Hayes, S. C., Hayes, L. J., & Reese, H. W. (1988). Finding the philosophical core: A review of Stephen C. Pepper's world hypotheses: A study in evidence. *Journal of the Experimental Analysis of Behavior, 50*, 97–111.

Hayes, S. C. & Wilson, K. G. (1993). Some applied implications of a contemporary behavior-analytic account of verbal events. *The Behavior Analyst, 16*, 283–301.

Hineline, P. N. (1990). The origins of environment-based psychological theory. *Journal of the Experimental Analysis of Behavior, 53*, 305–320.

Johnston, M. (1989). Did I begin? *New Scientist, Dec. 9*, 39–42.

Johnston, M. K. & Pennypacker, H. S. (1980). *Strategies and tactics of human behavioral research*. Hillsdale, NJ: Erlbaum.

Keenan, M. & Toal, L. (1991). Periodic reinforcement and second-order schedules. *The Psychological Record, 41*, 87–115.

Kohlenberg, B. S., Hayes, S. C., & Hayes, L. J. (1991). The transfer of contextual control over equivalence classes through equivalence classes: A possible model of social stereotyping. *Journal of the Experimental Analysis of Behavior, 56*, 505–518.

Kohlenberg, R. J., Tsai, M. & Dougher, M. J. (1993). The dimensions of clinical behavior analysis. *The Behavior Analyst, 16*, 271–282.

Krishnamurti, J. (1986). *The awakening of intelligence*. London: V. Gollancz.

Krishnamurti, J. (1988). *The first and last freedom*. London: V. Gollancz.

Lee, V. L. (1981). The operant as a class of responses. *Scandinavian Journal of Psychology, 22*, 215–221.

Lee, V. L. (1985). Scientific knowledge as rules that guide behavior. *The Psychological Record, 35*, 183–192.

Lee, V. L. (1988). *Beyond behaviorism*. Hillsdale, NJ: Lawrence Erlbaum.

Lee, V. L. (1989). Comments about the isolation of behavior analysis. *The Behavior Analyst, 12*, 85–87.

Leigland, S. (1989a). On the relation between radical behaviorism and the science of verbal behavior. *The Analysis of Verbal Behavior, 7*, 25–41.

Leigland, S. (1989b). A functional analysis of mentalistic terms in human observers. *The Analysis of Verbal Behavior, 7*, 5–18.

Lonigan, C. J. (1990). Which behaviorism? A Reply to Mahoney. *American Psychologist, 45*, 1179–1181.

MacLeod, R. B. (1964). Phenomenology: A challenge to experimental psychology. In T. W. Wann (Ed.) *Behaviorism and phenomenology: Contrasting bases for modern psychology*. University of Chicago Press.

Marr, J. (1983). Memory: Models and metaphors. *The Psychological Record, 33*, 12–19.

Michael, J. (1982). Distinguishing between discriminative and motivational functions of stimuli. *Journal of the Experimental Analysis of Behavior, 37*, 149–155.

Michael, J. (1993). Establishing operations. *The Behavior Analyst, 16*, 191–206.

Moore, J. (1975). On the principle of operationism in the science of behavior. *Behaviorism, 3*, 120–138.

Moore, J. (1980). On behaviorism and private events. *The Psychological Record, 30*, 459–475.

Moore, J. (1981). On mentalism, methodological behaviorism, and radical behaviorism. *Behaviorism, 9*, 55–77.

Moore, J. (1985). Some historical and conceptual relations among logical positivism, operationism, and behaviorism. *The Behavior Analyst, 8*, 53–63.

Morris, E. K. (1985). Public information, dissemination, and behavior analysis. *The Behavior Analyst, 8*, 95–110.

Morris, E. K. (1980). Contextualism: The world view of behavior analysis. *Journal of Experimental Child Psychology, 46*, 289–323.

Morris, E. K. (1990). What Mahoney 'knows'. *American Psychologist, 45*, 1178–1179.

Morris, E. K. (1992). The aim, progress, and evolution of behavior analysis. *The Behavior Analyst, 15*, 3–29.

Morris, E. K., Higgins, S. T., & Bickel, W. K. (1982). Comments on cognitive science in the experimental analysis of behavior. *The Behavior Analyst, 5*, 109–125

Neuringer, A. (1981). Self-experimentation: A call for change. *Behaviorism, 9*, 79–94.

Neuringer, A. (1984). Melioration and self-experimentation. *Journal of the Experimental Analysis of Behavior, 42*, 397–406.

Neuringer, A. (1991). Behaviorism: Methodological, radical, assertive, sceptical, ethological, modest, humble, and evolving. *The Behavior Analyst, 14*, 43–47.

Nicholl, M. (1984). *Psychological commentaries on the teachings of Gurdjieff and Ouspensky.* Boston: Shambhala Publications.

Schnaitter, R. (1987). Knowledge as action: The epistemology of radical behaviorism. In S. Modgil & C. Modgil (Eds), *B. F. Skinner: Consensus and controversy.* New York: Falmer Press.

Schneider, S. M. & Morris, E. K. (1987). The history of the term *Radical Behaviorism*: From Watson to Skinner. *The Behavior Analyst, 10*, 27–40.

Schoenfeld, W. N. & Farmer, J. (1970). Reinforcement schedules and the 'behavior stream.' In W. N. Schoenfeld (Ed.), *The theory of reinforcement schedules.* New York: Appleton

Schwenk, T. (1990). *Sensitive chaos.* London: Rudolf Steiner.

Skinner, B. F. (1945). The operational analysis of psychological terms. *Psychological Review, 42*, 270–277.

Skinner, B. F. (1953). *Science and human behavior. New York*: Free Press

Skinner, B. F. (1964). Behaviorism at fifty. In T. W. Wann (Ed.) *Behaviorism and phenomenology: Contrasting bases for modern psychology.* University of Chicago Press.

Skinner, B. F. (1966). What is the experimental analysis of behavior? *Journal of the Experimental Analysis of Behavior, 9*, 213–218.

Skinner, B. F. (1974). *About behaviorism.* New York: Knopf.

Skinner, B. F. (1977). Why I am not a cognitive psychologist. *Behaviorism, 5*, 1–10.

Skinner, B. F. (1985). Cognitive science and behaviorism. *British Journal of Psychology, 76*, 291–301.

Skinner, B. F. (1988). The operational analysis of psychological terms. In A. C. Catania & S. Harnard (Eds) *The selection of behavior: The operant behaviorism of B. F. Skinner: Comments and consequences.* New York: Cambridge University Press.

Skinner, B. F. (1989). *Recent issues in the analysis of behavior.* Ohio: Merrill.

Skinner, B. F. (1990). To know the future. *The Behavior Analyst, 13*, 103–106.

Smith, L. D. (1986). *Behaviorism and logical positivism: A reassessment of the alliance.* Stanford: Stanford University Press.

Smith, N. W. (1985). Heredity and environment revisited. *The Psychological Record, 35*, 173–176.

Spinelli, E. (1989). *The Interpreted world.* London: Sage.

Terrell, D. J., & Johnston, J. M. (1989). Logic, reasoning and verbal behavior. *The Behavior Analyst, 12*, 35–44.

Ulrich, R. (1975). Toward experimental living, phase II: 'Have you ever heard of a man named Frazier, Sir?' In E. Ramp & G. Semb (Eds.), *Behavior analysis: Areas of research and application.* Englewood Cliffs, NJ: Prentice-Hall.

Wann, T. W. (1964) (Ed.). *Behaviorism and phenomenology: Contrasting bases for modern psychology.* University of Chicago Press.

Watt, A., Keenan, M., Barnes, D., & Cairns, E. (1991). Social categorization and stimulus equivalence. *The Psychological Record, 41*, 33–50.

Williams, J. L. (1986). The behavioral and the mystical: Reflections on behaviorism and eastern thought. *The Behavior Analyst, 9*, 167–173.

Wyatt, W. J. (1990). Radical behaviorism misrepresented: A reply to Mahoney. *American Psychologist, 45*, 1181–1183.

Zuriff, G. E. (1985). *Behaviorism: A conceptual reconstruction.* New York: Columbia University Press.

4

What are the reinforcers for cognitivism in behaviour therapy?[1]

Kevin J. Tierney and John A. Smith[2]

Abstract

Despite the fact that the evidence for the effectiveness of cognitive procedures in behaviour therapy is far from conclusive, there has been a shift by clinical psychologists away from the use of behavioural procedures towards the use of cognitive ones. We attempt to account for this situation by proposing that this shift in therapeutic practices may be determined by sources of reinforcement that are unrelated to the effectiveness of therapeutic procedures. Possible sources of reinforcement identified are differential reinforcement of cognitive verbal behaviour, immediacy of reinforcement derived from apparent client improvement, the inconspicuous nature of the presumed controlling variables, the fun derived from exploring inner thoughts, and cognitive-behaviour therapy's greater consistency with prevailing political and religious ideologies.

Introduction

In the first edition of their authoritative book, *The effects of psychological therapies*, Rachman and Wilson (1971) concluded that:

(*a*) behaviour therapy is frequently more effective than other forms of therapy;

(*b*) behaviour therapy has never been shown to be inferior to any alternative form of therapy;

[1] This paper was first published in *The Irish Journal of Psychology*, 1990, 11, 1, 24–30. Reprinted with permission.

[2] We wish to express our thanks to Julian Leslie for his helpful comments on an earlier draft of this paper.

(*c*) behaviour therapy is applicable to a wider range of problems than alternative therapies.

In the second, enlarged edition of this book nine years later, Rachman and Wilson (1980) noted a considerable widening of the range of problems to which behaviour therapy had been successfully applied and a continued success in more traditional areas. The picture that emerged was one of an approach to treatment with a proven track record, which was being successfully applied to more and more clinical problems. It is surprising, therefore, that the nine years that elapsed between the publication of these two editions is notable not for a continued adherence to the principles of behaviour therapy, but for a shift by clinicians away from behaviour therapy towards the use of more cognitively oriented therapies and the emergence of a new approach known as cognitive-behaviour therapy (Latimer & Sweet, 1984).

The best known versions of cognitive-behaviour therapy are Beck's *Cognitive therapy* (Beck, 1976), Ellis's *Rational emotive therapy* (Ellis, 1970) and Meichenbaum's *Self instructional training* (Meichenbaum, 1977). Although these therapies differ in many respects, they share the following common features:

 (i) an assumption that emotional and behavioural problems are caused by maladaptive cognitions;

 (ii) an assumption that therapeutic change may be brought about by altering underlying maladaptive cognitions;

(iii) the use of both cognitive strategies (e.g., logical analysis, rational disputation) and behavioural strategies (e.g., behavioural rehearsal and reinforced practice) to alter cognitions.

The conclusions drawn by Rachman and Wilson (1980) concerning the effectiveness of cognitive-behaviour therapy were that, despite its heavy emphasis on the treatment of a limited range of psychological disturbances and an absence of adequate follow up studies, cognitively oriented interventions had 'chalked up some interesting results', although some writers had been far more critical of the approach (e.g., Ledwidge, 1978; Rachlin, 1977). Since 1980 there has been an accumulation of studies that form the basis of a good case for the effectiveness of cognitive-behaviour therapy; although the nature of the mechanism of change is still open to discussion.

The above sequence of events has been presented not to question the current status of cognitive-behaviour therapy, but to make the point that the cognitive revolution in behaviour therapy appears to have preceded the availability of a body of evidence that demonstrates the effectiveness of cognitive methods. In addition, it occurred at a time when the evidence for the effectiveness of behaviour therapy was very convincing.

In an attempt to account for this apparently paradoxical state of affairs, we propose to present a number of possible determinants of this change in therapeutic behaviour that are not based on the effectiveness of the treatment. To help organise this material we have adopted the framework of behavioural analysis.

The contingencies that we will discuss appear to operate at two distinct levels. The first involves contingencies of reinforcement that influence the behaviour of individual therapists on a day-to-day basis. The second level involves outcomes that are more remote from particular instances of therapeutic behaviour, but which result in the accrual of long-term benefits to individuals and groups who engage in particular therapeutic practices.

Day-to-day influences on behaviour

The first possible sources of reinforcement for cognitivism that we will consider act on the verbal behaviour of therapists. Working within the health services behaviour therapists are surrounded by verbal communities that are primarily mentalistic in their terminology; this is true in the case of both professional colleagues (e.g., psychiatrists, nursing staff, speech therapists) and clients. The effects of audiences on verbal behaviour are powerful and it is safe to conclude that audiences selectively reinforce verbal practices consistent with their own (Branch & Malagodi, 1980). The consequences of this for a behavioural therapist are that it may be difficult to sustain verbal behaviours consistent with behaviourism in most working environments. The verbal behaviours of cognitive-behaviour therapists are already mentalistic and are therefore consistent with the terminology of their fellow professionals and clients. Thus, behaviour therapists entering the health services may find their verbal behaviour shaped in a mentalistic direction and in the absence of easy access to a sympathetic audience the shift in verbal behaviour may go unchecked.

The second selective pressure that may favour the practice of cognitive behaviour therapy over that of behaviour therapy is a difference in the immediacy of reinforcement derived from apparent client improvement. Cognitive behaviour therapists attempt to alter the beliefs of their clients, by challenging existing assumptions and offering alternatives. The first indication that change has occurred is when the client's verbal behaviour changes, and the client begins to utilise the verbal formulations offered by the therapist. This takes place during the therapeutic session and is usually contiguous with therapeutic strategies used by the therapist. The same temporal proximity of therapeutic behaviour and outcome does not always obtain in the case of behaviour therapy. Behaviour therapists intervene by re-arranging contingencies of reinforcement in the lives of their clients, directly or through agents (e.g., parents). Therapeutic change is monitored by taking objective measures of the target behaviour before, during and after treatment. It often takes several weeks before therapeutic behaviours produce observable changes in client behaviours. Thus, although the changes may be contingent upon the therapeutic intervention, they are seldom contiguous with them.

It is a well-established finding that humans and other animals choose immediate, small reinforcers in preference to larger, delayed ones (e.g., Logue, 1988). Individuals differ in the degree to which temporal delay devalues a reinforcer (Rachlin, 1980) but it is probably safe to assume that delay of reinforcement effects reinforcer value for everybody— including therapists.

Applied to the present context it is apparent that for some therapists in some circumstances (perhaps even for most therapists in most circumstances), the immediate reinforcement of a client accepting a verbal formulation may be preferred to the more long term reinforcement derived from delayed changes in behaviour.

A further selective pressure that may have served to maintain the behaviour of cognitive-behaviour therapists is a general tendency to value change more when it is brought about by inconspicuous contingencies than when it is caused by overt contingencies. This point was made by Skinner in his book *Beyond freedom and dignity* (Skinner, 1972) and was well supported with examples from everyday life. For example, Skinner made the point that we commend those who behave well when unsupervised more than we commend those who need to be watched. Applied to a therapeutic situation, we are more likely to value behavioural changes that we attribute to internal unobservable causes than similar changes brought about by overt manipulations. Thus even when a cognitive-behaviour therapist and a behaviour therapist bring about a similar degree of therapeutic improvement, the change brought about by the former may be valued more, due to the inconspicuous nature of the presumed controlling variables.

Finally, it has been suggested (Ledwidge, 1978) that cognitive-behaviour therapy is not as bland or boring as behaviour therapy for the clinician to undertake; 'getting inside someone's head, sharing their innermost thoughts and feelings . . . and making wise sounding interpretations wins hands down' (i.e., is more reinforcing), when the alternative involves such mundane activities as frequent observation and recording, or the construction of anxiety hierarchies.

Remote contingencies operating on therapeutic behaviour

This section is concerned with selective pressures that operate at a cultural level. These pressures result in long-term advantages for individuals who engage in particular practices.

The first possible pressure of this type emanates from the funding of research and the direct involvement of the state in this activity. Cognitive-behaviour therapists view psychological problems as resulting primarily from the way people negatively perceive and interpret reality. For example, depression may be viewed as being the result of a negative view of the self, the world and the future (Beck, 1976). Although cognitive-behaviour therapists acknowledge that psychological problems may arise from imperfect living conditions their research is seldom concerned with these. Many research papers written from a cognitive-behavioural perspective report significant differences between the cognitions of the well and the unwell; few focus on the differences in the real-life circumstances that these two groups experience.

The attraction of such a focus for agencies of the state is obvious. By focusing on the deficiencies of individuals, attention is diverted away from deficiencies in the life circumstances that such individuals endure, and from the responsibility of the state to intervene and provide a better life for its citizens.

Behaviour therapy offers no such comfort for the state. By focusing on the contingencies that operate in the lives of people as the source of psychological problems, behaviour therapy often requires significant changes to be implemented to bring about therapeutic improvements. A therapy that concentrates on bringing about therapeutic changes by changing contingencies of reinforcement, sometimes requiring considerable changes in individual life circumstances – rather than changing minds – is bound to uncover deficiencies in people's circumstances and is, therefore, less likely to receive approval from the state and consequently may be less likely to be funded.

The next point is closely related to the last, and involves decisions made about recruitment and promotion within clinical psychology. In general, these decisions are made by interview panels comprising agents of the state and senior members of the clinical psychology profession. It seems plausible to assume that the same selection pressures that may favour research proposals that focus on the inadequacy of the individual operate in this context also. The likely result being the selection of candidates who attribute psychological problems to misinterpretations of reality rather than to genuine problems within that reality.

A further set of metacontingencies that may have served to shape the behaviour of behaviour therapists in a cognitive direction has been the ascendancy in the past decade of a political doctrine that is sympathetic with the basic tenets of a cognitive-behaviour therapy, and which may have nurtured its growth in popularity. In the British context this doctrine has been manifest as 'Thatcherism'. The aspect of Thatcherism with which we are concerned is its emphasis on the responsibility of individuals for their own well-being and its promotion of self-help. The focus on individual responsibility of the Thatcherist political ideology is similar to cognitive-behaviour therapy's emphasis on locating the causes of psychological problems within the individual (Beck, 1976; Ellis, 1970) and to the belief that therapeutic change must be brought about by individuals changing the way they perceive and interpret reality.

The relationship between the cultural practice of cognitive-behaviour therapy and Thatcherism is not very clear; that is, it is not clear how Thatcherism has contributed to the maintenance of cognitive-behaviour therapy, but it is probably safe to assume that a culture is more likely to maintain cultural practices that are consistent with it, rather than ones that are not.

Finally, cognitive-behaviour therapy is also consistent with another aspect of our culture that is even more powerful and enduring than Thatcherism, that is, the dominant set of religious beliefs and practices within Western society: the Judeo-Christian tradition. A central theme of this tradition is the notion of free will. A deterministic therapeutic perspective, such as Radical Behaviourism, which asserts that behaviour is caused primarily by previous experiences, is at variance with the notion of free will. Scientists who hold such views, if they are Christians, have to keep separate their religious and scientific beliefs. Far better for such Christian scientists if their approach to psychology is less obviously deterministic and better still if it is only partially deterministic. Few psychologists have articulated the friction between behaviourism's overtly deterministic approach and the notion of free will that is central to Christian faith. However, at least two eminent psychologists have clearly done so and have suggested that a resolution to this problem may be forthcoming from the cognitive revolution we have witnessed in psychology over the past two decades (Bergin, 1980; Sperry, 1988).

It is possible that similar factors operate in the cases of other psychologists who have 'gone cognitive'. Thus, the emergence of cognitivism in behaviour therapy may be partially caused by its greater apparent consistency with Christian beliefs, which are obviously caused in turn by factors unrelated to the scientific or therapeutic value of cognitivism.

Concluding comments

We have attempted to show that the maintaining factors for cognitive behaviour therapy may be independent of its scientific value, but rather could be derived from social and political factors that ideally should have no influence on scientific decisions. The history of science in general, and of psychology in particular, is full of examples of scientific theories being rejected and others being accepted, not because of their scientific value, but because they are reinforced by prevailing political ideologies and other external influences (Gould, 1981). These determinants cannot be rejected as being trivial; they probably rival acceptable scientific criteria in importance in determining the acceptability of scientific theories. We believe that this type of influence on scientific decisions is likely to be particularly potent in the therapeutic context. Unlike the behaviour of other applied scientists, the therapeutic behaviour of clinical psychologists involves social interaction with other human beings; and because of this their behaviour is more likely to be influenced by the determinants of social behaviour in other contexts.

References

Beck, A. T. (1976). *Cognitive therapy and the emotional disorders*. New York: International University Press.

Bergin, A. (1980). Psycho-therapy and religious values. *Journal of Consulting and Clinical Psychology*, *48*, 95–105.

Branch, M. & Malagodi, E. (1980). Where have all the behaviorists gone? *The Behavior Analyst*, *3*, 31–38.

Ellis, A. (1970). *The essence of rational emotive psychotherapy: A comprehensive approach to treatment*. New York: Institute for Rational Living.

Gould, S. J. (1981). *The mismeasure of man*. New York: Norton.

Latimer, P. R. & Sweet, A. A. (1984). Cognitive versus behavioral procedures in cognitive-behavioral therapy: A critical review. *Journal of Behavior Therapy and Experimental Psychology*, *15*, 9–22.

Ledwidge, B. (1978). Cognitive behavior modification: A step in the wrong direction? *Psychological Bulletin*, *85*, 353–375.

Logue, A. W. (1988). Research on self-control: An integrating framework. *Behavioral and Brain Sciences*, *11*, 665–709.

Meichenbaum, D. (1977). *Cognitive behavior modification: An integrated approach*. New York: Plenum.

Rachlin, H. (1977). A review of M. J. Mahoney's 'Cognition and behavior modification'. *Journal of Applied Behavior Analysis*, *10*, 369–374.

Rachman, S. J. & Wilson, G. T. (1971). *The effects of psychological therapies*. Oxford: Pergamon.

Rachman, S. J. & Wilson, G. T. (1980). *The effects of psychological therapies* (2nd ed.). Oxford: Pergamon.

Skinner, B. F. (1972). *Beyond freedom and dignity*. London: Jonathan Cape.

Sperry, R. W. (1988). Psychology's mentalist paradigm and the religious/science tension. *American Psychologist*, *43*, 607–613.

PART 2

APPLIED ISSUES

APPENDICES.

5

Bye-bye behaviour modification

Peter Walsh

Abstract

This paper discusses the current status of behaviour modification, or as it is more appropriately termed 'Applied Behaviour Analysis' as an accepted therapeutic procedure, particularly in the field of learning disability. The argument is put forward that behaviour modification has fallen into some disrepute in recent years and a number of hypotheses are proposed which may account for this.

Introduction

As a therapeutic approach, behaviour modification, or as it is more aptly, but less commonly, termed 'Applied Behaviour Analysis' (ABA), has evolved over the past thirty years from a position of having to fight tooth and nail for its acceptance to that of being one of the most commonly reported treatment techniques in a large number of the more established journals. For a time the application of the basic principles of Operant Psychology in applied fields appeared to gain almost universal acceptance and, as Baker (1984) said 'ABA is now recognised as a discipline that has much to offer and that has a widespread influence that is likely to continue to grow' (p. 165). This view was also expressed by Matson and Coe (1992) writing in the journal *Research in Developmental Disabilities* when they stated: 'For mental retardation services, the changes affected at that time [the sixties] were nothing less than remarkable. How conditioning procedures came to dominate the conceptualisation and treatment of mental retardation behaviour is a topic worthy of consideration' (p. 172).

The employment of behavioural principles in areas of human need has challenged many of the myths that became institutionalised over the preceding years. In the fields of mental health and learning disability it has demonstrated that nobody is 'beyond help', a 'hopeless case' or a 'lost cause'. The emphasis on the observable environment has resulted in a radically different view of the causes of psychiatric breakdown and the potential for learning of people who, not too long ago, would have been considered incapable of acquiring new skills, or improving upon skills already acquired. Whilst it could not be argued that the behavioural approach has been alone in affecting the way we view 'problem people', it is probable that by concentrating on the environment it has, for example, helped highlight the problems associated with institutional care and inappropriate interactions within families and has increased awareness of the fact that the individual person is not operating within a vacuum but is part of a social environment that to a large extent defines his or her behaviour. By demonstrating that the behaviour of people with disabilities is governed by the same rules as the behaviour of people not so labelled, the communality of human nature is brought to the fore.

In the early days of behaviour modification much time and effort was devoted to debating the underlying philosophy of behaviourism, but pragmatism appeared to win out and many practitioners were happy to apply behavioural techniques even though they may have viewed behaviourism as a somewhat shallow and inadequate philosophy. Whilst this may have benefited many service users it may have caused some damage in reinforcing in others' eyes the notion that behaviour modification is simply a collection of techniques and procedures to be called on as required. In more recent times, behaviour modification would appear to have fallen somewhat out of favour in some applied fields, including the field of learning disability, and this fall from grace would appear to be linked as much, or perhaps more, to philosophy than to pragmatics. We thus appear to have gone full circle and there are many echoes about today that remind one of the early debates between Rogers and Skinner.

In summary, it would appear that behaviour modification has evolved over the years, passing through various phases of acceptance or rejection. Despite its proven track record in dealing with areas of concern that have not been dealt with effectively by other approaches, behaviour modification has, I believe, passed through a period of crisis, particularly in the field of learning difficulties, during which it has been subjected to much criticism, some of which was warranted, but a lot of which was not. Whether behaviour modification will survive and whether behaviour modifiers and others benefit from the experience is open to question. Much of the criticism against behaviour modification was, and is, valid and needs to be taken on board by behaviour modifiers and much of the criticism was unfounded and this needs to be acknowledged by the critics. No good will come of throwing the baby out with the bath water. If behaviour modification does survive there remain many serious obstacles to overcome if it is to be applied to its full potential, a position which has never been realised. For example, Lovaas (1982), in a review of the literature relating to the experimental analysis of self-injurious behaviour, pointed out that our knowledge of functional technologies in this area far outstrips their use in the field and that a comprehensive implementation of what we already know about decreasing such behaviours would reduce their incidence by one half. David Fisher (1983), in a paper discussing the sociopolitics of behaviour change, has stated that: 'Over a quarter of a century has passed since the appearance of behavioural technology. However, this technology has found a permanent home at very few treatment facilities. The introduction occasionally led to a brief romance but rarely to a marriage' (p. 249). Fisher goes on to point out that many behavioural programmes have failed to take root because many behaviourists are innocent about the real world of applied psychology: a world in which behaviour analysts are enormously dependent upon others in the successful design and implementation of their programmes and which is full of extraneous variables, such as personnel rules, social stresses, anxious administrators, union stewards, political and economic pressures, inter- and intra-professional rivalry, staff turnover and diamond hard inertia.

This failure of behavioural principles to be applied is clear from the findings of a paper by Intagliata, Rinck and Calkins (1986) who carried out a survey into how direct care staff dealt with problem behaviours in people who had a learning difficulty. They reported clear evidence that behaviourally oriented strategies were more effective than other approaches but expressed concern over the large number of staff who reported using totally ineffective techniques and suspected such staff were not adequately prepared and trained to deal with such behaviours. It would appear, therefore, that there has been and continues to be a gross deficiency in the dissemination of behavioural techniques and findings. The finding by Cullen, Burton, Watts and Thomas (1984) that for the vast majority of the time the behaviour of people with learning difficulty goes totally unnoticed by anybody else would indicate that contingencies, a key concept in behaviour analysis, are more in the mind than in the environment.

So, 'where does behaviour modification go from here?' and, a related question, 'what future does it have as a meaningful intervention procedure in the field of learning disability?'.

I believe applied behavioural psychology is at a crossroads and which direction it takes will be crucial to the future viability of its practice. For the remainder of this paper I would like to try and give some ideas I have regarding the current status of behaviour modification and the difficulties it is facing if it is to continue to be one of the most effective psychological therapies to be implemented by large numbers of people in a wide variety of settings. Whilst I am looking at these issues primarily in the field of learning disability, I suspect similar issues arise in other applied fields.

As a starting point it may prove beneficial to examine some of the reasons as to why behaviour modification has not achieved widespread acceptance and support in organisations or by individuals providing services for those in need. These reasons are many and varied and the following hypotheses may help to shed some light on the issue:

Hypothesis one: There is an association of behaviour modification with the use of punishment procedures.

Hypothesis two: There is a separation between behaviour modification and its roots in the experimental analysis of behaviour.

Hypothesis three: There are many services catering for people with learning disability being run by management whose ethos and philosophies are fundamentally opposed to behaviourism and its associated determinism, as perceived.

Hypothesis four: There is extinction of behavioural behaviour in people working in human services.

Hypothesis five: Behavioural techniques are often applied by practitioners who naively believe that behaviour modification is a relatively simple approach to employ.

Hypothesis six: There are many people who work in the field of learning disability who lack the characteristics of being good behaviour change agents.

Hypothesis seven: There is a lack of adequate training in the field of behaviour analysis by both front-line, advisory and management personnel.

The above are just some factors which I believe combine and interact to have the overall effect of reducing the likelihood of behaviour modification being utilised as an intervention of choice in many service areas. I would now like to spend some time examining these various hypotheses in more detail.

Hypothesis one
There is an association of behaviour modification with punishment procedures.
In recent years there has been an enormous amount of debate on the use and misuse of punishment procedures both from ideological and practical view-points and the debate has been acrimonious and divisive. This debate, whilst mainly originating in the US has had an impact on the practice of psychology in Ireland, as illustrated by the following:

Behaviourists emphasise adaptive behaviours over maladaptive behaviours by dispensing positive reinforcers for compliance and punishment for non-compliance. They only contingently value the person. If a person follows the rules, value is given. If a person fails to obey, punishment is applied. . . . They (the behaviourists) manage behaviour through the total subjugation of people . . . their goal is to protect society from those whom it rejects and their treatment is a means of social domination. Restraint and restriction are a way of life (McGee, Menolascino, Hobbs & Menousek, 1987, p. 176).

Behaviour modification is the least appropriate method of treating people with learning difficulties (Brandon, 1990, Presentation to the Mental Handicap Group of PSI).

I began to see how behaviourism could be used as a political tool that really supported a hierarchy of power between therapist and those they ostensibly served. I began to feel that some of my colleagues were using behaviourism as a way to work on others while I had wanted to work with them (Lovett, 1985).

The relevance of these quotes is that McGee was invited to present the Mental Handicap Group of the Psychological Society of Ireland Annual Easter Workshop in 1989; Brandon did so in 1990 and Lovett did so in 1991. Thus, for three years running psychologists working in Ireland, where, to my knowledge, there is little use of aversive procedures, were basically being told that behaviourism was inherently evil and could never work for the benefit of people with learning disability. This is summed up concisely by Jones (1990) writing an account of his attendance at the workshop given by McGee.

Early in the workshop McGee presented us with a vision of behaviourism as an evil, soul-destroying activity based on punishment and fear. He then presented gentle teaching as a liberating, democratic and valuing activity which existed in opposition to the behavioural approach. I was starting to feel that I was at a sales presentation and that behavioural approach which I had believed in for years was being caricatured by someone who did not fully understand it. (p. 9)

In the *Irish Psychologist*, a report of the workshop presented by Brandon referring to his statement quoted above went: 'At that stage, the vast majority of the audience shuffled restlessly in an attempt to hide looks of guilt'. Interestingly, the Easter workshop in 1992 was addressing the issue of where Psychologists are going in the field of mental handicap. The crucial point here is that I believe the 'aversives debate', which is being debated within behavioural circles as much as outside of those circles, has been used (or rather misused) in an ideological way to indicate that behaviourism is necessarily repressive. Of the above quotes, the one by Lovett is true: behaviourism can be repressive, and on occasions quite definitely has been. However, this applies to any effective therapeutic approach. The word *can* is of central importance here as it indicates that whilst the potential for repression is there, this does not mean repression is inevitable. What appears to have been operating over recent years is ideology being considered as being the all-important factor in analysing the suitability or appropriateness of an intervention procedure. There is, however, a danger in this. As Jackson (1988) points out 'The problem with ideologies is that they invariably create ideologists, wedded to what they perceive as the fundamental purity of the principles enshrined in the ideology. Such people tend to make the greatest impact within professional groups whose members are unclear and/or uncertain of their professional raison d'être.' (p. 149)

A finding by Lennox, Miltenberger, Spengler and Erfranian (1988) is of some relevance here. In reviewing five years of treatment research with people having developmental disabilities, they found that the most common behaviour reduction procedure reported in the first half of the 1990s was differential reinforcement. No treatment, other than overcorrection, was used even 50 per cent as frequently.

Hypothesis two

There is separation between behaviour modification and its roots in the experimental analysis of behaviour.

Much has been written in the psychological literature of the relationship between pure and applied psychology (Claridge, 1976; Davidson, 1977; Feldman, 1977) and the specific relationship between pure and applied behavioural work has been ably documented by Baker (1984). Willems (1974) stated that behaviour modification is basically a technology in so far as it involves the systematic application of tested scientific principles to pragmatic real-life tasks and problems and that this close co-operation of treatment model to the research process (i.e., of technology to science) surrounds behaviour analysis with an enviable degree of explicitness.

Whilst such close co-ordination may have existed in the early days of Applied Behaviour Analysis (ABA), this gradually has become less evident as time has passed and the links between ABA and the Experimental Analysis of Behaviour (EAB) are becoming more and more tenuous. As Baker (1984) points out the applied sciences have been seen as part of a three stage development of a science (Bushell & Brigham, 1971; Brigham & Catania, 1978; Musterberg, 1914; Poffenberger, 1942). The first step is that in which the foundation science discovers and elaborates its principles; the second involves an elaboration of the procedures and the demonstration of their application and the third, the development of field applications themselves. It would appear at the present time that EAB, as pure research, is continuing to discover and elaborate its principles and improve its procedures, whilst ABA is largely concerned with demonstrating the application of procedures and principles discovered long ago and developing their field applications. Thus, workers in the two related areas can have little common interest and there is a tendency for those involved in EAB to be unconcerned about the applications of their work and those involved in ABA to be unconcerned about the theoretical basis for their work. The fundamental question for the worker in EAB is 'what controls behaviour?', whilst, for the worker in Applied Behaviour Analysis, the question is 'how do we bring this behaviour under control?'.

Whilst accepting the two fields are of necessity directing their energies to somewhat different questions and to very different problems, it is questionable as to whether either field has yet acquired the knowledge and expertise to relinquish its ties and obligations to the other. The pure researcher has an obligation to co-operate with the practitioner in further developing the technology and the practitioner has a duty to ensure that research findings are applied in ways beneficial to those seeking their expertise. At present it is not uncommon for many practitioners to believe that research in the Experimental Analysis of Behaviour is of absolutely no interest or relevance to them. They view the pure researcher as somebody pursuing areas of research that can be of no possible practical relevance and believe there are other more practical topics that should be researched – and perhaps there is some truth to this. The biologist, Rene Dubois (1970), for example, has stated that scientists tend to shy away from the problems posed by human life because they are not readily amenable to study by orthodox methods of science and, hence, are not likely to lead to clear results and professional advancement in academic circles. Thus, the way to scientific success is often through substituting for important problems which are overwhelmingly complex other less important problems that can be solved within a relatively short period of time (p. 156). For the practitioner, therefore, who is working in areas of public concern, and where results must be obtained, it is easy to sympathise with his or her view that those engaged in EAB research would be better off devoting their time and energy to answering basic questions that would help develop new, improved behavioural treatments. This attitude, is, however somewhat harsh and could be viewed as 'passing the buck'. The person who is best able to carry out applied research is not the laboratory based scientific researcher but the practitioner who is in daily contact with the subject he or she wishes to know more about and who is aware of what the problems are. There is a definite onus on practitioners to be involved in more research and, likewise, there is an onus to keep abreast of pure research related to one's field of work. A point of interest here is the existence in Ireland of an active group within the Psychological Society of Ireland (PSI) called Behaviour Analysis in Ireland (BAI). This group has been in existence since 1977, regularly presents a symposium at the PSI annual conference and has regular meetings throughout the year. Despite the fact that over half of the papers presented within this group have been of an applied nature, many in the field of learning disability, attendance is largely limited to academic psychologists who are university-based. This would hardly suggest that many applied psychologists are interested in cross-fertilisation of ideas. However, if psychologists employ behavioural principles and yet fail to keep abreast of developments in their base science they are in danger of becoming mere technologists.

Hypothesis three

Many services for people with learning disability are run by organisations whose ethos and philosophies are fundamentally opposed to behaviourism and its associated determinism, as perceived.

This hypothesis is simply that, a hypothesis, worthy perhaps of some empirical research which is currently lacking. I mention it because I suspect many agencies providing human services see behaviourism as counter to their ideals and goals. Thus, behaviourism can be perceived as not treating the whole person, or being deterministic, or ignoring spiritual needs, or running counter to normalisation (see Roos, 1972 for a detailed discussion on reconciling behaviour modification procedures with normalisation), or simply just lacking a sound ideological root (see Cullen, 1991 for discussion of this). Again, what appears to be in operation here is ideology being considered the all-important factor in analysing the suitability or appropriateness of intervention procedures. As indicated earlier, however, there is a danger to this (see earlier quote by Jackson, 1988). I am not saying here that organisations are explicitly rejecting of a behavioural approach, but rather, there is an implicit assumption that behavioural approaches may be useful in certain limited circumstances when other approaches have failed and, thus, behaviourism is taken on board begrudgingly and in a piecemeal manner. In other words, behaviour modification or behaviour analysis is frequently employed within a culture that does not hold a behavioural ethos. This has the effect of greatly diminishing the efficacy of the approach. One way of overcoming this difficulty is to employ a behavioural approach but call it something different.

Hypothesis four

There is extinction of behavioural behaviour in people working within the field of learning disability.

By behavioural behaviour I refer to behaviour on the part of the service provider which is conducive to client development and such behaviour includes: reinforcing certain behaviours in clients and colleagues, extinguishing certain others, setting up stimulus conditions and environmental circumstances that are appropriate for future development, tackling problems in a scientific and objective manner, and analysing the underlying causes of behaviour occurring. Unfortunately, such behaviour on the part of service providers frequently goes unreinforced and hence is extinguished and drops out of their repertoire. This is particularly the case in under-staffed, over-populated settings. A fundamental problem, particularly for people working on the front-line, is that administration of reinforcement would not appear to be a frequently used means of controlling behaviour in our society. Much of front-line workers' behaviour is controlled by aversive procedures, either by means of punishment for having done something incorrectly or by means of negative reinforcement.

Hypothesis five

Behavioural techniques are often applied by practitioners who naively believe that behaviour modification is a relatively simple approach to employ.

This rests on the premise that behaviour modification means one must reward good behaviour and not reward bad behaviour. Whilst one cannot disagree with this statement, it is hard to align this view with the voluminous amount of work published in the field of behaviour modification over the past thirty years. However, it is a perception that is adhered to by many, particularly by people not working on the front line. Those on the front-line are only too often very aware of how difficult it can be rewarding 'good behaviour', particularly in situations of overcrowding, poor staff:client ratios, and the presence of many other demands. Likewise, it is often difficult, maybe even unethical, at times not to reward bad behaviour – it is difficult not to respond to some extremely challenging behaviours, such as aggression or self-injury, in ways that are not reinforcing.

Hypothesis six

Many people working in the field of mental handicap lack the characteristics of being good behaviour change agents.

Foxx (1985) in a paper examining the question as to why behavioural programmes do not work any better than they do in many settings concluded that it was largely because we have ignored the behavioural characteristics of the behaviour change agent. We have failed to examine what makes a good behaviour change agent. Foxx then went on to list seven characteristics which he believed good behaviour change agents should possess and which he felt would distinguish between a behavioural technologist and a behavioural artist. This he felt could help explain programme failure. The seven characteristics he listed were:

- Having a bizarre sense of humour;
- Liking people;
- Possessing perceptive sensitivity, i.e., being sensitive to small changes in behaviour;
- Not liking to lose;
- Being an optimist;
- Being able to not take personally what clients may do to one;
- Being self-actualised.

Clearly, this is a somewhat demanding list of traits and yet if working with people, some of whom can be very demanding, they would appear to be necessary. But how many people working in stressful, applied settings can retain these characteristics over periods of years, or even decades; and that assuming they possessed them in the first place? Also of interest is the final characteristic Foxx mentions – being self-actualised. Foxx is referring here to the individual knowing him- or her- self and being at ease with oneself and is stating that this is a necessary condition for affecting behaviour change in others. This appears to be far removed from the picture of the behaviour modifier painted earlier by McGee.

Hypothesis seven

There is a lack of adequate training in the field of behaviour modification and particularly in behavioural analysis.

This is really one of the crucial issues in the success or failure of behavioural programmes and has been the subject of many papers (e.g., Cullen, 1988). Suffice to say, the people who are crucial to the success of behavioural intervention are those who are in daily contact with the client, as it is they who, if not initiating and planning interventions, will have to implement interventions and maintain any effects over time. It is crucial therefore that those in most frequent contact with clients are well acquainted with behavioural principles and procedures. However, whilst knowledge is essential, it is also essential that there is a system in place which ensures the knowledge is applied. Thus, in terms of staff training, although the front-line person is the key person, management and advisors also need to be well versed in procedures they expect staff to implement. Whilst many front-line staff do receive training in behaviour modification, people in senior management positions frequently do not. If this is the case it is unlikely that senior members in service organisations will reinforce behavioural behaviour in their staff. This may explain the finding of research that staff training rarely by itself results in noticeable improvements in the lives of people with learning disability (Cullen, 1988) and why it rarely has any long-term effects on staff behaviour.

Conclusion

From the foregoing it would appear that the future of applied behavioural psychology is somewhat uncertain. The successful application of behavioural principles is fraught with difficulties, particularly if effects are to be long-term. However, there would appear to be cause for optimism regarding the future.

Firstly, I believe the rejection of behavioural principles on ideological grounds is beginning to wane as realisation grows that the alternatives (e.g., gentle teaching) may not be as efficacious as once thought (Jones & McCaughey, 1992). Furthermore, much of the ideological debate surrounding the employment of aversive procedures has emanated from within the behavioural community. There are many behaviourists who would be totally opposed to the use of any aversive procedures. In conjunction with this, there is a growing technology of positive, non-aversive procedures for dealing with behaviours that were not widely available until relatively recently.

The ongoing development of ABA includes increased concentration on antecedents and setting events and the realisation within the behavioural literature that behaviour cannot be adequately explained by a simple ABC contingency. The behavioural literature is now far more questioning about environmental conditions and in viewing a person's behaviour in a wider context, both in environmental and temporal terms.

The increased acknowledgement of the need for positive programming, and for interventions to be based on detailed assessment and evaluation, means that applied behaviour analysis is finally beginning to live up to its name and become, not just applied and behavioural, but also analytic. In the early days behaviour modification was simply that: the act of modifying or changing behaviour or behaviours. Interventions were frequently implemented without any analysis or attempt at understanding underlying causes. The emphasis has shifted and this is not only scientifically sound, but also ideologically sound.

While much of this chapter has referred to 'behaviour modification', I believe the term should be laid to rest. Behaviour modification has played an important role in the evolution of behavioural psychology but it needs to be replaced by an approach that is applied, behavioural and analytic. Such an approach entails far more than changing behaviour. It entails understanding behaviour and the complexity of the interactions between individuals and their environment, particularly their social environment. I believe the result of such a change in emphasis will do much to overcome many of the obstacles to a wider acceptance and application of behavioural psychology, some of which have been touched on in this chapter.

References

Baker, L. J. V. (1984). Contemporary behaviour analysis: Pure and applied. *Irish Journal of Psychology, 6,* 156–168.

Brigham, T. A. & Catania, A. C. (1978). The behavior analysis technology. In A. C. Catania & T. A. Brigham (Eds), *Handbook of applied behavior analysis.* New York: Irvington.

Bushell, D. & Brigham, T. A. (1971). Educational technology. In M. C. Berman (Ed.), *Motivation and learning.* Engelwood Cliffs, N.J.: Educational Technology.

Claridge, G. (1976). Scientist or practitioner? A reactionary viewpoint. *Newsletter. Clinical Division, BPS,* 17, 12–15.

Cullen, C. (1988). A review of staff training: The emperor's old clothes. *Irish Journal of Psychology,* 9, 309–323.

Cullen, C. (1991). Experimentation and planning in community care. *Disability, Handicap and Society,* 6, 115–127.

Cullen, C., Burton, M. S., Watts, S., & Thomas, M. (1984). A preliminary report on the nature of interactions in a mental handicap institution. *Behavior Research and Therapy,* 21, 579–83.

Davidson, M. A. (1977). The scientific/applied debate in psychology: A contribution. *Bulletin British Psychological Society, 30,* 273–278.

Dubois, R. (1970). *So human and animal.* Abacus.

Feldman, M. P. (1976). Scientist or practitioner? A reactionary viewpoint. *Newsletter. Clinical Division, BPS, 17,* 12–15.

Fisher, D. (1983). The going gets tough when we descend from the ivory tower. *Analysis and Intervention in Developmental Disabilities, 3,* 249–255.

Foxx, R. M. (1985). The Jack Tizard Memorial Lecture. Decreasing behaviours: Clinical, ethical and environmental issues. *Australia and New Zealand Journal of Developmental Disabilities, 10,* 189–199.

Hale, P. (1990). Brokerage and counselling. *Irish Psychologist,* 16, 75.

Intagliata, J., Rinck, & Calkins, C. (1986). Staff response to maladaptive behaviour in public and community residential facilities. *Mental Retardation, 24,* 93–98.

Jackson, R. N. (1988). Perils of 'pseudonormalisation'. *Mental Handicap, 16,* 148–150.

Jones, R. S. P. (1990) Gentle teaching: Behaviourism at its best? *Community Living, 3,* 9–10.

Jones, R. S. P. & McCaughey, R. E. (1992). Gentle teaching and applied behavior analysis: A critical review. *Journal of Applied Behavior Analysis, 25,* 853–867.

Lennox, D. B., Miltenberger, R. G., Spengler, P., & Erfranian, N. (1988). Decelerative treatment practices with persons who have mental retardation: A review of five years of the literature. *American Journal on Mental Retardation, 92,* 492–501.

Lovaas, O. A. (1982). Comments on self-destructive behaviors. *Analysis and Intervention in Developmental Disabilities, 2,* 115–124.

Lovett, H. (1985). Cognitive counselling and persons with special needs: Adaptive behavior approaches to the social context. New York: Praeger.

McGee, J. J., Menolascino, F. J., Hobbs, D. C., & Menousek, P. E. (1987). *Gentle teaching: A nonaversive approach for helping persons with mental retardation.* New York: Human Sciences Press

Matson, J. L. & Coe, D. A. (1992). Applied behavior analysis: Its impact on the treatment of mentally retarded emotionally disturbed people. *Research in Developmental Disabilities. 13,* 171–189.

Musterberg, H. (1914). *Psychotechnik.* Leipzig: Barth.

Poffenberger, A. T. (1942). *Principles of applied psychology.* New York: Appleton-Century Crofts.

Roos, P. (1972). Reconciling behavior modification procedures with the principle of normalisation. In W. Wolfensberger *Normalisation: The principle of normalisation in Human Services.* Toronto: National Institute on Mental Retardation.

Willems, E. P. (1974). Behavioral technology and behavioral ecology. *Journal of Applied Behavior Analysis, 7,* 151–165.

6

Applied psychology from the standpoint of behavioural analysis

Julian C. Leslie

Abstract

Although the main impact of psychology is in the broad area of applied psychology, and the experimental analysis of behaviour is one of the main contributors to the range of methodologies used in applied psychology, applied behavioural analysis does not make up a very large part of the broad domain of applied psychology. An examination of the defining features of applied psychology suggests that behavioural analysis could be appropriately extended over the whole domain. Practitioners of applied psychology tend to have either an eclectic view of methodology, or one derived from the approach to general psychology in which they were originally trained. Using examples from the rapidly growing field of health psychology, and the less well-researched one of aviation psychology, it is argued that the evaluation of the effectiveness of the methodology used in any area of applied psychology should be given higher priority, and that if this were done techniques derived from the experimental analysis of behaviour would have greater importance in applied psychology. However, for applied behavioural analysis to have wider acceptability, it is also necessary that its long-standing narrow focus on specific target behaviours be abandoned in favour of an evaluation of the broad context in which that behaviour occurs. Very often such a strategy will involve promoting good practice rather than attempting to eliminate unwanted target behaviours. Recognition of the crucial role of establishing operations is also required.

The experimental analysis of behaviour has, since Skinner (1938), been concerned with the analysis of functional relationships between environmental variables and behaviour, and, since Skinner (1950) and Sidman (1960), it has emphasised the value of establishing a systematic body of data, through the replication and extension of experimental findings, rather than theory construction and testing. Arguably, it is these priorities that have led to applied behavioural analysis being a significant part of the broad field of applied psychology. The purposes of the present paper are to examine the uses of methodology and its relation to theory in applied psychology generally, and to suggest that the precepts of the experimental analysis of behaviour are of general relevance in applied psychology, and that their promotion in an appropriate form could lead to applied behavioural analysis making an even greater contribution. As a preliminary, it will be necessary to discuss the definition of applied psychology.

The definition of applied psychology

Although applied psychology is recognised as being of great importance, and is perhaps the main driving force that is moving psychology to a position of prominence in modern life (Leslie, 1995), it is not easy to define. Gale and Chapman (1984) pointed out that it generally means either a set of techniques devised by psychologists, or is used slightly differently as a generic term to refer to the work of all the well-known types of professional psychologists. A third possibility, but not one favoured by many psychologists, is to define it as those general principles of psychology that arise directly from everyday life or professional practice, rather than from attempts to generalise 'pure' psychological principles to real life contexts.

As an alternative to previous formulations (but one that is akin to the first type of definition suggested above), Gale and Chapman (1984) suggested that applied psychology should be defined by the range of skills used by psychologists working in applied contexts. They further suggested that there is a substantial number of common skills, but the relative importance of different skills varies a great deal across contexts. This scheme has the advantages that it defines applied psychology as a set of skills or techniques that can in principle be objectively measured, and that they have taken an initial step towards specifying those skills. In a brief form, a list of the skill areas Gale and Chapman identified appears in Table 1.

Let us concentrate on Skills 1 to 12 of this comprehensive list (of the remainder, Skills 13 to 15 could be said to be common to many professional groups, and I have recently discussed Skill 16 – which is sometimes seen as problematic for applied behavioural analysis – in detail elsewhere; see Leslie, in press). Of these, Skills 1, 2, 3, 4, 11 and 12 could be said to be defining features of applied behavioural analysis, while Skills 5, 6, 7, 8 and 9 should be included in the prospectus for the development of applied behavioural analysis. This alternative version of the list of skills appears as Table 2.

Table 1 *Gale and Chapman's (1984) list of skills of applied psychology*

1. Bringing about change.
2. Improving quality of life of individuals.
3. Using techniques of observation, measurement and report.
4. Resolving complex problems into constituent parts.
5. Awareness of socially-determined conception of the person.
6. Working within organisational contexts.
7. Allowing individuals to make decisions about own lives.
8. Recognising family and emotional ties of individuals.
9. Recognising effects of broader social context on individuals.
10. Assisting individuals in developing coping skills.
11. Providing education and training.
12. Evaluating the efficacy of intervention strategies.
13. Collaborating with other professionals.
14. Relating to government agencies.
15. Showing sensitivity to political issues.
16. Dealing ethically with individuals.

Table 2 *Defining Skills of Applied Behavioural Analysis*

1. Bringing about change.
2. Improving quality of life of individuals.
3. Using techniques of observation, measurement and report.
4. Resolving complex problems into constituent parts.
11. Providing education and training.
12. Evaluating the efficacy of intervention strategies.

Skills which Applied Behavioural Analysis should include

5. Awareness of socially-determined conception of the person.
6. Working within organisational contexts.
7. Allowing individuals to make decisions about own lives.
8. Recognising family and emotional ties of individuals.
9. Recognising effects of broader social context on individuals.

On this analysis, applied behavioural analysis readily subsumes 11 of the 12 core Gale-Chapman skills. The six that I take to be essential to applied behavioural analysis would stand as a large part of a defining statement, while many practitioners would argue that the other five have already been incorporated into current practice: four of them are concerned with putting an intervention into a broader context, while the other (Skill 7) is often regarded as a core skill of applied behavioural analysis (see, for example, Owens, 1995).

There is, then, little problem in demonstrating that applied behavioural analysis can match the general requirements of applied psychology. However, a complete definition of applied behavioural analysis would naturally make extensive reference to the use of behavioural principles derived from the experimental analysis of behaviour, in addition to the skills given, and it is this that most obviously distinguishes it from other approaches to applied psychology (see Leslie, 1996, for a recent review of basic behavioural principles). The origins of applied behavioural analysis lie in the early successes of behaviour therapy, and since then it has only been cautiously extended to other areas of application where 'learning processes' seem to have face validity. Currently, these areas include almost all areas of clinical psychology and educational psychology, and a smaller number of social problems.

I will return later to the question as to why applied behavioural analysis has only gradually been seen to apply to the broad domain of applied psychology. Over the same period that applied behavioural analysis has made only faltering progress, applied psychologists in general have been rapidly extending the field. They have used a diverse range of methodologies in many of the same areas as those current in applied behavioural analysis, and other areas where the methods chosen seem to have face validity. There is an informal and intuitively reasonable process involved here: psychologists seeking to conceptualise and investigate a new area look for a theoretical framework and a methodology that has been developed in an apparently related field and see what use they can make of these in the new case. However, there is a danger that unreliable and invalid data will be generated by this approach and will be accepted as giving the psychological characteristics of the new area. The crucial additional step is to ensure at an early stage that the methodology used is effective in the new area. This is Skill 12 – evaluating the efficacy of an intervention – in the tables presented earlier, and, importantly, is a high priority in applied behavioural analysis. Because applied behavioural analysis does not see behaviour as an indication of an underlying psychological process, but rather treats it as its essential subject matter, prediction and control of behaviour are always its first concern. It follows from this that specification of behavioural outcomes is a key feature of applied behavioural analysis, and workers in this tradition have always taken the demonstration of effectiveness to be their highest priority.

Methodological weakness in contemporary applied psychology

It might be objected at this point that I am making a lot of fuss about what is, at most, very little: is it not the commitment of psychology, whatever the specific approach adopted, to demonstrating the effectiveness of its methods that has lead to the current realisation that it might be effectively applied in many areas? I suggest that this commitment can be seen to have at least wavered when contemporary research literature is examined, and I will give illustrative examples from the rapidly burgeoning literature of health psychology.

A series of studies has looked at locus of control in insulin-dependent diabetic people, on the reasonable assumption that this personality dimension might predict the capacity of individuals to manage this serious medical condition. Lowery and DuCette (1976) used Rotter's (1966) scale with diabetics whose conditions had been diagnosed recently, for three years or for six years. They found some differences between those who perceived the locus of control of their problem to be internal and those who perceived it to be external. Harris, Linn, and Pollack (1984) suggested that Wallston, Kaplan and Maides' (1976) health-specific locus of control measure was more sensitive and appropriate for use with diabetics than Rotter's (1966) original measure. Bradley *et al.* (1984; 1987) further argued that there should be a diabetes-specific version of the scale. They devised such a scale, and used it in a substantial study with 286 diabetics. They claimed that their scale was a good predictor of choice of treatment type, and of physiological control one year later.

Coates (1993) sought to replicate Bradley *et al.*'s (1987) findings in a study of 264 insulin-dependent diabetics. Factor analysis of her data showed that all the constructs proposed by Bradley *et al.* (1984) were identified, thus enhancing construct validity, and acceptable reliability estimates were obtained. Measurement error was considered by conducting a second-order factor analysis in which each pair of constructs from the first-order factor analysis contributed to one second-order factor. In this analysis, the variance was separated into (*a*) common (valid) variance; (*b*) variance specific to one of the pair of constructs; (*c*) random error. This analysis showed that random error accounted generally for more than half the variance, while valid variance varied from less than a quarter to just over half the variance. Furthermore, locus of control was not a significant predictor of either of the outcome variables used, which were clinic attendance and glycosylated haemoglobin levels.

While it is always possible that the Coates study was flawed in some way, it appears more likely that the more rigorous data analysis she used revealed a lack of relationship between the proposed personality variable and the putatively-associated behaviour that might have been found in the earlier studies if they had been analysed in the same way. The series of studies examining locus of control in diabetes arose from a set of assumptions that had high face validity, but have not succeeded in demonstrating how the behaviour of diabetic patients is controlled. As this is essentially a behavioural management problem, one might reasonably ask whether applied behavioural analysis has been attempted. A recent literature review (Cox & Gonder Frederick, 1992) notes that over 4,000 articles relevant to behavioural aspects of diabetes could be identified in a ten-year period. Within the area of self-care, however, most studies are correlational or cross-sectional, limiting their interpretation. Cox and Gonder-Frederick identify only five involving behavioural interventions, and they report that all of these had beneficial outcomes.

From a behaviour-analytic standpoint, we are faced with a paradox: on the one hand, a great many studies have been carried out using a social cognition framework, although they have not contributed much to the management of the disease. On the other hand, virtually no behavioural management studies have been attempted, despite growing evidence that control of behaviour is crucial if long-term serious complications for insulin-dependent diabetics are to be avoided (DCCT Research Group, 1993). It seems likely that so many data have been published from a social-cognition perspective because relatively weak criteria for positive outcomes have been applied. Although measures of clinical effectiveness are increasingly used as a yardstick for the success of psychological studies, it remains the case that many data sets are published which reach only the lower threshold of containing differences between treatments which reach statistical significance. Such findings will generally be accepted for publication, provided they are related to a contemporary theoretical account.

The preference for theory-development over collection of 'good' data or, more importantly, successfully changing behaviour is not, of course, new (see Skinner, 1950), but is now deeply rooted in applied psychology. In health psychology, social-cognition approaches are almost invariably preferred to that of behavioural analysis (but see Leslie, 1988, for a discussion of the use of the behavioural analysis conceptual framework). The development of this preference is carefully explained in a recent keynote address by a distinguished health psychologist (Johnston, 1996). She wrote: 'I have used this [behavioural] model in working with a girl who was unable to take food by mouth... oral feeding was unsuccessful until a programme of social contingencies . . . was introduced. . . . Satisfactory drinking was achieved in four days and eating in eight days.' (p. 207). So far, so good, one might think, but she went on to say that using this behavioural model it was 'difficult to explain what had changed in the girl following the introduction of the programme and the contingencies.' This perceived gap in our knowledge, she said, has been the subject of more recent cognitive theorising. Of the various cognitive models applied to disability, her particular health psychology research interest, she preferred to use the Theory of Planned Behaviour (Azjen, 1988), which contains four entities, or constructs, which have to be inferred (these are attitudes, subjective norms, perceived control and behavioural intention) with the addition of two more (the internal representation of behaviour, and eliciting external cues). There are thus six variables intervening between the impairment of function by disease or disorder and the behaviour of disability in Johnston's (1996) model, and her paper charted a twenty-year journey away from an interest in the determinants of behaviour to one in the development of a model that could not possibly be regarded as testable using the methodologies currently or prospectively available to health psychology.

Theory versus methodology

The examples given above illustrate the strong link between theory and methodology in contemporary psychology, rather than their independence. Workers in health psychology have tended to abandon methods derived from behavioural analysis not because they have been shown to be ineffective, but because they believe that there are theoretical shortcomings in behavioural analysis which preclude its effective application to health issues. Something similar has happened in the less-studied field of aviation psychology.

Human factors are increasingly recognised as crucial in aviation, although recent authors note that in many aviation industrial concerns there are still very few psychologists employed. Fuller (1994) pointed out that there are many straightforward possible applications of behavioural analysis in aviation, but very few have yet been attempted. He attributed this to the prevailing cognitivist *Zeitgeist*, and there is certainly interest in applying notions of mental models to the highly complex tasks involved.

Safety is a major concern within many complex human-machine systems. In this context, I reviewed (Leslie, 1995) the aviation-related contributions to a Royal Society symposium on human factors in hazardous situations (Broadbent, Reason, & Baddeley, 1990). While none of these was presented in a behavioural framework, I was able to identify a general concern with complex systems as sets of contingencies within which humans operate. Furthermore, many of the safety concerns could be construed as the failure of operators to be sensitive to long-term contingencies, in situations where both short term and long-term contingencies exist. This is, of course, a familiar issue in applied behavioural analysis and its resolution has been undertaken in many other contexts (cf., Rachlin & Green, 1972; Rachlin, 1989). Another theme I identified in Broadbent *et al.* (1990) was that 'human error' was not seen as an important category of human behaviour. Rather, it was recognised that errors in complex systems can come about in unforeseen ways at many levels in complex systems. Consequently, the best intervention strategy must be to promote good practice in human behaviour at all levels and aspects of the system. Again, such a strategy readily translates into a behavioural management package.

In aviation psychology, as in health psychology, the methodology used appears to have been determined by the prevailing *Zeitgeist*, not by a careful, or even occasional, examination of the effectiveness of alternative methodologies. Given the richness and diversity of the overall body of method and data in psychology in the last fifty years, there are obviously many possible starting points for the development of new areas of application. That is, if we wish to consider the management of a particular disease or the avoidance of a catastrophic accident in a particular system in the aviation industry, we can conceptualise issues and devise related methods from a number of different psychological perspectives. This, however, only increases the importance of relentless attention to the effectiveness of the methods adopted. Otherwise we risk extrapolating from weak findings and never gaining control of the phenomena of interest.

As has been shown, applied behavioural analysis has not been extensively investigated in these contexts, despite its track record elsewhere (see Kazdin, 1994, for an account of applications in clinical psychology and the *Journal of Applied Behavior Analysis* for many other areas of application). In the final part of this paper, I turn to a consideration of those factors or beliefs that currently persuade so many applied psychologists not to use behavioural approaches or methods.

Giving behaviour analysis away

It has been documented elsewhere that behavioural analysis and applied behavioural analysis have had a bad press, at least in earlier decades (Carey, Carey, & Turkat, 1983; Turkat & Feuerstein, 1978). A number of issues need to be emphasised to counter this and to facilitate the broader adoption of behavioural methods. Below I briefly mention a selection of these; the ones that I have selected concern the alleged 'narrowness' of behavioural analysis.

Analysis can occur at the level of large categories of behaviour

Although behavioural programmes have generally dealt with precise, small-scale categories of behaviour, this is not a necessary feature and there is no reason why higher-level skills cannot be the target.

Behavioural analysis should be placed in a professional context

Relatedly, even when a narrowly-defined behavioural category is the focus of interest, the programme of work with an individual client (for instance) must be seen in a broader context. Bernstein (1982) outlined a 'behavioural services model' with four elements; as well as the client and the 'manager' (who implements the programme), there must be an 'engineer' to design the programme and, crucially, a 'consultant' who provides resources for the programme. This is a helpful scheme, because it moves away from the traditional position of presenting applied behavioural analysis without its professional context.

Behavioural analysis is readily placed in its social context

Since Wolf (1978), behaviour analysts have been concerned with the social validity of their work. This can involve assessing public opinion as to the social significance of goals, the appropriateness of procedures and the importance of the effects of behavioural programmes. This is a process of explicitly identifying the social context, and it also addresses some of the ethical issues inherent in behavioural analysis (Leslie, in press).

The effectiveness of reinforcement contingencies varies with context

Behavioural interventions have largely been concerned with the identification and alteration of reinforcement contingencies. While it has always been stressed that three terms are required to define contingencies (the discriminative stimulus must be specified as well as the response and reinforcer), sometimes little attention has been paid to the important fact that these three elements will only function together under certain prevailing conditions or contexts. Michael (1993) has revived the term 'establishing operations' to describe this type of relationship, and it is important that the role of establishing operations both receives attention within behavioural analysis and is understood in applied behavioural analysis. That is, it must be realised that more effective behavioural change may sometimes be produced by altering prevailing conditions (that is, by changing establishing operations) than by altering contingencies.

These issues are amongst those that must be addressed if applied behavioural analysis, the most successful general strategy for modifying human behaviour, is to be 'given away' across the broad domain of applied psychology. Even the best products need appropriate marketing.

References

Azjen, I. (1988). *Attitudes, personality and behaviour*. Milton Keynes: Open University Press.

Bernstein, G. S. (1982). Training behavior change agents. *Behavior Therapy*, 13, 1–23.

Bradley, C., Brewin, C. R., Gamsu, D. R. & Moses, J. L. (1984). Development of scales to measure perceived control of diabetes mellitus and diabetes-related health beliefs. *Diabetic Medicine*, 1, 213–218.

Bradley, C., Gamsu, S., Moses, J. L., Knight, G., Boulton, A. J. M., Drury, J., & Ward, J. D. (1987). The use of diabetes-specific perceived control and health belief measures to predict treatment choice and efficacy in a feasibility study of continuous and subcutaneous insulin pumps. *Psychology and Health, 1*, 133–146.

Broadbent, D. E., Reason, J., & Baddeley, A. (Eds) (1990). *Human factors in hazardous situations*. Oxford: Clarendon.

Carey, K. B., Carey, M. P., & Turkat, I. D.(1983). Behavior modification in the media: A five-year follow-up. *American Psychologist, 38*, 498–500.

Coates, V. E. (1993). Beliefs, knowledge, and the self-management of diabetes. Unpublished DPhil thesis, University of Ulster.

Cox, D. J. & Gonder-Frederick, L. (1992). Major developments in behavioral diabetes research. *Journal of Consulting and Clinical Psychology, 60*, 628–638.

DCCT Research group (1993). The effect of intensive treatment of diabetes on the development of long-term complications in insulin-dependent diabetes mellitus. *New England Journal of Medicine*, 329, 977–986.

Fuller, R. (1994). Behaviour analysis and aviation safety. In N. Johnston, R. G. C. Fuller, & N. MacDonald (Eds), *Aviation psychology in practice* (pp. 173–189). Aldershot: Avebury.

Gale, A. & Chapman, A. J. (1984). The nature of applied psychology. In A. Gale & A. J. Chapman (Eds), *Psychology and social problems* Chichester: Wiley (pp. 1–26).

Harris, R., Linn, M. W., & Pollack, L. (1984). Relationship between health beliefs and psychological variables in diabetic patients. *British Journal of Medical Psychology, 57*, 253–259.

Johnston, M. (1996). Models of disability. *Psychologist, 9*, 205–10.

Kazdin, A.E. (1994). *Behavior modification in applied settings*. Fifth edition. Pacific Grove, California: Brooks/Cole.

Leslie, J. C. (1988). Behavioural analysis of professional competence. In R. Ellis (Ed.), *Professional competence and quality assurance in the caring professions* (pp. 179–198). London: Croom Helm.

Leslie, J. C. (1993). The Kraken wakes: Behaviourism in the twenty-first century. *Irish Journal of Psychology, 14*, 219–232.

Leslie, J. C. (1995). Behavioural theory and behavioural technology in the design of safe systems. In N. McDonald, N. Johnston, & R. Fuller (Eds), *Applications of psychology to the aviation system: Proceedings of the 21st Conference of the European Association for Aviation Psychology (EAAP)*, (pp. 209–215), Volume 1.

Leslie, J. C. (1996). *Principles of behavioral analysis*. Third Edition. Amsterdam: Harwood

Leslie, J. C. (in press). Ethical implications of behavior modification: Historical and conceptual issues. *Psychological Record*.

Lowery, B. J. & DuCette, J. P. (1976). Disease-related learning and disease control in diabetics as a function of locus of control. *Nursing Research, 25*, 358–362.

Michael, J. (1993). Establishing operations. *The Behavior Analyst, 16*, 191–206.

Owens, R. G. (1995). Radical behaviourism and life-death decisions. *Clinical Psychology Forum, 80*, 12–16.

Rachlin, H. (1989). *Judgement, decision and choice: A cognitive/behavioral synthesis*. New York: Freeman.

Rachlin, H. & Green, L. (1972). Commitment, choice, and self-control. *Journal of the Experimental Analysis of Behavior, 17*, 15–22.

Rotter, J. B. (1966). Generalised expectancies for internal versus external control of reinforcement. *Psychological Monographs, 80*, 1–28.

Sidman, M. (1960). *Tactics of scientific research*. New York: Basic Books.

Skinner, B. F. (1938). *The behavior of organisms*. New York: Appleton Century.

Skinner, B. F. (1950). Are theories of learning necessary? *Psychological Review, 57*, 193–216.

Turkat, I. D. & Feuerstein, M. (1978). Behavior modification and the public misconception. *American Psychologist, 33*, 194.

Wallston, K. A., Wallston, B. S., Kaplan, G. D., & Maides, S. A. (1976). Development and validation of the health locus of control scale. *Journal of Consulting and Clinical Psychology, 44*, 580–585.

Wolf, M. M. (1978). Social validity: The case for subjective measurement or how applied behavioral analysis is finding its heart. *Journal of Applied Behavior Analysis, 11*, 203–214.

7

The behavioural self-control of study in third-level students: A review

Samuel D Cromie and Leo J.V. Baker

Abstract

The applied behavioural literature on study is examined in the light of the theory of rule-governed behaviour. Self-control interventions are conceptualised as rules which specify, or imply, the self-control behaviours to be performed, the occasions for performing them and the consequences which will ensue.

Fourteen studies which used group designs to evaluate the relative efficacy of self-control interventions are reviewed. However, particular attention is given to five studies which employed single-subject designs since the data they provide are the most useful for getting a grasp of the precise behavioural processes that may be occurring. The interventions used included stimulus control, planning, contingency contracting, self-instructions, and self-consequation (encompassing self-reward, self-punishment and self-monitoring).

The chapter concludes that much of the literature operates with an inadequate, 'tool-box', conception of self-control. Self-reinforcement, self-monitoring and stimulus control are seen as unitary, distinct therapeutic devices which each work in some mysterious way but must, it is presumed, all work better together. Research has focused on which tools in the package are the 'active ingredients' with little regard for the fact that many of the procedures overlap considerably. What is needed is not more stimulus-control-versus-planning-versus-both-together-across-high-and-low-ability-students, controlled-outcome studies, but a coherent and comprehensive conceptual account of the behavioural processes involved in studying and improving studying. The theory of rule-governed behaviour provides a potent paradigm for providing such an account.

Introduction

The set of behaviours that we label as study has received little attention from pure behaviour analysts, rather it has been investigated as problem of applied behavioural analysis. This is probably because the analysis of human operant behaviour was not sufficiently developed to accommodate an account of such a complex human, social-behavioural phenomenon. However, with the advancement in the understanding of the apparently unique role of verbal behaviour in the determination of human behaviour, it is now necessary to scrutinise the literature in applied behavioural analysis to revise concepts, techniques and strategies which may have been inappropriately or crudely applied.

Rule-governed behaviour and self-control

Rule-governed behaviour is a theoretical concept that has been around for a long time, indeed since Skinner used it in 1953. However, it is only in recent years that it has come to take a significant place in behavioural theory, a milestone marked by Hayes (1989). It is this development in behaviour theory which, in particular, provides the scope for a more sophisticated account of self-control. It furnishes us with a means of analysing planning, self-instruction, contingency contracting, intentions statements and other behaviours associated with self-control, without recourse to mentalistic terminology. It can be argued that the theory of rule-governed behaviour has enriched the radical-behaviour perspective to the point where it can rival the explanatory scope of social-cognitive theory without relaxing its own conceptual rigour.

Mallot (1989) has taken up the task of integrating rule-governed behaviour into accounts of self-control. He argued that many of the goals towards which we work are too delayed, improbable or cumulative to directly reinforce behaviour. For example, tooth-brushing cannot be directly maintained by avoidance of tooth decay and gum disease, since these consequences generally occur years later, if they do, and each brushing of the teeth has only a tiny impact on the probability of their occurrence. Rather, he argues, the contingency acts indirectly through the mediation of rules.

Rules are descriptions of contingencies. They may specify all three components of the three term contingency, for example, 'If you brush your teeth (the behaviour) every morning and night (the antecedent) then you will not get gum disease (the consequence).' Often they only specify one or two of these components, with the other two being implicit. Thus 'Clean your teeth!' specifies only the behaviour. The implicit antecedents and the consequences derive from the listener's previous experience of that and similar rules, from that speaker, in that tone of voice.

Study as a problem of behavioural self-control

Several authors have offered behavioural analyses of the problem of insufficient and/or delayed study in third-level students. Early analyses (Rachlin, 1978; Whaley & Mallot, 1971) emphasised that the positive consequences that follow study, e.g., exam success, are *delayed*, while the reinforcers for alternative behaviours, e.g., social interaction and/or leisure activities are *immediate*. This temporal issue has long been seen as the nub of all self-control problems. Self-control interventions such as self-reinforcement were seen as means of making the positive consequences of study more immediate.

Rachlin (1978) saw self-control of study as equivalent to the self-control paradigm used in laboratory studies with non-humans (Rachlin & Green, 1972, for example). More recently, Mallot (1986; 1989) argued that the delayed consequences maintaining study behaviour, by contrast to those maintaining the pigeon's choice behaviours, are not direct acting but are mediated by rules. He insisted that outcomes of study, such as exam success, are too delayed, improbable and cumulative to directly reinforce behaviour. Rather, study is governed by rules, e.g., 'If you study now, then you will pass your exams in June.'

Self-control interventions

Self-control interventions in study have arisen out of the general behavioural self-control literature and have thus applied most of the techniques from this general literature. The most commonly researched techniques are self-monitoring and self-reward but stimulus control, planning, self-punishment, self-instructions and contingency-contracting have also been examined. This review will start with a survey of studies which used a group design before examining in more detail those which employed a single-subject design.

Group designs

Fourteen studies published between 1972 and 1985 used group designs to evaluate the relative efficacy of the various self-control procedures with third-level students. Some of them did not use study itself as a dependent variable, relying instead on grades and/or survey of study habits and attitudes (SSHA) scores as measures of academic competence and behaviours respectively (Greiner & Karoly, 1976; Groveman, Richards & Caple, 1977; Richards & Perri, 1978; Van Zoost & Jackson, 1974). Several studies used fairly sophisticated control groups (Kirschenbaum, Tomarken, & Ordman, 1982), while others simply compared specific self-control procedures with each other or manipulated particular dimensions of one procedure (Tichenor, 1977).

Stimulus control

Two studies examined stimulus control treatments (Richards, 1975; Ziesat & Rosenthal, 1978). Richards found that stimulus control as a treatment-addition to a study-skills advice programme actually produced deleterious effects on final-exam grades as compared with study-skills advice alone or study-skills advice plus self-monitoring. Ziesat and Rosenthal found no difference between stimulus control, self-reward and a combination of both procedures on study time or grade point averages, although all three self-control groups showed a greater increase in study time, but not in grade point average (GPA), over control groups.

The results of these two studies appear equivocal with regard to stimulus control until their methods are examined. While providing similar advice – setting aside times and a place exclusively for study and avoiding distracting stimuli – Richards's intervention consisted of two handouts while Ziesat and Rosenthal's subjects received two training sessions, either individually or in four-person groups. In these sessions, the subjects stated their chosen study place, block of time and daily quota of study time, which the experimenter noted, they committed themselves to this plan and were given tally sheets to self-record daily study time. Thus, Ziesat and Rosenthal's procedure included the extra components of personal instruction, forced statement of plans, public commitment to them, and self-monitoring. The social context of this intervention, rather than the advice itself, may have been responsible for its effectiveness although the fact that the increase in study time was not reflected in GPA gains leaves open the possibility that Richards's grade data may have missed actual changes in study.

Stimulus control is a very general term for an intervention. In behavioural terms, it covers not only the time and place of study but external and self-instructions, statements, rules and plans. It also makes little sense when treated in isolation from the consequences of the behaviour. That is preceding stimuli do not control behaviour except when they differentially predict the consequences, positive or negative, of the behaviour. This is the potential of public, social standard setting (Hayes, Rosenfarb, Wulfert, Munt, Korn, & Zettle, 1985) in that it establishes external consequences for standard following and breaking that are not easily retracted.

Self-consequation

Nine studies used interventions explicitly examining some form of *self-consequation*: self-reward, self-punishment, self-monitoring, or self-recording. These components are considered together since they all employ similar procedures – rules are stated which establish the students' study or non-study behaviours as cues (S^D) for performance of other behaviours (R) – self-consequating responses, and may describe or imply externally mediated social consequences (S^+/S^-). They differ in the nature of the consequences used, the consequences of following or not following the intervention rules, in how explicitly they specify the three terms of this contingency, the cue for the self-consequating behaviour, the self-consequating behaviour itself and the consequences that attend it, and the social context of the intervention.

Bristol and Sloane (1974) used recording and graphing as a baseline condition against which to compare the effects of contingency contracting on study time in a combined single-subject (ABAB) and group design. They also included a no-treatment control group who were only requested to follow the recording and graphing procedure for the initial pre-assignment baseline.

Study time in the contracting group increased 100 per cent during the contracting phases while that of the self-monitoring group rose 30 per cent. This 30 per cent increase was probably due to the fact that two of the three tests during that quarter occurred while the experimental group was in a contracting phase and the self-monitoring groups showed a pronounced scalloping pattern in plotted study time prior to tests. Perhaps the most important finding of this study regarding self-monitoring was that recording and graphing maintained by experimental contingencies did not negate the scalloping effect, although study-time data from the no-recording control group are not available.

Greiner and Karoly (1976) found that neither training in self-monitoring nor the addition of self-reward led to significant improvements over a study-skills training programme alone while the further addition of planning strategies did. This finding emerged in two outcome measures – psychology-quiz scores and SSHA scores. Most significant for the purposes of this review are the data from the self-monitoring records of the self-control groups. Subjects trained in planning strategies studied more and spread their study more evenly over the days of the experiment than those trained only in self-monitoring or self-monitoring and self-reward. There was no difference between these latter two groups.

Subjects were trained either individually or in small groups in most of the studies on self-control of study. Two studies, however, utilised a bibliotherapy intervention – training consisted primarily of typed handouts (Richards, 1975; Richards, McReynolds, Holt, & Sexton, 1976). The significance of this procedure may be that minimising experimenter-subject interaction may also have minimised implicit social contingencies.

Richards (1975) found that the inclusion of a stimulus control component did not lead to a greater number of pages read or hours studied than study-skills advice and self-monitoring alone (self-monitored data). Results from other outcome variables, psychology course final-exam scores and final grades and scores on a therapist-developed, multiple-choice test similar to the final course exam, led him to conclude that self-monitoring is an effective treatment addition to study-skills advice.

Richards, McReynolds, Holt, and Sexton (1976) attempted to replicate the findings of Richards (1975) to evaluate the efficacy of low and high information feedback in self-monitoring and to investigate whether the addition of self-administered covert and overt consequences would augment the behaviour change. They were also interested in whether uninformed students whose estimates of their own study time prior to self-monitoring were inaccurate would benefit more from self-monitoring than informed students whose estimates were more accurate.

All the self-monitoring plus study-skills advice groups showed superior exam grades compared with the study-skills advice alone group. Neither high-information feedback nor self-administered consequences enhanced the effectiveness of self-monitoring on this dependent variable (results were not presented for self-monitored study time). Uninformed students benefited more from self-monitoring than informed ones: they increased their study time more, showed greater increase in exam scores and were more likely to report that the self-monitoring techniques helped and to request extra self-monitoring sheets after treatment.

Tichenor (1977) attempted to experimentally separate out the effects of self-monitoring and self- and external reinforcement, while also examining the effects of delayed versus immediate reinforcement *in situ* or in the experimenter's office. Only groups using *in situ* self-reinforcement (immediate or delayed) reported significantly more minutes studied than the self-monitoring-only group; there was no significant difference between the groups on test scores. Tichenor concluded that reinforcing oneself in the natural environment is an important determinant of the efficacy of the reinforcement while immediacy of reinforcement is not and suggested that this may be because the stimuli associated with the reinforcer acquire discriminative stimulus properties which cue further studying.

Jackson and Van Zoost (1972) set out to compare the relative efficacy of self-reinforcement, external reinforcement and no reinforcement in enhancing learning of good study habits from a study-skills course. In two different studies they found that both self- and external reinforcement of correct performance of study-skills exercises in the training situation significantly increased study-habits scores on the SSHA, while there was no significant difference between the two experimental groups. The authors concluded that self-regulated evaluation and reinforcement is at least as effective as externally governed assessment and reward. Jackson and Van Zoost raise the question of whether the change in reported study habits was due to self-evaluation and self-administration or simply enhanced self-observation.

Van Zoost and Jackson (1974) instructed students in self-reinforcement of self-monitoring behaviours rather than of study itself, reasoning that a common deficit in study-skills is the student's inability to monitor his own behaviour. They found, however, that self-reinforced monitoring of study behaviour or library behaviour in conjunction with a study-skills programme did not yield increases in SSHA scores significantly greater than the study-skills programme alone.

Ziesat and Rosenthal (1978) compared the effects of self-reward with stimulus control alone and a combination of the two treatments and also divided subjects between individual and group treatments with or without a self-punishment procedure. All three self-control groups increased their study time significantly over the control group which received non-directive counselling as a placebo treatment, though no significant effects were observed in GPA scores. Neither individual treatment nor self-punishment enhanced study on any of the dependent variables used: study time, attitudes toward studying, or GPA.

Hayes *et al.* (1985) critically examined the literature of self-reinforcement and proposed that the reported empirical effects operate through the mechanism of social standard setting. That is, the observed effects are due not to self-consequation nor to goal setting per se but to the establishment of a socially available standard against which their performance can be evaluated.

Hayes *et al.* tested this hypothesis in a group-design study using students studying for the Graduate Record's Exam on a teaching machine on which they read passages, answered subsequent questions and checked their answers by advancing the machine. They used a 2 by 2 by 2 (public or private, goal setting with or without self-delivery of external consequences, their favourite edibles, baseline or experimental) factorial design, plus a feedback-only control. Self-consequating groups were given control of the edible and told that they were expected to consume a predetermined amount of it if they met their goal for the number of correct answers to each passage. Private goal-setting groups wrote down their goals on a piece of paper and posted them in a box, having been led to believe that no-one would know which goal was theirs while those in the public goal-setting conditions gave the paper to the experimenter who read it back to them as if to confirm it.

Public goal-setting groups showed the greatest increase in the average number of answers correct per passage from baseline to treatment phase. Self-reinforcement enhanced the increase for public goal-setters but not for subjects led to believe that their goals were private.

An important implication of Hayes *et al.*'s analysis is that social standard setting may be a principle mechanism underlying the effectiveness not just of self-reinforcement but also of goal setting and more elaborate planning interventions. In fact, they conducted an applied extension of the above experiment as part of a study-skills programme. Students in the public goal-setting group wrote down and announced to the rest of the group their goals for the number of modules they would study and the score they would receive on a subsequent test of study-skills knowledge (all subjects took such a test prior to the first treatment session). The private goal-setting group anonymously posted their written goals in a box while the control group was not asked to set any goals.

Students in the public goal-setting group improved significantly more on the test of study-skills knowledge than the other two groups, though they did not study more modules. They also came closer to meeting their stated goals than those in the private goal-setting group. Hayes *et al.* suggested that, rather than goal-setting automatically inducing a process of self-evaluation and self-consequation, it establishes a social standard with which 'one strives to perform consistently . . . based on a past history of socially based reinforcement for doing so' (p. 212).

Planning

Kirschenbaum and his colleagues (Kirschenbaum, Humphrey, & Malett, 1981; Kirschenbaum, Tomarken, & Ordman, 1982) built on the finding of Greiner and Karoly (1976) that the addition of a *planning* component was a critical component in raising the performance of students receiving self-control training above that of those only trained in study-skills. They set out to identify some critical variables determining the efficacy of a planning intervention. The variables they examined were specificity of planning (Kirschenbaum *et al.*, 1981) and choice (Kirschenbaum *et al.*, 1982). The planning intervention in all three studies consisted in instructing the subjects in the following planning strategies: breaking difficult tasks down into smaller units, setting an achievable standard for reward, and being specific about the task size and rewards.

Kirschenbaum *et al.* (1981) found, contrary to expectation, that monthly rather than daily planning increased study time and improved study habits, compared with controls. Kirschenbaum *et al.* (1982) subsequently found that subjects who received the planning intervention (daily or monthly) of their choice out-performed those who did not and the control groups, on most measures. They also replicated the finding that monthly planning interventions are, generally, more effective than daily ones. In particular, students in the group who used a monthly plan by choice showed less of a cramming pattern in their self-reported study time than those who used daily plans by choice, though the latter group reported more study time overall. The empirical data on planning indicate it to be a useful addition to a self-control package, particularly if the planning strategy used can be chosen by the subject.

Contingency-contracting

Contingency-contracting was included by Kirschenbaum and Perri (1982) as a behavioural rather than a self-control intervention, although it can be viewed from a self-control perspective as a pre-commitment strategy. Bristol and Sloane (1974) showed contingency contracting to be more powerful than recording and graphing alone in increasing study times, but only below-average students improved their test grades. This study is examined in more detail later.

Self-instructions

Miller and Gimpl (1972) reported the only group-design study in the literature explicitly using *self-instructions* as an intervention. The self-instruction intervention, which followed one week's self-recording baseline, required the subject to read 'the appropriate instructions' aloud to himself three times a day (morning, noon and evening) using an observer of his choice as his witness. It is unclear exactly what the instructions were but they probably consisted of a statement of the experimenter-defined study time target for the day and/or the subject's own plan for distributing this time during the day. In the third week, differential reinforcement contingencies were introduced to five groups using course points as reinforcers.

Differences in study time between the five groups only emerged in the third week. Group 1, who received no reinforcement and followed the same procedure as in Week 2, studied significantly less than all other groups. Group 5, which received course points for *tandem self-instruction and study*, studied significantly more than the three other reinforcement groups who gained course points for self-instructions, study, or both. Miller and Gimpl made the tentative generalisation that 'self-instructions are most effective when reinforcement contingencies involve a complete sequence of self-instructions and behaviour consistent with them' (p. 498).

Case studies and single-subject designs

Few single-subject design studies have been reported in the literature. However, since the data they provide are the most useful for getting a grasp of the precise behavioural processes that may be occurring, they are presented below in some detail. Case studies are also valuable from another perspective: if an adequate behavioural account is to be offered, it needs to explain the specific behavioural patterns of the individual, especially those which diverge from the norm, and not the average behaviour of a group of students.

The first single-subject design using a self-control intervention to improve academic competence that is reported in the literature was by Fox (1962). He did not provide study data for the five students in his pilot study but he reported that they all improved their average grade by at least one letter grade. His study was split into two phases, the first concerned with study quantity, the second with quality.

In Phase 1, he attempted to establish stimulus control of studying by requiring his subjects to conduct the designated study sessions only in one room in the library and to leave that room when they stopped studying. Initially, he dealt only with one course per student, asking him to go to the study room at the same specified time each day to study that course.

To maintain these study periods as positive events, subjects were to leave the room immediately they felt discomfort or began day dreaming. To maximise the use of available reinforcers, Fox instructed them that before they left they were to perform one specified short study behaviour, e.g., reading a page of text, and then to go and do whatever pleased them.

The principle of successive approximations was used. The amount of this behaviour that was required was increased each day until the student spent a full hour studying. Then the experimenter switched his focus to another course, applying the same procedure to bring it up to criterion and so on until the student was spending an hour a day on every course.

The procedure in Phase 2 involved training the subjects in study-skills using Robinson's (1946) SQ3R technique. However, training was not just instruction as is most common in study-skills training. Fox again used the principle of successive approximation. He started by teaching what he considered the easiest task, surveying, and worked up to the hardest, recitation. With each task he initially instructed the subject to perform a minimal form of the study skill and then gradually increased the demands until the student reached what the experimenter deemed an optimal level.

In addition to the specific interventions outlined above, there were several other aspects of the procedure which may have had considerable influence on the success of the programme. On being recruited, subjects were told that, not only would the method improve their grades, but it would require them only to study in the day time and leave evenings and weekends free – quite an attractive offer and a strong positive expectancy manipulation.

Subjects met with the experimenter individually every day for five or ten minutes, a high frequency of contact which could in itself be a powerful variable. Although Fox suggests reducing time with a professional counsellor in similar programmes in the future by utilising other students or written or computerised instructions, it is difficult to imagine the social contingencies of these alternatives being as powerful as those in the original high-contact intervention. This is especially the case when the means used to maintain the following of instructions are examined.

The experimental instructions were written down for the subject and it was stressed that he should follow them to the letter and that failure to do so might lead to the counsellor's refusal to work with him. Each day students were asked in detail what they had done the previous day and, if they had violated the instruction in any way, they were warned that further violations might lead to the termination of counselling. No other study in the literature appears to have used such stringent censure for noncompliance with experimental instructions. The characteristics of this study appear to be ideally suited to maximising the demand characteristics that Kanfer, Cox, Greiner & Karoly (1974) showed to be powerful in influencing self-control behaviours.

Goldiamond (1965) reported two case studies of individuals referred to him with study problems with whom he used what he called 'self-control interventions'. The first case was one in which the problem was handwriting illegibility which is not relevant to the present review. The second client came to him for advice because of his poor academic record.

Goldiamond identified the problem as one of not merely insufficient study but of no study at all. How he ascertained this baseline of zero was not made clear but the first intervention he made was daily self-recording of the number of hours spent studying for each course and the total for the day.

Goldiamond presented daily study charts for two courses. For a language class with daily recitations, the subject reported studying an average of over one hour per day, fairly evenly distributed over a 37-day period, while for another class he studied 'minimally' except for one day immediately prior to a test on which he studied three hours.

These data prompted Goldiamond to institute daily quizzes in his classes and he reported that the averages rose. However, it is not clear if the averages he refers to are study times for the subject, for his class as a whole, or another type of average, e.g., grade point averages, as no data were presented.

Goldiamond introduced several other interventions with this subject but they fit more into the category of study-skills interventions, outlining texts, and creating flash cards.

In summary, Goldiamond introduced one self-control intervention with this client, self-recording, however he provided baseline data and subsequent intervention data only at an anecdotal level so little can be concluded about the efficacy of the procedure. The apparent control over the rate of studying exerted by external contingencies (tests and recitations) is suggested by the data he does report, but since the data came from two entirely different courses, rates may have been affected by a variety of other variables.

Goldiamond's paper is of value as a source for self-control and other behavioural-intervention ideas for personal behaviour problems and has certainly been cited extensively in the subsequent literature. But it provides no firm evidence for the efficacy of self-recording as a self-control intervention with inadequate study.

Bristol and Sloane (1974) used a combined individual and group design to investigate the effects of contingency-contracting on study rate and test performance. The individual aspect of the study was a time-sample, ABAB design, the baseline condition being recording and graphing of study time for an introductory psychology course and the intervention being contingency contracts specifying on daily task cards the amount of time subjects were to spend studying introductory psychology and the monetary reward to be earned for achieving the target. The target criterion was faded in, increasing by 10 minutes per day for the subsequent week if the target was achieved on four of the five previous days.

All twelve students who received the contingency contracting intervention reported a significantly higher mean study time during the contracting phases than during the recording and graphing phases. These results were highly consistent across individuals and are some of the most clear and consistent single-subject data in the literature.

The question arises as to why contingency contracting had such a powerful effect on reported study times. Bristol and Sloane pointed out three aspects of the contracting procedure that may have played a role in its effectiveness: the monetary reinforcers, the recording and feedback, and the social reinforcement from the experimenter.

What exactly Bristol and Sloane meant by recording and feedback and how it differs from the recording and graphing of the baseline is not entirely clear. One difference that is clear is that targets were set in the contracting phases but not in the baseline phases. Thus, a public social standard was set which Hayes *et al.* (1985) have shown powerfully influences study behaviour. This would seem to be the fundamental difference between the phases, the monetary and social reinforcers only making sense with respect to the social standard set.

Looked at from this perspective the contingency contract is a rule-based intervention. A rule was stated describing a contingency: the amount of time introductory psychology must be studied (R), on a particular day (S^D) to receive a particular sum (S^+). Since the experimenter's approval and monetary reward were received weekly rather than immediately on completion of the target time, it would seem that these contingencies were not direct acting but were mediated by rules that described them (Mallot, 1989).

The implication of this analysis is that to explain the increase in study time we need not look primarily at the social and monetary consequences but at the rules that were stated to the subjects and at their previous history of rule-following and rule-breaking. Particularly we need to examine the specific context in which the rules were stated: introductory psychology students received rules from a research psychologist, they were explicitly stated on task cards, some of their classmates received this contracting procedure, others did not. The context was also one of a psychology experiment.

Cohen, De James, Nocera and Ramberger (1980) reported two case studies using a 'simple self-instruction procedure'. The goal was to increase physical exercising in one subject and studying in the other.

The first study used an ABC design, 'A' being the baseline when Sally, the subject, recorded how much she exercised each evening at home in her living room. Her exercise regimen was clearly specified. During the experimental demand phase (B), Sally wrote a series of instructions on an index card telling herself exactly what routine to follow while exercising. She agreed to read the card sub-vocally every evening immediately prior to exercising. In the self-instruction intervention (C), Sally wrote an additional set of instructions describing not *what* she was to do while exercising, but *why*, e.g., 'I would like to appear "slim and trim" when wearing slacks and as summer approaches I would like to feel comfortable wearing a two-piece bathing suit'. These instructions were to be read at four specified times during the day for the next 27 days, while continuing to follow the experimental demand procedure.

Sally recorded her own exercising by using one-minute momentary time sampling for 20 minutes per evening in which she recorded the presence or absence of exercise behaviours. How she recorded this without interrupting the exercises is not reported. Her mother on nine occasions made reliability checks, achieving an inter-observer reliability of 96 per cent.

Cohen *et al.* took the unusual step of reporting a critical part of the procedure in the results section. It is only here that it emerges that a changing-criterion design was used during the self-instruction condition, eight criterion phases, specifying the number of minutes of exercise to be done, led up to the target of 20 minutes. It is unclear what these criteria involved, i.e., how explicit or important they were in Sally's instructions.

'Experimental demands' increased exercise time somewhat and Sally reached her target of 20 minutes' exercise on two days at the end of the self-instruction condition. But there was a serious confounding of the self-instruction intervention with the criterion-setting procedure. The close control exerted by the criteria implicates the criterion-setting procedure as a critical variable. It is possible that self-instructions may have enhanced the control exerted by the criteria but the design of the study precludes this analysis.

This case report is a clear demonstration of how verbal behaviour can govern non-verbal behaviour in an applied setting. Cohen *et al.* focused on two types of verbal interventions which they call experimental demands and self-instructions. Their choice of terminology is questionable as both procedures seem to use explicit self-instructional interventions which differ in the content of the instructions, the former specifying the exact behaviours to be performed and the latter focusing on the consequences (S^+/S^-) of performing and not performing the behaviours.

Two other classes of verbal behaviour in this case to which the authors gave less attention were the basic exercise regimen and the criterion-setting procedure. The basic exercise regimen, presumably introduced at the start of the baseline phase, was virtually identical to the experimental demand procedure except that in the latter Sally wrote the instructions out explicitly herself and agreed to read them daily at the specified time. This is the self-instructional aspect of the experimental demand phase which was included in the design to ensure that the changes in the subsequent self-instruction phase were due to the content of the instructions rather than the self-instructing procedure itself.

The verbal behaviour involved in criterion setting was not explicitly described but it would appear to fall into the category of social standard setting (Hayes *et al.*, 1985). It specified a certain quantity of the behaviour that would lead to positive social consequences (experimenter approval) if achieved and negative social consequences if not achieved. These consequences were probably not explicitly stated but the previous history of most socialised humans would include more or less frequent contact with the consequences of reaching or failing to reach social standards.

The second case study Cohen *et al.* (1980) reported used an ABCAC design to modify the study behaviour of a college student, Betty. The conditions again were baseline (A), experimental demands (B) and self-instructions (C), respectively. Betty identified her problem as one of numerous distractions while studying (reading) at home, an apartment which she shared with two others. While she was supposedly studying she frequently talked on the telephone or to her roommates, listened to music, or snacked on 'junk' foods.

The dependent variables used were percentage time on task, self-recording using a five-minute, momentary time-sampling procedure for approximately one hour per evening, five evenings a week, and the number of sentences she underlined per day. One of Betty's room-mates conducted reliability checks on 16 occasions, yielding an inter-observer reliability of 96 per cent.

During the baseline phase the only intervention made was self-recording of study behaviour. As in the previous case report (on Sally), both the experimental demands and the self-instruction phases involved instructions about studying written on index cards, the former to be read once before commencing study and the latter every 15 minutes during study. The difference between the type of instructions in the two conditions for Betty is even less obvious than in the case of Sally. Both sets of instructions describe the behaviour to be engaged in (study), and those to be avoided (snacking, etc.), and the consequences of studying and of the other behaviours. The only difference seems to be that the instructions in the self-instruction condition were more explicit about the positive consequences of study, good grades.

The outstanding procedural differences between the two intervention conditions were not in the nature of the self-instructions but in the frequency with which they were to be repeated and in the self-instructions phases containing the two sets of instructions. The experimental-demands procedure remained in effect while the self-instruction procedure was added.

There was an increase in study time over the baseline level in the experimental-demand phase, a further increase in the self-instructions phases and then a drop in the withdrawal period. The results for the number of sentences underlined were not as expected as a clear increase over the baseline level was observable only for the second self-instructions period and a decrease occurred in the experimental-demand phase.

This case study is another demonstration of the verbal control of behaviour, both experimental demands and self-instructions being verbal interventions whatever the supposed difference between them. The fact that these interventions increased percentage time on task more than sentence-underlining did supports an analysis in terms of rule governance, since the instructions were specifically directed at maximising the former variable, percentage time on task, rather than increasing the latter, sentence underlining.

Cohen *et al.* pointed out that they did not collect data on how frequently Betty and Sally actually used the self-instructions; only the frequency with which they were instructed to use them was stated. Thus, it is not entirely clear whether the effects observed were those of self-instructions or external instructions alone. It also raises the question of whether the two can be separated in verbally proficient humans, i.e., do external instructions generally cue self instructions anyway?

Green (1982) used a single-subject, multiple-intervention design to differentiate the effects of self-monitoring and self-reward on study behaviours of six 'academically disadvantaged minority students' enrolled in a reading improvement class. Two weeks of baseline data were recorded prior to a two-week, self-monitoring phase and, finally, a six-week condition in which self-reward was added to the self-monitoring procedure.

The primary dependent variables were externally recorded *academic behaviours*, attendance, prompt completion of assignments, and study time in the study centre. Complementary to these variables, three *procrastinative behaviours* were recorded, tardiness (the number of minutes the subject arrived after a class began), postponed assignments (the number of days an assignment was late), and postponed studying (the number of days that passed before a subject commenced studying).

A major advantage of the use of externally-recorded dependent variables is that the baseline is a true baseline, i.e., not affected by self-recording reactivity and thus the efficacy of self-monitoring can be evaluated in a single-subject design using actual study behaviours as a dependent variable. The self-monitoring intervention entailed instructing the subjects on how to observe and record the same academic behaviours recorded by the external observers and using the same behavioural definitions. Self-monitoring did not, however, include recording procrastinative behaviours.

The self-monitoring plus self-reward condition was divided into three two-week periods. A new self-reward contract commenced at the start of each period and continued to the end of the study. The self-reward intervention involved instructing subjects in how to arrange contingencies and reward themselves. For each self-reward contract they selected the reinforcer to be used from a list of favourite activities using the following three criteria: the activity was accessible and controllable, it was rated with a high reward value, and its preferred frequency was higher than its current frequency. The contract stated that the subject was making a binding contract with himself or herself to partake in a specified activity contingent on and immediately following his or her performance of specified academic behaviours. Subjects also recorded whether they met the criterion for self-reward and whether they engaged in the reward activity. The order of the use of the three academic behaviours in the self-reward contracts was varied across subjects.

A further outcome measure used was the percentage of initial contract maintenance, whether the level of the dependent variables was increased or decreased between the initial week and subsequent weeks. Grades achieved on assignments were also used as an outcome measure.

Two process measures were used. The percentage of accurate self-monitoring was calculated as the agreement between subjects' and observers' observations of each behaviour. The percentage of self-reward was the percentage of occasions on which the subject reached the reward criterion that he or she self-rewarded.

The results reported for the whole group on academic behaviours, procrastinative behaviours, and grades on both assignments and passages were remarkably consistent. On each of these eight dependent variables the self-monitoring plus self-reward condition showed significant improvement over both the self-monitoring and baseline conditions while no significant difference was found between self-monitoring and baseline conditions.

Green concluded that self-reward plus self-monitoring is an effective self-control strategy for the intervention to improve the academic competence of minority students. He did not address the question of which components of the combined procedure were effective. The major issue is whether the self-reward worked because of genuine self-reinforcement or because of other aspects of the intervention.

The reward procedure given to the subjects in this study was based on Premack's principle (Premack, 1965) of making preferred behaviours contingent on performance of less-preferred behaviours to increase the frequency of the latter. Green provided a process measure, percentage of self-reward, which indicated that the students gave themselves the specified reward on between 58 per cent and 98 per cent of occasions when it was earned. However, he provided no process measure relating to non-contingent consumption of the reward. Reinforcement, according to Premack's principle, would require both a high percentage self-reward and a low non-contingent consumption. Given that the rewards were favourite activities, watching television, listening to records, for example, it is doubtful whether this second criterion was met.

The self-reward condition also included a contracting intervention, the subject met with the experimenter, specified the contingencies, and included them in a specific contract. Exactly how specific the contracts were is not stated by Green, but it is clear that this procedure involved some form of public goal setting, which may itself be a potent component of self-reinforcement procedures (Hayes *et al.*, 1985). Thus, even though the contract was made by the subject with himself or herself, the presence of the experimenter made it, to some degree, a public contingency contract.

In addition to this public statement of the contract, the subjects were also required to provide the experimenter with records of when they met the performance criterion and when they self-rewarded. Thus, keeping to the contract, or at least putting oneself frequently in contact with the rules of the contract, was maintained by an external social contingency. Green concluded from his data showing a high percentage of initial contract maintenance that (minority) 'students are able to enact several self-reward contracts for different academic behaviours and continue these self-reward contingencies simultaneously' (p.642). But it may be that the self-recording procedures he initiated as process measures maintained the contracts rather than the 'abilities' of the students.

The self-monitoring procedure was not effective in producing significant changes in academic behaviours. Green cited previous research that suggested that self-monitoring is more effective if it is continuous rather than intermittent (Mahoney, Moore, & Moura, 1973) and uses a number of different self-monitoring methods. This suggests a further confound in the self-monitoring plus self-reward condition: that self-monitoring of contract keeping and self-rewarding behaviours may have been sufficient extra self-monitoring to make the intervention effective.

In summary, the clear and consistent improvement in the self-monitoring plus self-reward condition relative to the baseline and self-monitoring conditions may be attributable to any one of four components of the procedure: self-reinforcement, public goal-setting through contracting, social reinforcement of contract re-reading, and self-monitoring of contract keeping. Thus, not only did the students follow their study behaviours with rewards but they also publicly stated the contingencies and were socially reinforced for restating the rules to themselves and for recording the correspondence of their behaviour to those rules.

Non-intervention studies of self-control of study

Two studies have investigated the self-control strategies used by students who were identified as successful or unsuccessful self-controllers (Heffernon & Richards, 1982; Perri & Richards, 1977). Perri and Richards found that successful self-controllers used more self-control techniques for a longer period of time and in particular were more likely to have used written self-monitoring and self-reinforcement procedures. Heffernon and Richards replicated these findings and found in addition that 'planned schedules' were used more frequently by successful self-controllers. 'Planned schedules' referred to students setting aside specific blocks of time each week for certain study activities and simply monitoring whether they followed their plan or not.

Irving Wallace (1977) presents samples of the self-monitoring diaries he kept for many years while writing his novels. Each day he would record the number of pages he wrote and note occasional reasons why he wrote little or nothing on a particular day. His self-monitoring graphs are strikingly similar to the respond-pause-respond pattern observed on fixed-ratio schedules (Ferster & Skinner, 1957) with finishing a chapter apparently functioning as the reinforcer.

These data are seductive in that it is tempting to assume functional equivalence from topographical similarity. However, human rule-governed performance can also resemble animal schedule-shaped performance (Lowe, 1979). The question remains: was Wallace's respond-pause pattern shaped directly by the reinforcer of finishing a chapter or mediated by self-generated rules, either in tact or mand form (Zettle & Hayes, 1982). It is also unclear whether self-monitoring was functionally crucial in forming and maintaining this work pattern or simply an adjunct to it.

Implications

This review has raised a number of methodological and theoretical issues which are relevant to the conduct and analysis of research in self-control of study. Most of these issues also have wider application for the field of self-control.

The paucity of good single-subject data is remarkable in this field. Although they were collected in a lot of these studies, they have rarely been reported. This does not allow for a fine-grain analysis of the behavioural processes involved. Discussion of self-reinforcement as an intervention depends to a large extent on group averages, whereas the theoretical and practical issues concern what is actually happening at the individual behavioural level. Are subjects reinforcing their own study behaviour? Do they consume reinforcers non-contingently?

A related issue is the widespread use of the grade point average as a dependent variable. A grade point average is not a direct study variable. It is an assessment of a behavioural repertoire that, it is assumed, is acquired partly by studying. It is also an infrequently sampled behaviour lacking the continuity of day-to-day study data that permits fine-grain behavioural analysis.

Another limitation of existing research is that many studies either gave course credits for participation or paid subjects. No experiment which involves conscious participation can exclude the influence of demand characteristics altogether. However, the inclusion of such external incentives must remove the behaviour further from the setting in which it naturally occurs, or does not occur, that is, when the students attempt to control themselves. A completely ecologically valid self-control intervention study may be impossible. However, whereas advice and self-help techniques are commonly received from friends, books and parents, the student is rarely paid to follow them or to record his study. He may be paid to *succeed* in study but not to perform the behaviours someone else thinks will make him succeed.

This methodological limitation is indicative of a wider problem, that of undue focus on the *content* of interventions, with little regard for their *context*. Much of the literature, particularly the counselling literature, operates with a 'tool-box' conception of self-control. Self-reinforcement, self-monitoring and stimulus control are seen as unitary, distinct therapeutic devices which each work in some mysterious way but must surely all work better together. Research has focused on which tools in the package are the 'active ingredients' with little regard for the fact that many of the procedures overlap considerably. What is needed is not more stimulus-control-versus-planning-versus-both-together-across-high-and-low-ability-students, controlled-outcome studies, but a coherent and comprehensive conceptual account of the behavioural processes involved in studying and improving studying. Rather than just analysing programmes to determine which strategies were effective, the critical dimensions of effective strategies need to be identified.

To achieve this, studies need to give more comprehensive accounts of the actual procedures entailed in interventions. Analysis of a number of the studies reported here have been hampered by inadequate reporting of method. Particular aspects of the study which warrant description are: the method of recruitment of subjects and the incentives for participation, the social context of the study, the exact nature of the instructions, whether plans are publicly stated, and the pattern of explicit external contingencies on study (exam deadlines, etc.).

The social context is the broadest of these. It includes the nature of the relationship between students and experimenter whether the experimenter is a lecturer, post-graduate, friend or acquaintance of the student. Also important is the relationship between subjects. If they are friends, classmates or likely to have regular contact the context is different than if they are unacquainted. Similarly the context of meetings with the experimenter is relevant, whether they are group of individual, formal or informal. These three aspects of the social context all are relevant to the implicit social contingencies that may attend both study and adherence to the intervention.

This review has highlighted some critical features for an adequate theoretical analysis of studies in self-control of study. The verbal components of instructions and interventions need to be examined. They can best be conceptualised as rules which describe contingencies on study and on following the intervention. In tandem with this it is critical to examine the contingencies that attend rule-following and breaking, both in the experimental context and in the wider social environment. In sum, rules are central to self-control interventions and rules derive their power from their social context. To ignore rules or the social context is to limit the scope of the analysis.

The focus of this review has been on theoretical and methodological issues, rather than on practical effectiveness. Thus it does not bring any answers to the question, 'which is the most effective strategy?' Instead it has argued that the development of more effective self-control strategies demands a more sophisticated theoretical analysis and methodological approach.

References

Bristol, M. M. & Sloane, H. N. (1974). Effects of contingency contracting on study rate and test performance. *Journal of Applied Behavior Analysis, 7,* 271–285.

Cohen, R., De James, P., Nocera, B., & Ramberger, M. (1980). Application of a simple self-instruction procedure on clients' exercise and studying: 2 case reports. *Psychological Reports, 46,* 443–451.

Ferster, C. B. & Skinner, B. F. (1957). *Schedules of reinforcement.* New York: Appleton-Century-Crofts.

Fox, L. (1962). Effecting the use of efficient study habits. *Journal of Mathematics, 1,* 75–86.

Goldiamond (1965). Self-control procedures in personal behavior problems. *Psychological Reports, 17,* 851–868.

Green, L. (1982). Minority students; self-control of procrastination. *Journal of Counselling Psychology, 29,* 636–644.

Greiner, J. M. & Karoly, P. (1976). Effects of self-control training on study activity and academic performance: An analysis of the effects of self-monitoring, self-reinforcement and systematic planning components. *Journal of Counselling Psychology, 23,* 495–502.

Groveman, A. M., Richards, C. S., & Caple, R. B. (1977). Effects of study skills counselling versus behavioral self-control techniques in the treatment of academic performance. *Psychological Reports, 41,* 186.

Hayes, S. C. (Ed.) (1989). *Rule-governed behavior: Cognition, contingencies, and instructional control.* New York: Plenum.

Hayes, S. C., Rosenfarb, I., Wulfert, E., Munt, E., Korn, Z. & Zettle, R. D. (1985). Self-reinforcement effects: An artifact of social standard setting? *Journal of Applied Behavior Analysis, 18* (3), 201–214.

Heffernon, T. & Richards, C. S. (1981). Self-control of study behavior: Identification and evaluation of natural methods. *Journal of Counselling Psychology, 28,* 361–364.

Jackson, B. & Van Zoost, B. (1972). Changing study behaviours through reinforcement contingencies. *Journal of Counselling Psychology, 19* (3), 192–195.

Kanfer, F. H., Cox, L. E., Greiner, J. M., & Karoly, P. (1974). Contracts, demand characteristics and self-control. *Journal of Personality and Social Psychology, 30* (5), 605–619.

Kirschenbaum, D. S., Humphrey, L. L., & Malett, S. D. (1981). Specificity of planning in adult self-control: An applied investigation. *Journal of Personality and Social Psychology, 43,* 941–950.

Kirschenbaum, D. S. & Perri, M. G. (1982). Improving academic competence in adults: A review of recent literature. *Journal of Counselling Psychology, 29,* 76–94.

Kirschenbaum, D. S., Tomarken, A. J., & Ordman, A. M. (1982). Specificity of planning and choice applied to adult self-control. *Journal of Personality and Social Psychology, 42,* 576–585.

Lowe, C. F. (1979). Determinants of human operant behavior. In M. D. Zeiler & P. Harzem (Eds), *Reinforcement and the organisation of behavior.* Chichester: John Wiley.

Mahoney, M. J., Moore, B. S., Wade, T. C., & Moura, N. G. M. (1973). The effects of continuous or intermittent self-monitoring on academic behavior. *Journal of Consulting and Clinical Psychology, 42,* 65–69.

Mallot, R. W. (1986). Self-management, rule-governed behavior and everyday life. In H. W. Reese & L. J. Parrot (Eds), *Behavior science: Philosophical, methodological and empirical advances* (pp. 207–228). Hillsdale, NJ: Lawrence Erlbaum.

Mallot, R. W. (1989). The achievement of evasive goals: Control by rules describing contingencies that are not direct acting. In S. C. Hayes (Ed.). *Rule-governed behavior: Cognition, contingencies, and instructional control* (pp. 85–96). New York: Plenum.

Miller, A. & Gimpl, M. P. (1972). Operant verbal self-control of studying. *Psychological Reports, 30,* 495–498.

Perri, M. G. & Richards, C. S. (1977). An investigation of naturally occurring episodes of self-controlled behavior. *Journal of Counselling Psychology 24,* 178–183.

Premack, D. (1965). Reinforcement theory. In D. Levine (Ed.), *Nebraska Symposium on Motivation* (pp. 123–180). Lincoln: University of Nebraska.

Rachlin, H. (1978). Self-control: Part I. In A. C. Catania & T. A. Brigham (Eds). *Handbook of applied behavior analysis* (pp. 259–274). New York: Irvington.

Rachlin, H. & Green, L. (1972). Commitment, choice and self-control. *Journal of the Experimental Analysis of Behavior, 17,* 15–22.

Richards, C. S. (1975). Behavior modification of studying through study-skills advice and self-control procedures. *Journal of Counselling Psychology, 22,* 431–436.

Richards, C. S., McReynolds, W. T., Holt, S., & Sexton, T. (1976). Effects of information feedback and self-administered consequences on self-monitoring study behaviors. *Journal of Counselling Psychology, 23,* 316–321.

Richards, C. S. & Perri, M. G. (1978). Do self-control procedures last? An evaluation of behavioral problem solving and faded counsellor contract as treatment maintenance strategies. *Journal of Counselling Psychology, 25,* 376–383.

Robinson, F. P., (1946). *Effective study*, New York: Harper & Row.

Skinner, B. F. (1953). *Science and human behavior.* New York: The Free Press.

Tichenor, J. L. (1977). Self-monitoring and self-reinforcement of studying by college students. *Psychological Reports, 40,* 103–108.

Van Zoost, B. L. & Jackson, B. T. (1974). Effects of self-monitoring and self-administration of reinforcement on study behaviors. *Journal of Educational Research, 67,* 216–218.

Wallace, I. (1977). Self-control techniques of famous novelists. *Journal of Applied Behavior Analysis, 10,* 515–525.

Whaley, D. L. & Mallot, R. W. (1971). *Elementary principles of behavior.* New York: Appleton-Century-Crofts.

Zettle, R. D. & Hayes, S. C. (1982). Rule-governed behavior: A potential theoretical framework for cognitive-behavioral therapy. In P. C. Kendall (Ed.), *Advances in cognitive-behavioral research and therapy* (pp. 76–120). New York: Academic Press.

Ziesat, H. A., & Rosenthal, T. L. (1978). Behavioral self-control in treating procrastination of studying. *Psychological Reports, 42,* 59–69.

8

Compliance training as an intervention strategy for antisocial behaviour: A pilot study

Dermot O'Reilly and Karola Dillenburger[1]

Abstract

By the time we reach adulthood most of us have engaged in some kind of behaviour that involves the infringement of family or community values or rules, such as hitting, cheating, stealing, truancy or lying. While these behaviours can be termed antisocial they are usually short lived and do not attract clinical attention. They are clearly distinguished from patterns of persistent antisocial behaviour that are displayed by children who are referred for clinical intervention. Kazdin (1987) introduced the term 'Conduct Disorder' for children who break family or societal rules to this extent. In this chapter we will discuss the concept of conduct disorder and its utility for clinical intervention. We will outline treatment approaches such as parent management training, compliance training and planned activity programmes. We will conclude with an example of these applied to the case of a seven-year-old boy and his mother. The results indicate an increase in the mother's appropriate instruction giving, contingent attention, and correct programme implementation, and an increase in the child's compliance. Although these increases were rather small, they indicate that compliance training and planned activity programmes are a useful strategy for dealing with children who display antisocial behaviours in a pro-active, positive way.

Introduction

Most children, at one time or another, behave in ways that can be termed anti-social because they involve the infringement of family or community values or

[1] The authors wish to acknowledge and thank Patricia Byrne (MSW) for her contributions in the development of the coding schema and data collection.

rules. Antisocial behaviours such as hitting, cheating, stealing, truancy or lying are usually short lived and, in the main, do not attract clinical attention. However, children for whom these behaviours persist and become more serious will usually come to the attention of professionals and may eventually be referred for clinical intervention. Kazdin (1987) introduced the term 'Conduct Disorder' for children who break family or societal rules to this extent. He defined the term as follows:

The term *Conduct Disorder* is used to refer to instances when the children evidence a pattern of antisocial behavior, when there is significant impairment in everyday functioning at home or school, or when the behaviors are regarded as unmanageable by significant others. (p. 187)

On the surface the terms 'antisocial behaviours' and 'conduct disorder' thus appear to refer to two distinct patterns of behaviour, but the description and classification of child behaviour disturbance is by no means straightforward. There is some debate about whether the kind of behaviour problems described above can be classified with the same degree of rigour as other clinical syndromes. Usually clinical syndromes are categorised either by the occurrence of clusters of common symptoms or by a single conspicuous symptom. For example, children may be categorised as autistic because they present a cluster of common symptoms, such as ecolelia or mutism, stereotypical behaviours, lack of social behaviours and fixation on particular objects. On the other hand, children may be labelled, for example as encopretic if they show the single symptom of soiling.

In relation to conduct disorder the boundaries are not as clear cut. Behaviours displayed by children who are labelled as conduct disordered vary considerably. In an attempt to draw some kind of diagnostic distinction, Wolff (1977) looked at the boundary between delinquent and nondelinquent disturbances of conduct. However, due to the occurrence of very broad ranges of behaviour patterns she could not identify separate clinical syndromes. Wolff concluded that it is not possible to distinguish between delinquent and nondelinquent conduct disorder. In fact, she went as far as saying that in the case of conduct disordered children

. . . we shall have to do without specific syndromes and limit ourselves instead to considerations of the general associated, antecedent and outcome factors related to children who, whatever else may be the matter with them, also display aggressive, acting-out but non delinquent behavior. (p. 490)

The term conduct disorder, then, does not refer to a clinical syndrome in the traditional sense. It is, however, useful as a diagnostic category as long as we keep in mind that the '. . . correlates of such behavior are likely to be less valuable in the management of the individual case than if we were dealing with a more specific clinical syndrome' (Wolff, 1977, p. 490).

Conduct disorder

As a diagnostic category the term conduct disorder represents certain methods of classifying child behaviour disturbance. In all there are three distinct methods of classifying child behaviour disturbance, all of which are relevant to research and clinical intervention (Sanders & Dadds, 1993). These are:

1. Diagnostic taxonomy

2. Dimensions of dysfunction

3. Behavioural approach

1. *A diagnostic taxonomy* (of which the term 'conduct disorder' is an example) summarises symptom clusters by giving them a common label. This is the approach usually taken in the diagnosis of psychopathology. While, as stated above, conduct disorder cannot be delineated as clearly as other clinical syndromes, the following general characteristics have been identified:

. . . all children with Conduct Disorders of whatever kind share certain characteristics; they are predominantly boys, they tend to come from lower socio-economic backgrounds, they frequently have educational difficulties and their future outlook is less good than that of children without antisocial behavior. (Wolff, 1977, p. 490)

In so far as the term conduct disorder is used as a description of the kind of behaviours that can be expected from a child it may be a useful summary label. It is important to point out though that a summary label is not to be confused with an explanation of the behaviour in question (Grant & Evans, 1994).

2. *The dimensions of dysfunction approach* identifies the degree to which a child's behaviour varies from that of a normative comparison group across a range of dimensions of dysfunction, such as aggression, anxiety or depression. This approach is characterised by the use of behavioural checklists, such as the Child Behavior Checklist (Achenbach, 1991) in which behaviour is charted and then compared with normative data.

In relation to conduct disorder the dimensions of dysfunction vary considerably. As mentioned earlier the behaviours in question can range from delinquent to nondelinquent disturbances of conduct. However, it is difficult to establish concrete normative data of antisocial or conduct disordered behaviours as family and cultural norms and values differ considerably and what is deemed antisocial in one family or culture may well be acceptable in another.

3. *The behavioural approach* relies on a clear description of the individual's repertoire and focuses on excesses or deficits of behaviour in the context in which the behaviour is performed. Specific behaviours are of interest in their own right and assumptions about the extent that they are symptomatic of an

underlying disorder or dysfunction are avoided. In fact, the usual inferential process which characterises diagnostic taxonomies such as the Diagnostic and Statistical Manual of Mental Disorders (DSM–111–R) (American Psychiatric Association, 1987) is viewed as hindering the process of identifying the causes for the behavioural excess or deficit. Baum (1994) considered this point when he stated that because '. . . mental fictions give the appearance of explanations, they tend to impede the inquiry into environmental origins, which would lead to a satisfactory scientific explanation' (p. 46).

A behavioural approach to conduct disorder focuses on the actual behaviours of the child in question rather than on hypothetical inferences. For example, the behaviour of stealing would be analysed in terms of distal as well as proximal antecedents and consequences. The emotional state of the child during the stealing episode would be analysed in similar terms (Skinner, 1953). Reference to hypothetical inferences regarding the underlying motivation for the action is avoided, because the actions of a person, which include emotions and thoughts, are viewed as dependent variables that are a function of contingencies of reinforcement and punishment.[2]

The main advantage in diagnosis and classification of clinical syndromes is that labels are provided which describe and classify child behaviour disturbance in general terms. The utility of such a system is that clinicians and researchers can share in a common international language of child psychopathology (Sanders & Dadds, 1993) and as such a common basis of epidemiological studies is established (e.g., Robins, 1991).

Diagnosis alone, however, does not provide clues to the management of specific cases (Wolff, 1977). Terms used in diagnosis and classification are summary labels of certain behavioural patterns that can be useful in the identification of problem situations of social value but should not be confused with the aetiology of the behaviour. At the clinical level the patterns of deviant behaviour which are exhibited by individual children are of primary concern. 'If a behavior is socially important, the usual behavior analysis will aim at its improvement. The social value dictating this choice is obvious' (Baer, Wolf & Risley, 1968, p. 91). Behavioural assessment leads to a detailed description of the child's behavioural repertoire and treatment then focuses on changing specific patterns of behaviour, such as increasing pro-social behaviour and decreasing anti-social behaviour. This approach has been applied in parent management training, functional family therapy, cognitive problem-solving skills training and community-based interventions (Kazdin, 1987). On the basis of published research, parent management training is the most effective

---

[2] 'Reinforcement' and 'punishment' are terms used to describe functional relations between behaviour and consequences. The term 'reinforcement' is used if consequences function to increase behaviour in frequency, duration, intensity, etc. The term 'punishment' is used if consequences function to decrease behaviour along any of the same dimensions.

treatment method for conduct disordered children. Kazdin (1987) found that none of the other interventions for antisocial children have '. . . been investigated as thoroughly and shown as favourable results'. (p. 192)

Parent management training

In parent management training parents are taught to alter their interactions with their children. This form of treatment is based on knowledge gained from the thorough scientific analysis of behaviour. An individual's behaviour is viewed as a function of ontogenetic as well as phylogenetic contingencies, that is to say, human conduct is determined by genetic selection during the evolution of the species as well as behavioural selection during an individual's lifetime (Skinner, 1981). The latter obviously is the focus of parent management training because, during each individual's lifetime, behaviours are selected through contingencies of reinforcement and punishment. Knowingly or unknowingly parents as well as other relevant adults arrange most of these contingencies for young children.

Patterson's (1982) research into childhood aggression illustrates this point. Patterson undertook direct observations of children in their home environment in order to examine patterns of interaction in families who had been referred to the Oregon Social Learning Centre because of antisocial child behaviour. He found that when the behaviour of each family member was compared with non-problematic controls, family members of children with antisocial behaviour were significantly more likely than controls to exhibit coercive behaviour. Roughly one third of antisocial child behaviours in these families occurred in response to aversive or coercive behaviour of another family member. Patterson (1982) surmised the following:

In effect, a sizeable proportion of coercive child behaviours could be thought of as *counterattacks*, i.e., they were reactions to noxious intrusions. . . . Clearly, then, much of children's aggression is not attack but *counter*attack behavior. (p. 148)

Patterson found that coercive behaviours tend to be performed by other family members besides the target child and that the performance of coercive behaviour by one family member serves to increase the likelihood that other family members will perform further coercive acts. He refers to the self-reinforcing pattern of coercive interactions in these families as the 'Negative Reinforcement Trap'. Parent management training attempts to interrupt the cycle of mutually reinforcing coercive events by training parents to elicit and reinforce prosocial child behaviour and by using mild but effective forms of punishment for antisocial behaviours. For example, Forehand and McMahon (1981) devised a clinic-based parent training programme in which the parent is trained to implement specified skills such as attending, praising, ignoring, commanding and the use of time-out from positive reinforcement procedures

(Martin & Pear, 1992). During the first half of the programme parents are trained to become effective reinforcement agents. A central tenet of the programme is that parents should attend to and reinforce prosocial child behaviour rather than concentrating primarily on punishing deviant child behaviour. The motto is to 'Catch your child being good' (Forehand & McMahon, 1981, p. 62). The parents are trained to implement time-out from positive reinforcement procedures only when they have acquired the skills of attending, praising, giving instructions and ignoring.

Parent management training has been demonstrably effective in achieving behaviour change with a wide range of discrete child behaviour problems including hair-pulling, thumb-sucking, psychogenic vomiting and stealing (Moreland, Schwebel, Beck, & Wells, 1982). It has also made a contribution to the treatment of childhood disorders such as autism (Breiner & Beck, 1984). However, although parent management training has been shown to be effective in achieving behaviour change, the positive treatment effect has not always generalised.

Generalisation of treatment effects

The generalisation of treatment effects is an important issue because treatment is successful only when the desired change is achieved in the relevant setting or in the presence of relevant persons. 'If the application of behavioral techniques does not produce large enough effects for practical value, then application has failed' (Baer, Wolf, & Risley, 1968, p. 7). For example, if behavioural change is achieved in the clinic setting but does not generalise to the home setting, treatment cannot not be considered complete or successful. Without due consideration of the generalisation of treatment effects, treatment becomes unnecessarily prolonged and relapse is much more likely. Generalisation, according to Stokes and Baer (1977), is defined as the

. . . occurrence of relevant behavior under different, non-training conditions (i.e., across subjects, settings, people, behaviors and/or time without the scheduling of the same events in those conditions as had been scheduled in the training conditions). (p. 350)

While the importance of generalisation of treatment effects seems to go without saying, it is only recently that it has attracted significant amounts of attention. In the early 1980s, Moreland *et al.* (1982) reviewed parent management training studies that were published between 1975 and 1981 and concluded that the question of treatment generalisation had not received sufficient attention. In fact, they called for a concentration on this issue in future studies:

Since there now appears to be substantial evidence that parent training procedures do reduce targeted children's behavior problems, future studies should focus upon evaluating factors which may facilitate the generalization of parent training effects. (p. 269)

Since then many researchers have heeded their recommendation and an increasing number of studies in parent management training include a direct consideration of the generality of treatment effects. Wiese (1992) reviewed 148 parent training studies and found that between 1975 and 1984 only 51 per cent of studies included consideration of generalisation effects; since than (between 1984 and 1990) 63 per cent of the studies included generalisation information.

There are two main strategies that have been adopted in parent management training for the enhancement of treatment generalisation (Cataldo, 1985). On one hand, specific procedures are applied to the target problem behaviours in a range of settings. This approach can, however, present certain problems, especially when as Cataldo put it, the '. . . consequence is that parents then seek additional behavioral programmes for each succeeding problem' (p. 340). The other approach to enhance generalisation effects in parent management training is not to deal with the target problem immediately, but instead to teach parents general behavioural principles first. This approach is based on the assumption that if parents are '. . . well versed in the principles, generalization of techniques to successive behavior problems is supposed to be enhanced' (Cataldo, 1985, p. 340). In most studies this assumption is not explicitly tested In fact, this approach is so unpredictable that Stokes and Baer (1977) refer to it as the 'Train and Hope' strategy for promoting generalisation.

A much more reliable approach to enhance generalisation of treatment effects in parent management training seems to be compliance training. Here parents are taught to '. . . reinforce compliance using a standard, specific set of techniques. Since almost any behavior problem can be identified as a compliance problem, an immediate solution is provided for the target or referred problem. . . . Generalization is inherent in the procedure instead of a process that parents must extrapolate from successive behavior programmes or from being taught principles' (Cataldo, 1985, p. 340).

Compliance training

Compliance training refers to a set of procedures where the child is reinforced for responding appropriately to parental instructions. Ducharme and Popynick (1993) describe compliance as a 'keystone behaviour', because an increase in compliant responding has been associated with an increase in non-targeted pro-social behaviours, a phenomenon which is termed 'Behavioural Covariation'. The behavioural covariation effect of compliance training has been examined in a number of studies. Russo, Cataldo and Cushing (1981) examined changes in the aberrant behaviour of three children (between three and five years of age) with developmental disabilities in response to contingent reinforcement of compliance to adult instruction. Although there was some variation between subjects, compliant responding was accompanied by a reduction in aberrant behaviour even though these behaviours had not been targeted directly.

In a later study, Parish, Cataldo, Kolko, Neef and Egel (1986) examined whether functional relations existed between compliance to adult instruction and maladaptive behaviours. Four developmentally disabled children (three to five years of age) who had been identified as exhibiting non-compliance and inappropriate behaviours were studied. Results indicated that compliant and maladaptive behaviours varied inversely; contingent reinforcement of compliant behaviour decreased inappropriate behaviour and contingent punishment of inappropriate behaviour increased compliant behaviour.

Cataldo, Ward, Russo, Riordan and Bennett (1986) found in their study that compliance to adult instruction weakened when it was not followed by explicit consequences. They acknowledge a number of features of the study that might restrict the clinical implications of the results:

1. Observations of the children were conducted in a residential setting with clinic staff, rather than with parents.

2. The children were developmentally disabled.

3. In discrete trials the children were given five specified instructions, such as 'Sit down/Stand up'. These were repeated three times during each training session during each phase of the study. The precision of this kind of procedure would be difficult to achieve within a home setting with non-delayed children.

Despite these misgivings, the authors conclude that, the results '. . . lend strong support for a clinical treatment strategy based on reinforcing children for complying with instructions in order to also modify a variety of problem behaviors in addition to non-compliance' (Cataldo *et al.*, 1986, p. 279).

Although all these studies suggest that compliance training may enhance generalisation of treatment effects by leading to a reduction in non-targeted problem behaviours, there are a number of ethical considerations to be considered. Firstly, it is important to establish that compliance to instruction is not a terminal goal (LaVigna & Donnellan, 1986). Compliance training takes place within the context of a programme that also includes other prosocial components. Secondly, some compliance training programmes have advocated the use of physical management in response to persistent non-compliance (Forehand & McMahon, 1981; LaVigna & Donnellan, 1986). The physical management of severely oppositional and aggressive children within the context of a compliance training programme can lead to confrontational parent-child interactions (Ducharme & Popynick, 1993). Since abusive parents have been found to engage in more physical discipline strategies than do non-abusive parents (Urquiza & McNiell, 1996) and physical abuse of children often takes place in the context of disciplinary confrontations (Bourne, 1993) there are risks associated with advocating physical management of conduct disordered children.

Alternative behaviour reduction strategies, such as extinction, are not without problems within the context of compliance training. Patterson (1982) argues that due to the patterns of mutual reinforcement that occur in family interactions, planned non-reinforcement (extinction) of aggressive behaviour by parents may serve to induce further aggressive behaviour. He concludes, that for '. . . child management purposes, extinction of coercive behavior is not a useful concept' (p. 147).

Still, in most cases compliance training programmes for the treatment of antisocial behaviour in children will not be effective unless they include some form of behaviour reduction strategies for non-compliant behaviours. Little and Kelley (1989) suggest that response-cost procedures can be used effectively with this client group. One important aspect of these procedures is that it seems that parents find them more acceptable than time-out from positive reinforcement or physical punishment. Thus, they are more likely to be implemented by parents on a consistent basis. In response-cost procedures, similar to standard token systems, children may be awarded points that can be exchanged for treats, activities, privileges, or other previously identified reinforcers. Points can then be deducted contingent upon non-compliant behaviour. Results from Little and Kelley's (1989) study suggest that, given its efficacy and its acceptability to parents, the procedure represents an viable alternative to procedures that include physical management.

Background to pilot study

The compliance training programme that is described here is a modification of a child management programme reported by Sanders and Dadds (1982). Their child management programme was based primarily on a behaviour reduction strategy, that is parents were trained to apply a behaviour correction procedure to specified problem behaviours such as demanding, aggressing, tantruming, interrupting and non-complying. Treatment generalisation was assessed in 'problem settings'. These were settings which had been identified by parents as being associated with child problem behaviour. The authors reported that while change in parent behaviours, such as increased use of praise and non-aversive attention, did occur these were not strongly related to treatment outcome.

In order to improve on these results, Sanders and colleagues (Sanders & Dadds, 1982; Sanders & Christensen, 1985) developed an aspect of their compliance training programme that specifically aimed to emphasise positive, pro-social aspects of the parent-child relationship. They called the procedure 'planned activities'. The idea of planned activities is that the parent preplans activities with the child, thus setting the stimulus context for the intervention. Furthermore, this procedure creates a situation in which the parent can give constructive instructions to the child and the child is likely to comply, thus offering opportunities for positive reinforcement of prosocial behaviours. The procedure introduces parents to new educational and relational skills and ultimately, '. . . such strategies may be seen as more acceptable solutions to problem behaviors than are approaches that focus exclusively on contingency management' (Sanders & Christensen, 1985, p. 116).

The aim of the pilot project described here was to examine whether a parent management training programme that comprised planned activities, instruction-giving and response cost was feasible as a treatment strategy for antisocial behaviour within the home setting.

Method

Screening

Given the range of referrals that are received daily in a child guidance clinic it was necessary to include an initial screening of cases prior to inclusion in the programme. The following criteria were set for inclusion in the study:

1. The subject had to be between three and seven years of age and not suffering from an organic condition which was directly associated with behaviour problems.

2. During a pre-baseline assessment interview parents had to report that child behaviour problems included antisocial behaviour.

3. On the Child Behavior Checklist (CBCL) (Achenbach, 1991) the child had to have scored within a clinically significant range for externalising behaviour. The CBCL is a questionnaire which consists of 118 items. It measures parents' perceptions of their children's behaviour problems. Each item contributes to a specific dimension of dysfunction (e.g., delinquent, withdrawn) which in turn contributes to two global dimensions of disturbance (internalising behaviour and externalising behaviour), and a total behaviour problem score. It has been tested for reliability and validity.

4. On the Parenting Stress Index (PSI) (Abidin, 1990) the score had to indicate stress within the parent–child dyad. The PSI is a questionnaire that is designed to measure the relative components of stress in the parent–child system. It has 101 items and has been tested for reliability and validity. The child domain includes items on adaptability, acceptability, demandingness, mood and distractibility-hyperactivity. The parent domain includes items on depression, attachment, restriction of role, sense of competence, social isolation, relationship with spouse and parental health.

5. During one pre-baseline observation session in the home non–compliance to parental instructions had to be 50 per cent or less.

Subject

Kevin C. (not his real name), a seven-year-old boy, was the subject in this study. He had been referred to the child guidance clinic because of behaviour problems at home. Kevin's mother, Mrs C., reported that he had recently begun to destroy her personal belongings. He had thrown items of her jewellery in the bin and had emptied shampoo on her bed. She reported that these incidents had occurred following disciplinary confrontations and she complained that 'he will not take correction'.

Kevin lived at home with his mother and his three-year-old brother. Mr C. had left the home six months previously in order to undergo a residential treatment programme for drug addiction. Mrs C. acknowledged that the atmosphere in the home during the previous two years, when Kevin's father had become addicted to heroin, had been marked by tension and unhappiness. At the time of referral Mr C. had relocated to another part of the country in order to avoid the drug subculture with which he had been associated. He visited the home on a regular basis but did not participate in the parent management training programme. By the time that the programme was completed, Mr C.'s visits to the home had become irregular, and Mrs C. acknowledged that she was very uncertain as to whether he would rejoin the family.

The scores on the CBCL indicated that Kevin was within borderline clinical range on the withdrawn and aggressive subscales. Scores on the PSI indicated that while the total score was within normal range, there were high scores within the child domain subscales for demandingness and non-adaptability. Within the parent domain subscales, there were high scores (indicating dysfunction) for parent attachment and for parent's sense of competence. During the screening observation session in the home environment, Kevin complied with 84 per cent of parental instructions. His mother, however, did not respond with contingent attention (praise) to a single instance of compliant behaviour. It was therefore decided that although Kevin did not present as clinically non-compliant, a compliance training programme would help his mother to reinforce compliant responding, to attend to child prosocial behaviour and to punish aversive behaviour effectively.

Settings

All interviews and training took place in the child guidance clinic to which Kevin had been referred. Clinic-based training sessions were supplemented with training feedback sessions that were conducted in the home. Direct observations of mother and child behaviours were conducted in the home environment at pre-arranged times. The following criteria for observation sessions were implemented:

1. Mother, son and observer remained in an identified area of the house (kitchen or sitting room).

2. Television set was switched off.

3. Visitors and phone calls were kept to a minimum.

Observation procedures.

Observations of mother–child interactions were conducted in two different settings within the home:

1. Training setting (once a week). Observation was carried out by the first author (who acted as therapist).

2. Generalisation setting (twice a week). Observation was carried out by a trained observer.

Each observation session was pre-scheduled, of 30 minutes duration and was carried out in the home using a time sampling procedure (30-seconds). The observer was cued by an audio tape to observe Mrs C. and Kevin during a 20-second 'observe' phase, and to record one category each of parent and child behaviour during a 10-second 'record' phase. The observer was a social work trainee (Master's level) who had received training in the use of the coding schedule. This training included sample vignettes and sequences from video-tapes. The observer attended weekly recalibration sessions with the first author during each phase of the study. During these sessions video sequences were reviewed and decisions about coding were discussed.

Behaviour categories.

The observational coding schedule was based on the Family Observation Schedule-V [FOS-5] (Dadds & Sanders, 1996). This schedule includes behaviour categories for the instructional sequence (Table 1) as well as categories for specific parental behaviours (Table 2) and child behaviours (Table 3). For the present study an antecedent, behaviour, consequence (ABC) contingency record was added. Antecedent (parental instruction), behaviour (child response) and consequence (parent contingent attention) were recorded during each interval in which the parent issued an instruction.

A summary measure called 'programme implementation', was formulated in order to assess the effects of parent management training. Correct programme implementation was defined by intervals in which two specific parent behaviours (Alpha instruction and contingent attention) and one specific child behaviour (compliance) had been recorded. Alpha negative, Beta and negative instructions were not deemed to constitute correct programme implementation.

Table 1 *Instructional sequence*

Category	Symbol	Definition
Alpha instruction	1a	An order, suggestion, rule or question to which a motor response is feasible, and which is presented in a non-aversive manner.
Aversive Alpha instruction	1a–	An Alpha instruction which is presented aversively.
Beta instruction	1b	A command to which the child has no opportunity to comply due to vagueness or due to lack of opportunity to respond.
Aversive Beta instruction	1b–	A Beta instruction which is delivered in an aversive manner.
Compliance	c	Compliance or attempt to comply with parental instruction within 5 seconds.
Non-compliance	nc	Non-compliance to parental instruction within 5 seconds.
Praise	P	Positive descriptive comment about child or behaviour.
Response cost	RC	Parent issues warning that a privilege will be lost in response to non-compliance.

Inter-observer reliability

Inter-observer reliability was assessed on 25 per cent of observation sessions in the generalisation settings. The first author acted as the second observer. Inter-observer reliability were calculated interval-by-interval, using the following formula:

$$\frac{\text{agreement intervals}}{\text{agreement} + \text{disagreement intervals}} \times 100 = \% \text{ agreement}$$

(Cooper, Heron & Heward, 1987).

Inter-observer reliability was assessed for each category of behaviour comprising the instructional sequence, parental behaviour and child behaviour. Overall agreement ranged from 81 per cent for the child oppositional behaviour

Table 2 *Parent behaviour categories*

Category	Symbol	Definition
Aversive contact	C–	Parental physical contact with the child in an aversive fashion which causes pain or physical discomfort to the child.
Aversive social attention	S–	Social attention which is deemed to be aversive due to content and/or tone of voice.
Contact	C+	Parental physical contact with the child in a friendly, affectionate manner.
Social attention	S+	Pro-social, verbal or non-verbal parental attention to the child.
Non-attention	NA	Parent does not attend to target child.

Table 3 *Child behaviour categories*

Category	Symbol	Definition
Physical negative	p–	Actual or threatened motor movement in relation to another person that involves infiltrating physical pain. Also destruction of objects.
Complaint	ct	Whining, crying, protesting, temper tantrums.
Demand	d	An instruction or command which is aversive due to tone and/or content.
Oppositional	o	Inappropriate child behaviour that cannot be included readily into any other categories.
Contact	c+	Child physical contact in a friendly, affectionate manner.
Social attention	s+	Pro-social, verbal or non-verbal child attention to parent or sibling.
Appropriate behaviour	a	Non-social, constructive behaviour.
Withdrawal	w	Absence of interaction with objects or persons, or self-stimulation.

category to 100 per cent for the implementation of response-cost and the child withdraw behaviour category.

Design

A single–case–study design (AB) was used during this study.

Baseline

Four baseline points were collected on each of the parent and child behaviour categories mentioned above.

Compliance Training

The compliance training was based on three procedures: 1. activity planning, 2. instruction-giving and 3. response-cost procedure.

1. Activity planning

The parent completed an activity planning checklist on a daily basis. This checklist was designed to prompt the parent to specify:

- (*a*) three activities that she wants the child to engage in during the practice session;
- (*b*) three steps that she can take in order to leave herself free to give direction as necessary during the training period;
- (*c*) whether she had prepared the child by telling him of the plan for the 30-minute session;
- (*d*) her feedback to the child on how he has performed during the session.

2. Instructional procedure

The instructional procedure involved the following steps:

- (*a*) get the child's attention.
- (*b*) issue a single instruction calmly, with one behavioural referent.
- (*c*) pause five seconds to assess child's response.
- (*d*) respond appropriately in the case of

Compliance:	make a statement of descriptive praise.
Non-Compliance:	repeat steps (*a*) and (*b*), but insert a prompt. If the child complies, make a statement of descriptive praise.
Non-Compliance:	issue a warning calmly that a response cost will be implemented. If the child does not comply, implement response cost procedure.

3. Response-cost procedure

At the beginning of the training session, the child was awarded points in the form of a row of five smiling faces printed on a sheet of paper. If the child failed to comply with an instruction after having been given a warning, one of the faces was turned over. At the end of the training session the points were exchanged for preferred items which had been specified at the outset of the session (e.g., four faces earns four sweets).

The compliance training programme lasted four weeks and was divided into two phases. The first training phase lasted two weeks and included one introductory clinic-based training session at which the overall rationale of the programme was outlined, followed by weekly sessions in which the three compliance training procedures were introduced. During the following two weeks (training phase 2) weekly training sessions were continued and a review of video material taken during observation sessions was included. Particular attention was paid to correct programme implementation. During the four weeks of compliance training the therapist called to the home once each week to conduct an observation session and to provide feedback on the implementation of the programme.

Post-training phase

The post-training phase lasted two weeks and was used to assess maintenance of intervention effects. During this phase Mrs C. did not complete any further practice session checklists, though two observation sessions were conducted per week as during the baseline phase.

Results

Alpha instructions

The rate of parental Alpha instruction (Figure 1) during baseline averaged 11.7% of intervals. The introduction of Phase 1 of the compliance training programme was associated with a significant increase in the rate of parent Alpha instructions and averaged 32.3% of intervals. The rate of Alpha instruction decreased somewhat during Phase 2 to an average of 28.5% of intervals. An average of 36.4% Alpha instructions was recorded during the post-training phase.

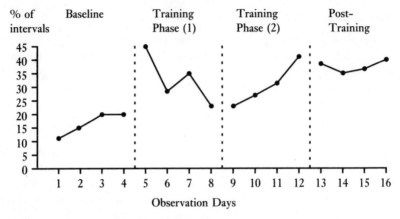

Figure 1. Percent of parental Alpha instructions across sessions.

Contingent attention

The rate of parental contingent attention (praise and implementation of response cost procedure) (Figure 2) averaged 2.3% of intervals during baseline. The introduction of Phase 1 of the compliance training programme was not associated with a significant increase in the rate of parent contingent attention; an average of 5.6% parental contingent attention was recorded. However, the introduction of Phase 2 led to an increase in the rate of parent contingent attention, and an average of 18.3% was recorded. The increase was maintained during the post-training phase, when an average of 30.8% parental contingent attention was recorded.

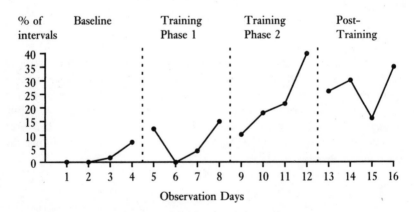

Figure 2. Percent of parental contingent attention across sessions.

Correct programme implementation

The rate of parent correct programme implementation (Figure 3) during baseline averaged 1% of intervals. The introduction of Phase 1 of the compliance training programme led to an increase in the rate of parent correct programme implementation. The introduction of Phase 2 led to a further increase. During the post-training phase this increase was maintained.

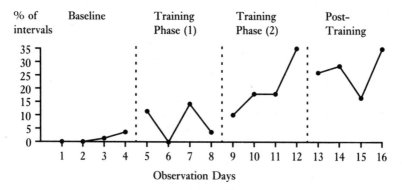

Figure 3. Percent of parental correct programme implementation across sessions.

Child compliance

The rate of child compliance (Figure 4) during baseline averaged 18.7% of intervals. The introduction of Phase 1 of the compliance training programme led to a significant increase in the rate of child compliance. During Phase 2 and post-training, this increase was maintained.

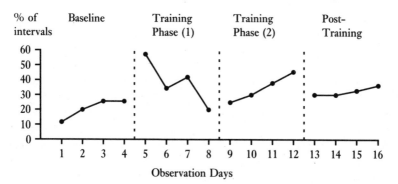

Figure 4. Percent of child compliance across sessions.

Discussion

A parent management programme was implemented with one parent-child dyad, a seven-year-old boy and his mother. The programme was based on compliance training including planned activity procedures, instruction giving and contingent response training. The results from this study showed an increase in the use of non-aversive instructions (Alpha instructions) by the parent, an increase in contingent attention by the parent, an overall increase in correct programme implementation by the parent and an increase in compliant behaviours by the child. Most of these increases were rather small and therefore only allow for tentative conclusions about the efficacy of the procedures.

The study reported here does, however, corroborate previous research that indicates that home-based parent management programmes for families with conduct-disordered children are a viable alternative to clinic-based intervention (Herbert & Iwaniec, 1981). On the other hand there are problems with home-based interventions. The interpersonal nature of parent management training means that it can be difficult to identify the exact variables that make it effective particularly in a home-based training setting. Home-based intervention is very labour intensive and unwelcome interruptions, such as telephone calls or visitors, can often not be prevented. As such, clinic-based training enables the therapist to be in control of the manipulation of contingencies much more rigorously.

Before discussing these points in detail it is important to note that in this study not only child behaviours but also parental behaviours were observed and recorded. All too often researchers of parent management programmes assume that parents implement the training content without collecting data to evidence changes in parental behaviour. As Stokes and Baer (1977) put it, a 'Train and Hope' strategy prevails. In order to assess the effect of treatment, research into parent management programmes should include evidence that parental behaviours have indeed changed.

The advantages of home-based training are, firstly, that the therapist is able to reinforce changes in parental behaviour in vivo; secondly, while reaching a steady baseline may be problematic, ultimately observations are likely to be more accurate due to the fact that they are taken in the environment where the problem behaviour usually occurs; thirdly, generalisation is more easily achieved due to the fact that training takes place in the setting in which the behaviour change is desired; and fourthly, behavioural maintenance can be achieved more readily when natural contingencies gain control over the newly acquired behaviours.

1. Reinforcing changes in parental behaviour in vivo

The parent in this study reported that she enjoyed the contact with the therapist and the observer. The effect that the presence of a therapist or observer has on parent and child behaviours is difficult to assess. However, the parent's implementation of the procedures improved during phase two of training, when weekly video reviews were included in the training. While this represents a greater investment of therapist time than that reported by Sanders and Dadds (1982), increased therapist attention and feed-back had a reinforcing effect on parent programme implementation. The emphasis of most parent training programmes is to teach parents how to reinforce their children's pro-social behaviours. In the main not enough attention is paid to the need to reinforce changes in parental behaviours. It is usually assumed that improved child compliance or an increase in desired behaviours in the child automatically has a reinforcing effect on parent programme implementation. The effect of a reinforcer can, however, only be measured by the function it has on the future probability of the behaviour. The study reported here showed that changes in parent behaviours could not be solely achieved or maintained by therapist instruction and changes in child behaviours. Additional reinforcement (i.e., therapist attention and positive feedback), especially in the early stages of intervention, was necessary to establish parent behaviour change. The increase in changes in parent programme implementation, as well as in the use of Alpha instructions and contingent attention during the post-treatment phase in this study, however, showed that once parent behaviours were fully established, child behaviour changes functioned effectively as reinforcers for parental behaviours.

2. Establishing a steady state

According to Johnston and Pennypecker (1993) it is important to achieve a steady baseline prior to intervention.

As a result of considerable experience and practice, behavioral researchers have learnt that if a properly defined and accurately measured behavior is repeatedly measured under conditions that are held constant from session to session (which often means that extraneous influences are absent, held constant, or at least have only very weak effects), the data will usually become relatively steady. (p. 190)

Achieving a steady state, while important in terms of full experimental control, can be difficult in home-based parent training settings (Herbert & Iwaniec, 1981). While defining and accurately measuring the targeted behaviour in a home-based training setting should not cause any particular difficulties, the level of extraneous influences is usually not fully under the control of the observer. Disruptions such as telephone calls and unexpected visitors may interrupt the observation session and influence the data. It may therefore be nearly impossible to hold conditions constant from session to session in a family home. This effect could be controlled if baseline observations were prolonged until a steady state is reached. However, in reality there is a limit to how long parents of conduct disordered children are prepared to wait for treatment to begin. In order to prevent parents from becoming disenfranchised it may at times not be possible to continue baseline observation until it is fully stabilised.

3. Achieving generality

Home-based training has a great advantage over clinic-based training in that the desired behaviour changes are achieved in the setting in which they are to be performed in the future. Generalisation of appropriate parent management is therefore usually achieved much more effectively in home-based training settings. In order to assess generalisation in the study reported here a distinction was made between training and generalisation settings during data collection. Both child and parent behaviours were observed in both settings. In the training setting the parent was to issue specified instructions during planned activities. Unspecified instructions were to be introduced only after a certain level of efficacy of parent management skills had been achieved. Generalisation was measured by the extent to which the parent used unspecified instructions in the generalisation setting.

However, the rate of unspecified instructions in the training as well as the generalisation settings increased quickly. In fact, the parent reported that she considered the observer as an integral part of the training programme. This comment suggested that treatment generalisation was taking place and confirms the findings of previous research that generalisation may be a function of the compliance training procedure in a home-based setting. Whether or not training for generalisation as a separate training component is necessary given the above procedure can only be assessed if generalisation is monitored throughout the study. As mentioned earlier this is not always the case in parent management research. The results of this pilot study suggest strongly that measurement of generalisation should become a matter of routine in future studies.

4. Achieving behavioural maintenance

Whether or not behavioural maintenance is achieved can only be assessed if observations continue after treatment is finished. Results of this study showed that treatment effect was maintained over time. Assessment of behavioural maintenance is often neglected in research in this area. The fact that the treatment effect was maintained in the present study without explicit training for maintenance indicates the effectiveness of home-based rather than the clinic-based parent management programmes. In home-based treatment natural contingencies can take over and ensure maintenance of treatment effects.

Conclusion

Even in families with severely conduct-disordered children not all interaction is conflicted and although behaviour reduction procedures were included in this study, the main intervention concentrated on the increase of pro-social behaviours in parent and child. Arranging contingencies to increase these pro-social behaviours must be the aim of parent management training. The study reported here shows that this kind of intervention is ethically sound and easily acceptable by all participants. Furthermore, it does not only improve targeted behaviours, but also has a positive influence on the atmosphere in the home. This is important in particular when working with children at risk of abuse.

References

Abidin, R. R. (1990) *Parenting Stress Index* (3rd ed.). Charlottesville: Paediatric Psychology Press.

Achenbach, T. M. (1991). *Manual for the Child Behavior Checklist/4–18 and 1991 Profile*. Burlington, VT: University of Vermont Department of Psychiatry.

American Psychiatric Association. (1987). *Diagnostic and statistical manual of mental disorders* (3rd ed.). Washington DC: Author.

Baer, D. M., Wolf, M. M., & Risley, T. R. (1968). Some current dimensions of applied behavior analysis. *Journal of Applied Behavior Analysis, 1*, 91–97. Reprinted in B.A. Iwata, J. S. Bailey, R. W. Fuqua, N. A. Neef, T. J. Page, D. H. Reid (Eds.). (1989) *Methodological and conceptual issues in applied behavior analysis*. Reprint Series, Volume 4. (pp. 1–7). Lawrence: Society for the Experimental Analysis of Behavior, Inc.

Baum, W. M. (1994). *Understanding behaviorism: Science, behavior, and culture*. New York: Harper Collins.

Bourne, D. F. (1993) Over chastisement, child non-compliance and parenting skills: A behavioural intervention by a family centre social worker. *British Journal of Social Work, 23*, 481–499.

Breiner, J. & Beck, S. (1984). Parents as change agents in the management of their developmentally delayed children's non compliant behaviors: A critical review. *Applied Research in Mental Retardation, 5*, 259–278.

Cataldo, M. F. (1984). Clinical considerations in training parents of children with special problems. In R. E. Dangel & R. A. Polster (Eds) *Parent training: Foundations of research and practice*. New York: Guilford Press.

Cataldo, M., Ward, E., Russo, D., Riordan, M., & Bennett, D. (1986). Analysis and intervention. *Developmental Disabilities, 6*, 265–282.

Cooper, J. O., Heron, T. E., & Heward, W.L. (1987). *Applied behavior analysis*. New York: Macmillan.

Dadds, M. R. & Sanders, M. R. (1996). *Family observation schedule-V [FOS-5]*. unpublished, personal communication.

Ducharme, J. M. & Popynick, M. (1993). Errorless compliance to parental requests: Treatment effects and generalization. *Behavior Therapy, 24*, 209–226.

Forehand, R. & McMahon, R. J. (1981). *Helping the non compliant child: A clinician's guide to parent training*. New York: Guilford Press.

Grant, L. & Evans, A. (1994). *Principles of behavior analysis*. New York: Harper Collins.

Herbert, M. & Iwaniec, D. (1981). Behavioural psychotherapy in natural home-settings: An empirical study applied to conduct disordered and incontinent children. *Behavioural Psychotherapy, 9,* 55–76.

Johnston, J. M. & Pennypecker, H. S. (1993). *Strategies and tactics of human behavioral research* (2nd ed.). London: Erlbaum.

Kazdin, A.E. (1987). Treatment of antisocial behavior in children: Current status and future directions. *Psychological Bulletin, 2,* 187–203.

LaVigna, G. W. & Donnellan, A. M.(1986). *Alternatives to punishment: Solving behavior problems with non-aversive strategies.* New York: Irvington.

Little, L. M. & Kelley, M. L. (1989). The efficacy of response cost procedures for reducing children's non-compliance to parental instructions. *Behavior Therapy, 20,* 525–534.

Martin, G. & Pear, J. (1992). *Behavior modification. What it is and how to do it.* New York: Simon & Shuster.

Moreland, J. R., Schwebel, A. I., Beck, S., & Wells, R. (1982). Parents as therapists: A review of behavior therapy parent training literature – 1975 to 1981. *Behavior Modification, 6,* 250–276.

Parish, J. M., Cataldo, M. F., Kolko, D. J., Neef, N. A., & Egel, A. L. (1986). Experimental analysis of response covariation among compliant and inappropriate behaviors. *Journal of Applied Behavior Analysis, 19,* 241–254.

Patterson, G. R. (1982). *Coercive family process.* Castalia: Eugene, Oregon.

Robins, L. B. (1991) Conduct disorder. *Journal of Child Psychology and Psychiatry, 20,* 566–680.

Russo, D. C., Cataldo, M. F., & Cushing, P. J. (1981). Compliance training and behavioral covariation in the treatment of multiple behavior problems. *Journal of Applied Behavior Analysis, 14,* 209–222.

Sanders, M. R. & Christensen, A. P. (1985). A comparison of the effects of child management and planned activities training in five parent environments. *Journal of Abnormal Child Psychology, 13,* 101–117.

Sanders, M. R. & Dadds, M. R. (1982). The effects of planned activities and child management procedures in parent training: An analysis of setting generality. *Behavior Therapy, 13,* 452–461.

Sanders, M. R., & Dadds, M. R. (1993). *Behavioural family intervention.* London: Allyn & Bacon.

Skinner, B. F. (1953). *Science and human behavior.* New York: Macmillan.

Skinner, B. F. (1981). Selection by consequences. *Science, 213,* 501–504.

Stokes, T. F. & Baer, D. M. (1977). An implicit technology of generalization. *Journal of Applied Behavior Analysis, 10,* 349–367.

Urquiza, A. J. & McNiel, C. B. (1996). Parent-child interaction therapy: An intensive dyadic intervention for physically abusive families. *Child Maltreatment, 2,* 132–141.

Wiese, M. R. (1992). A critical review of parent training research. *Psychology in the Schools, 29,* 229–236.

Wolff, S. (1977). Non delinquent disturbances of conduct. In M. Rutter & L. Hersov (Eds), *Child psychiatry: Modern approaches.* London: Blackwell.

9

Assessing challenging behaviour of persons with severe mental disabilities

Mark F. O'Reilly

Abstract

There has been a proliferation of research in recent years which has outlined assessment procedures to be used in the identification of the operant function of problem behaviour (i.e., aggression and self-injury) for persons with severe mental disabilities. These procedures can be divided into two catagories – functional assessment and functional analysis techniques. Functional assessment protocol provide correlative information regarding controlling variables. Functional analysis techniques involve the systematic manipulation of hypothesised variables in order to empirically verify the existance of causal relationships. This article reviews the use of these assessment procedures with people with severe mental disabilities who exhibit challenging behaviours.

Introduction

One of the dominant themes in the applied behaviour analysis literature over the last 20 years has been the identification of effective methods to treat problem behaviour in persons with severe mental disabilities (O'Reilly, O'Kane, & Taylor, 1994). There is now an abundance of effective treatment methods available for the practitioner (e.g., Jones & Baker, 1990; Repp & Singh, 1990). However, selecting the most appropriate treatment for an individual continues to be a complex and often difficult process requiring the consideration of a number of issues (Lovaas & Favel, 1987; Mace, Lalli, & Lalli, 1991).

The initial and important step in selecting an appropriate treatment involves the accurate identification of variables that are eliciting and maintaining the target behaviour. The term *functional assessment* has been used to describe a variety of systematic procedures to determine antecedent and consequent variables which occasion and maintain operant responding. Functional assessment typically involves a process whereby targeted operant classes are defined by interviewing significant others and are subsequently observed in naturalistic contexts (i.e., where the behaviour has been described as problematic). This form of assessment reveals correlational information regarding establishing/discriminative conditions and consequences for the targeted operant class. Assessment procedures may also involve the systematic manipulation of hypothesised controlling variables to empirically demonstrate causal relationships. This latter assessment technique is typically referred to as a *functional analysis* (Axelrod 1987; Iwata, Dorsey, Slifer, Bauman, & Richman, 1982; O'Reilly & Halle, 1993).

A knowledge of controlling variables derived from such an assessment protocol assists in the development of effective treatment procedures in a number of ways (Lennox & Miltenberger, 1989). First, assessment may identify reinforcing consequences (positive or negative) contingent upon target behaviour performance which can subsequently be eliminated or prevented (Carr, Newsom, & Binkoff, 1980; Rincover, Cook, Peoples, & Packard, 1979). Second, an assessment may identify motivational (Michael, 1982, 1993) and/or discriminative (Skinner, 1935) conditions that evoke the target behaviour. By removing or altering these conditions the behaviour may be prevented (Dunlap, Kern-Dunlap, Clarke, & Robbins, 1991; O'Kane & O'Reilly, 1994). Finally such pre-intervention assessments may allow the practitioner to identify more efficient and socially appropriate responses to access similar consequences as the problematic behaviours (i.e., functionally equivalent responses) (Carr & Durand, 1985; Durand & Carr, 1987).

While there is a growing literature base of empirical evidence for the validity of functionally based treatment procedures (e.g., Iwata, Vollmer, & Zarcone, 1990; Mace, Lalli, & Lalli, 1991), until recently few published reports have based treatment selection on functional assessment strategies. The behaviour of many researchers and practitioners alike seems to have been controlled by the structure (i.e., topography) of the presenting problem behaviours rather than by the operant function of these behaviours. This approach contradicts a fundamental premise of behavioural psychology which describes the operant primarily in terms of its function (Catania, 1992; Skinner, 1938; Skinner, 1957). In a similar vein, Lennox and Miltenberger (1989) have hypothesised that the traditional practice of treatment selection has been based on the direction of behaviour change desired rather than on the contingencies which maintain that behaviour. Lennox and Miltenberger (1989) note that practitioners often 'select a treatment designed to be decelerative or suppressive in function, but not necessarily related to the controlling variables of the target behaviour' (p. 305). This misinformed strategy of treatment selection may have been shaped by the multitude of introductory textbooks in applied behaviour analysis which classify and review specific treatment procedures based on the outcomes they produce (e.g., Alberto & Troutman, 1990; Martin & Pear, 1983). Fortunately, recent texts are now beginning to include a chapter on the functional assessment of behaviour (e.g., Snell, 1993).

The selection of treatment protocol that are not determined by functional assessment may expose the client to a number of risks (Lennox & Miltenberger, 1989). The client may be exposed to an ineffective treatment, thereby delaying the application of effective protocol. This inability of poorly selected treatments to produce desired changes can also negatively affect staff perceptions of behavioural techniques – leading to rejection of systematic behavioural approaches (O'Reilly, 1993). Clients may also be exposed to unnecessarily aversive and restrictive procedures.

This article outlines the major approaches of functional assessment and analysis identified in the literature. Key references which are accessible to the general practitioner are highlighted. The review will begin with a description of the various functional assessment approaches. Finally, experimental approaches to the analysis of behaviour will be described.

Functional assessment

This section will include a brief review of behavioural interviews and direct observation methods (i.e., scatterplot and ABC assessment).

Behavioural interview

Behavioural interviews rely on subjective verbal reports to identify the nature of the behaviour problem and the environmental conditions which are controlling it (Cone, 1987). Those who are interviewed (e.g., parents, teachers, vocational or residential staff) should be in daily contact with the client and are therefore in a position to describe events as they have witnessed them in the past and draw conclusions about the causes of an individual's behaviour (Iwata, et al., 1990). There are three main objectives of the behavioural interview: 1) definition of the behaviour(s); 2) identification of those physical and environmental factor(s) predictive of the problem behaviour(s); 3) identification of the potential functions of behaviour(s) in terms of their maintaining consequences.

To achieve these outcomes, a complete interview should include questions which probe the informant about the topography of the behaviour, the situations in which it does or does not occur and the typical reactions of others in response to the targeted behaviour. In essence, the behavioural interview attempts to review a large number of potential variables and narrow the focus to those that appear to be of some importance in occasioning and maintaining the undesirable behaviour. A number of behavioural rating scales, checklists, and questionnaires are commercially available and can be used to guide the interview process. For example, one of the most frequently used instruments is the *Motivation Assessment Scale* developed by Durand and Crimmins (1988) which provides a specific description of the targeted problem behaviour and attempts to isolate one of four possible reasons for this behaviour: positive reinforcement through attention, positive reinforcement through access to materials, negative reinforcement through escape, or sensory reinforcement.

Conclusion

There are a number of advantages to the interview approach including ease of application, cost and efficiency (administration takes only a brief period). On the reverse side of the coin, there are a number of inherent difficulties. Such methods do not allow for direct access to the relevant behaviours or their controlling variables and are therefore subject to a variety of difficulties including faulty recollection of events, observer bias and observer expectation (Kazdin, 1980). As such, information gained through these methods may provide unreliable estimates of behaviour and lead to invalid conclusions about its controlling variables (Iwata *et al.*, 1990).

Direct observation assessment

A more objective and systematic approach to assessment involves first-hand observation of an individual's behaviour in environmental contexts that are relevant to the problem. The individual is observed in their typical daily routine in as many settings and across as much time per day as is possible for a minimum period of 2–5 days (O'Neill, Horner, Albin, Storey, & Sprague, 1990). Notably, there is little, if any, control exerted over the environmental conditions during assessment (Sasso, Reiners, Coopers, Wacker, Berg, Steege, Kelly, & Allaire, 1992). Such direct observations should be based upon information gleaned from the interview process (i.e., behaviours and situations which have been identified as problematic are observed). The process is usually carried out by those parents, teachers, and support staff who already work with the individual and is conducted in a manner that does not require extensive time or training on their part. Two general classes of descriptive analyses have been forwarded in the literature and each will be discussed.

The Antecedent-Behaviour-Consequence (ABC) observation method attempts to evaluate the immediate antecedent and consequent events surrounding the target behaviour and assess the extent to which these specific events may be related to the occurrance of behaviour. This assessment usually entails a narrative account of directly observed behaviour and temporally related environmental events (Bijou, Petersen, & Ault, 1968; Kazdin, 1980).

Those working with the individual exhibiting the undesirable behaviour write brief descriptors of what occurs immediately prior to and following a behaviour occurrence. Such accounts are usually recorded on an ABC or sequence analysis chart (Sulzer-Azaroff & Mayer, 1977). Although the procedure is relatively easy to learn it requires extensive effort to implement (Pyles & Bailey, 1990). Further, such a procedure often leads to subjective interpretation of events rather than objective descriptions (Lerman & Iwata, 1993).

To overcome such difficulties a number of approaches have been recommended. It is essential that observers are aware of the temporal parameters involved in ABC assessment to combat the temptation to record global environmental events that are far removed from the target behaviour (Lennox & Miltenberger, 1989). In a practical measure to overcome this difficulty of subjective interpretation, Pyles and Bailey (1990) have developed the 'inappropriate record form' which lists pre-specified preceding and consequential events coupled with the problem behaviour. Staff are therefore cued to record pre-specified antecedent and consequent events upon the occurrence of the target behaviour. A less formal measure is simply to train observers not to infer motivation from an observation but to describe events clearly and accurately (Lennox & Miltenberger, 1989). For a review Cooper, Heron, and Heward (1987) provide extensive practical guidelines which if followed should produce a useful account of implicated variables.

The most recent and simplest direct observation method is the scatterplot assessment which records temporal distributions of behaviour (Touchette, MacDonald, & Langer, 1985). Staff are trained to record the time of day of the occurrence of each instance of the target behaviour on a grid which identifies time of day on the ordinate (usually in 30-minute segments) and consecutive days on the abcissa. As the behaviours are repeatedly observed and plotted, correlations between particular times of day and differential rates of behaviour usually become evident. This data allows for more detailed observational analyses (e.g., ABC assessments) during those time periods in which the behaviour has been identified as most probable. An example of a scatterplot data sheet used by staff to identify the temporal distribution of 'scratching other clients' by an adult with severe mental disabilities in a group home is presented in Figure 1 (O'Reilly, 1994). This scatterplot shows that the target behaviour clusters around certain time periods during the day when the client was required to engage in task-related activities.

Conclusion

Direct observation methods have a number of advantages. They allow direct access to problem behaviour in the natural environment and therefore are more objective in that they reflect current behaviour and not recall of past

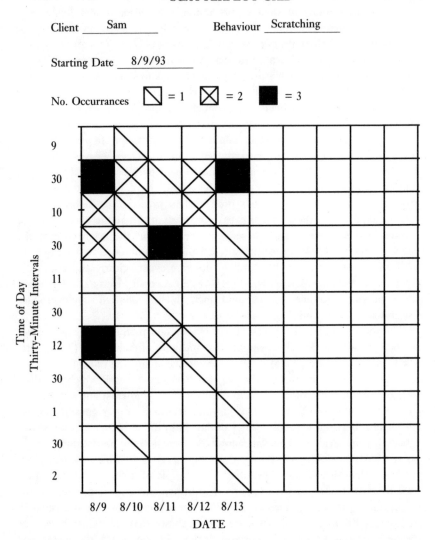

SCATTERPLOT GRID

Client ____Sam____ Behaviour __Scratching__

Starting Date __8/9/93__

No. Occurrances ◺ = 1 ⊠ = 2 ■ = 3

(Time of Day / Thirty-Minute Intervals on vertical axis: 9, 30, 10, 30, 11, 30, 12, 30, 1, 30, 2)

(DATE on horizontal axis: 8/9, 8/10, 8/11, 8/12, 8/13)

Figure 1: A scatterplot assessment grid which was used by staff to identify the number of occurrences of scratching others for a client with severe mental disabilities across a one-week period. This particular grid is sensitive to three occurrences of the target behaviour in a thirty-minute time period. It is evident from the distribution of the behaviour that the client is aggressive when involved in vocational (9:30–11:00) and domestic tasks (12:00–1:00) which involve considerable physical demands (woodwork, table setting etc.). One could therefore hypothesise that negative reinforcement (aggress to avoid demand) could be maintaining this operant class (O'Reilly, 1994). (Adapted from Touchette *et al.*, 1985).

observations. Like most procedures, direct observation procedures have a number of limitations. Relative to indirect methods such procedures are time consuming. The need to intervene immediately with particularly severe self-injury would not lend itself to such lengthy pre-assessment. More important perhaps is that these procedures do not necessarily reveal functional relationships (Iwata *et al.*, 1990). For example, it may be difficult to identify the consequences of behaviour maintained by intermittent reinforcement schedules (Lerman & Iwata, 1993).

Functional analysis approaches

Experimental analyses of behaviour constitute the final means of conducting an assessment of problem behaviours. The most distinguishing feature of this method of analysis lies in its direct and systematic manipulation of variables that potentially maintain the problem behaviour (Iwata *et al.*, 1990). Of the many assessment techniques to evolve from the literature in recent years, functional or experimental analyses have perhaps been used most frequently. This approach has been used successfully in the analysis and treatment of such behaviour problems as stereotypic behaviour (Durand & Carr, 1987; Sturmey, Carlsen, Crisp, & Newton, 1988), disruption (Carr & Durand, 1985), aggression (Slifer, Ivanic, Parrish, Page, & Burgio, 1986), pica (Mace & Knight, 1986), and self-injurious behaviour (e.g., Day, Rea, Schussler, Larsen, & Johnson, 1988; Lerman & Iwata, 1993; Steege *et al.*, 1990; Symons, Delaney, Brown, & Thompson, 1994). The rationale behind conducting an experimental analysis of behaviour is that variables, which are functionally related to the target behaviour, can be identified by recording changes in behaviour that occur when various antecedent and consequent events are introduced to and removed from the individual (Lennox & Miltenberger, 1989).

This form of analysis is important for many reasons. First, it emphasises the importance of gaining information about the contingencies maintaining behaviour rather than merely describing the topographical features (e.g., 'biting' or 'hitting'). It also explains how topographically similiar behaviours can serve different functions for any given individual. For example, one individual may engage in self-injurious behaviour (SIB) to gain access to attention and therefore may have their behaviour maintained by positive reinforcement. On the other hand, another individual's self-injury may be negatively reinforced and serve to escape from an aversive situation. It is through a realisation of these differing functions of topographically similiar behaviour(s) that researchers have recognised the need to develop highly individualised treatment programs which are tailored to the specific functions of problem behaviour.

Methods of conducting such an in-depth analysis of the functions of behaviour is a relatively recent advance, with the degree of rigour and sophistication of the different methods varying. The control necessary to adequately demonstrate functional relationships in an experimental analysis is often difficult to obtain in the natural environment. Functional relationships are therefore often verified in an analogue setting which approximates the natural environment. Once the conditions which control the behaviour are identified, these contingencies can then be manipulated in the natural environment. Iwata *et al.* (1990) describe this model as involving at least one condition (experimental) in which the variable of interest is present and another condition (control) in which the variable is absent. These conditions are then alternated in a multielement or reversal design while the behaviour of interest is observed.

There are two variations of this model which can be found in the literature. One approach involves demonstration of the effects of a single hypothetical controlling variable (for example, attention) on a particular operant class. An early example of this method was conducted by Lovaas and Simmons (1969) in which a subject who exhibited SIB was exposed to several conditions differing on the variable attention (social deprivation, non-contingent delivery of attention, and social attention contingent on occurances of self-injurious behaviour) and demonstrated that SIB was higher during the contingent attention condition. Similarly Carr, Newsom, and Binkoff (1976) compared levels of SIB and aggression with conditions involving either demands or no–demands.

More recent research, however, has shown that the functions of a behavioural problem may be multiply controlled and therefore a second model has developed in which several variables are compared to determine the behavioural function. One of the most frequently cited studies based on this model was carried out by Iwata, Dorsey, Slifer, Bauman, and Richman (1982) in which they used a multielement design to compare four conditions to assess the function of SIB: positive reinforcement (attention contingent on SIB), negative reinforcement (escape from demands contingent on SIB), automatic reinforcement (placement in a barren environment with no access to either attention or toys) and a control (no attention for SIB, no demands, play materials available and attention contingent on the absence of SIB). Their results showed higher SIB in a specific condition for six of the nine subjects.

Among the strengths of an experimental functional analysis are its objectivity and quantitative precision and its ability to analyse the effects of several variables either individually or in combination (Iwata *et al.* 1990). It has also been noted that the control condition included in an experimental analysis may indicate some temporary intervention strategies which can be implemented until the treatment program is designed and put into effect (Iwata *et al.*, 1990).

Although providing more conclusive data, one potential disadvantage in conducting such an assessment is that it may be difficult or impractical for use in many applied settings due to the stringent control necessary and also the limitations of staff, time and facilities (Lennox & Miltenberger, 1989). However, Iwata *et al.* (1990) point out that 'this criticism is unwarranted because precisely the same requirements must be met in order to implement most treatment programs with any degree of consistency' (p. 310). In recent years, Cooper (1989), Steege (1989) and Northup, Wacker, Sasso, Cigrand, Cook and DeRaad (1991) have shown how such analyses of problem behaviour may be successfully carried out during one 90-minute outpatient clinic session. O'Kane and O'Reilly (1994) used a mini-reversal design during a 60-minute therapy session to empirically establish antecedent eliciting variables of challenging behaviour for a client with severe brain injuries. This research overcomes the potential problem of an extended experimental analysis delaying the implementation of an effective treatment.

Another disadvantage which has been suggested by La Vigna and Donnellan (1986) is that the analogue analysis may not be ecologically valid (i.e., it may not mirror exactly the variables operating in the natural environment). This problem has been overcome in studies where experimental analyses have successfully been conducted in natural settings such as classrooms (Sasso & Reimers, 1988) and outpatient clinics with parents present (Northup *et al.*, 1991). Additionally, Iwata *et al.* (1990) point out that a functional analysis does not reveal the functional variables involved for a given behaviour but merely tests those variables that have been proposed through prior functional assessments. Hypothesised contingencies must be systematically identified prior to an experimental analysis. Therefore, all functional analyses must encompass additional information from background sources to facilitate how best to construct the analysis (i.e., to identify which variables to manipulate).

Conclusion

The data resulting from each of the experimental analyses described is used as a means of identifying the most effective intervention to be implemented. The identification of the current function of any given behaviour will allow the treatment to be uniquely matched to its particular function. Through analysing the current functions of a behavioural problem, effective behavioural programming may be facilitated without the need for more intrusive and restrictive crisis management approaches to be used (cf. O'Neill *et al.*, 1990).

References

Alberto, P. A., & Troutman, A. C. (1990). *Applied behavior analysis for teachers* (3rd ed.). New York: Macmillan.

Axelrod, S. (1987). Functional and structural analysis of behavior: Approaches leading to reduced use of punishment procedures? *Research in Developmental Disabilities*, 8, 165–178.

Bijou, S. W., Peterson, R. F., & Ault M. H. (1968). A method to integrate descriptive and experimental field studies at the level of data and empirical concepts. *Journal of Applied Behavior Analysis*, *1*, 175–191.

Carr, E. G., (1977). The motivation of self-injurious behavior: A review of some hypotheses. *Psychological Bulletin, 84,* 800–816.

Carr, E. G. & Durand, V. M. (1985). Reducing behavior problems through functional communication training. *Journal of Applied Behavior Analysis, 18,* 111–126.

Carr, E. G., Newsom, C. D., & Binkoff, J.A. (1976). Stimulus control of self-destructive behaviour in a psychotic child. *Journal of Abnormal Child Psychology, 4,* 139–153.

Carr, E. G., Newsom, C. D., & Binkoff, J. A. (1980). Escape as a factor in the aggressive behavior of two retarded children. *Journal of Applied Behavior Analysis, 13,* 101–117.

Catania, A. C. (1992). *Learning* (3rd ed.). Englewood Cliffs, NJ.: Prentice-Hall.

Cone, J. D. (1987). *Behavioral assessment with children and adolescents: A clinical approach.* New York: Wiley.

Cooper, L. J. (1989, May). Functional analysis of conduct disorders in an outclinic setting. In D. Wacker (Chair), Functional analysis of severe behaviour problems; Recent applications and novel approaches. *Symposium presented at the 15th Annual Conference of the Association for Behavior Analysis. Milwaukee. WI.*

Cooper, J. D., Heron, T. E., & Heward, W. L. (1987). *Applied behavior analysis.* Columbus, OH: Merrill.

Day, R. M., Rea, J. A., Schussler, N. G., Larsen, S. E., & Johnson, W. L. (1988). A functionally based approach to the treatment of self-injurious behaviour. *Behavior Modification, 12,* 565–589.

Dunlap, G., Kern-Dunlap, L. K., Clarke, S., & Robbins, F. R. (1990). Functional assessment, curricular revision, and severe behavior problems. *Journal of Applied Behavior Analysis, 24,* 387–397.

Durand, V. M. & Carr, E. G. (1987). Social influences on 'self-stimulatory' behavior: Analysis and treatment application. *Journal of Applied Behavior Analysis, 20,* 119–132.

Durand, V. M. & Crimmins, D. B. (1988). Identifying the variables maintaining self-injurious behavior. *Journal of Autism and Developmental Disorders, 18,* 99–117.

Evans, I. A. & Meyer, L. (1985). *An educative approach to behaviors: A practical decision model for interventions with severely handicapped learners.* Baltimore: Paul H. Brookes.

Iwata, B. A., Dorsey, M. F., Slifer, K. J., Bauman, K. E. & Richman, G. S. (1982). Toward a functional analysis of self-injury. *Analysis and Intervention in Developmental Disabilities, 2,* 1–20.

Iwata, B. A., Pace, G., Kalsher, M., Cowdery, G., & Cataldo, M. (1990). Experimental analyses and extinction of self-injurious escape behavior. *Journal of Applied Behavior Analysis, 23,* 11–27.

Iwata, B. A., Vollmer, T. R., & Zarcone, J. R. (1990). The experimental (functional) analysis of behavior disorders: Methodology, applications and limitations. In A. C. Repp & N. N. Singh (Eds) *Perspectives on the use of aversive and non-aversive interventions for persons with developmental disabilities* (pp. 301–330). Sycamore, Illinois. Sycamore Publishing.

Jones, R. S. P. & Baker, L. J. V. (1990). Differential reinforcement and challenging behavior. A critical review of the DRI schedule. *Behavioural Psychotherapy, 18,* 35–7.

Kazdin A. E. (1980). *Behavior modification in applied settings.* Homewood, Illinois: Dorsey.

Lalli, J. S., Browder, D. M., Mace, F. C., & Brown, D. K. (1993). Teacher use of descriptive analysis data to implement interventions to decrease students' problem behaviors. *Journal of Applied Behavior Analysis, 26,* 227–238.

La Vigna, G. D. & Donnellan, A. (1986). *Alternatives to punishment: Solving behavior problems with non-aversive strategies.* New York: Irvington.

Lennox, D. B. & Miltenberger, R. G., (1989). Conducting a functional assessment of problem behavior in applied settings. *Journal of the Association for Persons with Severe Handicaps, 14(4),* 304–311.

Lerman, D. C. & Iwata, B. A. (1993). Descriptive and experimental analysis of variables maintaining self-injurious behavior. *Journal of Applied Behavior Analysis, 26,* 292–319.

Lovaas, O. I. & Favel, J. E. (1987). Protection for clients undergoing aversive/restrictive interventions. *Education and Treatment of Children, 10,* 311–325.

Lovaas, O. I. & Simmons, J. Q. (1969). Manipulation of self-destruction in three retarded children. *Journal of Applied Behavior Analysis, 2,* 143–157.

Mace, F. C. & Knight, D. (1986). Functional analysis and treatment of severe pica. *Journal of Applied Behavior Analysis, 19,* 411–416.

Mace, F. C. & Lalli, J. S. (1991). Linking descriptive and experimental analyses in the treatment of bizarre speech. *Journal of Applied Behavior Analysis, 24,* 553–562.

Mace, F. C., Lalli, J. S., & Lalli, E. P. (1991). Functional analysis and treatment of aberrant behavior. *Research in Developmental Disabilities, 12,* 155–180.

Martin, G. & Pear, J. (1983). *Behavior Modification: What it is and how to do it.* Englewood Cliffs, NJ: Prentice-Hall.

Michael, J. (1982). Distinguishing between discriminative and motivational functions of stimuli. *Journal of the Experimental Analysis of Behavior 37,* 149–155.

Michael, J. (1993). Establishing operations. *The Behavior Analyst, 16,* 191–206.

Newton, J. T. & Sturmey, P. (1991). The Motivation Assessment Scale: Inter-rater reliability and internal consistency in a British sample. *Journal of Mental Deficiency Research, 35,* 472–474.

Northup, J., Wacker, D., Sasso, G., Steege, M., Cigrand, K., Cook, J., & DeRaad, A. (1991). A brief functional analysis of aggressive and alternative behavior in an outclinic setting. *Journal of Applied Behavior Analysis, 24,* 509–522.

O'Kane, N. P. & O'Reilly, M. F. (1994). *Increasing the predictabiity of therapeutic interactions for a client with short term memory deficits: An analysis of the effects on challenging behaviour.* Manuscript submitted for publication.

O'Neill, R. E., Horner, R. H., Albin R. W., Storey, K., & Sprague, J. R. (1990). *Functional analysis: A practical assessment guide.* Sycamore. Illinois: Sycamore Publishing.

O'Reilly, M. F. (1993). Aversive interventions. *The Irish Psychologist, 19,* 82.

O'Reilly, M. F. (1994). Examining the role of establishing operations in severe aggression. *Paper presented at the Experimental Analysis of Behaviour Group Annual Conference, University College, London.*

O'Reilly, M. F., & Halle, J. (1993). Stimulus control. In M. D. Smith, *Behavior modification for exceptional children and youth* (pp. 119–138). Andover Medical Publishers.

O'Reilly, M. F., O'Kane, N. P., & Taylor, I. (1994). Current trends in behavioural assessment of problem behaviour. *The Thornfield Journal, 17,* 18–23.

Pyles, D. A. & Bailey, J. S. (1990). Diagnosing severe behavior problems. In A. C. Repp & N. N. Singh (Eds) *Perspectives on the use of nonaversive and aversive interventions for persons with developmental disabilities* (pp. 381–401). Sycamore, Illinois. Sycamore Publishing.

Repp, A. C., Felce, D., & Barton, L. E. (1988). Basing the treatment of stereotypic and self-injurious behaviors on hypotheses of their causes. *Journal of Applied Behavior Analysis, 21,* 281–289.

Repp, A. C. & Singh, N. N. (1990). *Perspectives on the use of nonaversive and aversive interventions for persons with developmental disabilities.* Sycamore, Illinois. Sycamore Publishing.

Rincover, A., Cook, R., Peoples, A., & Packard, D. (1979). Sensory extinction and sensory reinforcement principles for programming multiple-adaptive behavior change. *Journal of Applied Behavior Analysis, 12,* 221–233.

Sasso, G. M. & Reimers, T. M. (1988). Assessing the functional properties of behavior: Implications and applications for the classroom. *Focus on Autistic Behavior, 3,* 1–15.

Sasso, G. M., Reimers, T. M., Copper, L. J., Wacker, D., Berg, W., Steege, M., Kelly, L., & Allaire, A. (1992). Use of descriptive and experimental analysis to identify the functional properties of aberrant behavior in school settings. *Journal of Applied Behavior Analysis, 25,* 809–82.

Skinner, B. F. (1935). The generic nature of the concepts of stimulus and response. *Journal of General Psychology, 12,* 40–65.

Skinner, B. F. (1938). *The behavior of organisms.* Englewood Cliffs, NJ: Prentice-Hall.

Skinner, B. F. (1957). *Verbal behavior.* New York: Appleton-Century-Crofts.

Slifer, K. J., Ivanic, M. T., Parrish, J. M., Page, T. J., & Burgio, L. D. (1986). Assessment and treatment of multiple behaviour problems exhibited by a profoundly retarded adolescent. *Journal of Behavior Therapy and Experimental Psychiatry, 17,* 203–213.

Snell, M. E. (1993). *Instruction of students with severe disabilities.* (4th Ed.). New York: Macmillan.

Steege, M. W. (1989, May). Functional analysis of self-injurious behavior in an outclinic setting. In D. Wacker (Chair), Functional analysis of severe behavior problems; Recent applications and novel approaches. *Symposium presented at the 15th Annual Conference of the Association for Behaviour Analysis, Milwaukee, Wl.*

Steege, M. V., Wacker, D. P., Cigrand, K. C., Berg, W. K., Novak, C. G., Reimers, T. M., Sasso, G. M., & DeRaad, A. (1990). Use of negative reinforcement in the treatment of self-injurious behavior. *Journal of Applied Behavior Analysis, 23,* 459–467.

Sturmey, P., Carlsen, A., Crisp, A. G., & Newton, J. T. (1988). A functional analysis of multiple aberrant responses: A refinement and extension of Iwata *et al.*'s methodology. *Journal of Mental Deficiency Research, 32,* 31–46.

Sulzer-Azaroff, B. & Mayer, G. R. (1977). *Applying behavior analysis procedures with children and youth.* New York: Holt, Rinehart, and Winston.

Symons, F., Delaney, D., Brown, B. & Thompson, T. (1994). Assessment of behavioural and opiod mechanisms in self-injurious behaviour. In M. F. O'Reilly (Chair), Assessment and Intervention in Developmental Disabilities. *Symposium convened for the Experimental Analysis of Behaviour Group Annual Conference. University College. London.*

Touchette, P. E., MacDonald, R. F., & Langer, S. N. (1985). A scatterplot for identifying stimulus control of problem behavior. *Journal of Applied Behavior Analysis, 18,* 343–351.

Zarcone, J. R., Rodgers, T. A., Iwata, B. A., Rourke, D. A., & Dorsey, M. F. (1991). Reliability analysis of the motivation assessment scale: A failure to replicate. *Research in Developmental Disabilities, 12,* 349–360.

10

Optimising winter-housing systems for dairy cattle

Janet M. O'Connell and Finola C. Leonard

Abstract

Understanding behavioural patterns of dairy cows can lead to more effective housing systems. Lying and resting are important behavioural activities for dairy cows as they are necessary for restorative processes. The objectives of the study reported here were to establish (i) the relationship between cubicle design and bedding and lying behaviour of dairy cows in winter housing, and (ii) the relationship between lying behaviour in different cubicle conditions and claw health of dairy cows. A general survey of housing and management status on farms indicated that small cubicles contribute to cubicle refusal. Using behavioural criteria, various cubicle designs were then evaluated experimentally. Percentage occupancy and lying time were used as indicators of the acceptability and comfort of five different cubicle designs in a series of preference tests. The results indicated that (*a*) cows lay longer in some designs than others, and (*b*) chose cubicle designs which allowed more space sharing. The provision of bedding increased lying time and was useful in training animals in the use of cubicles. A number of experiments on the relationship between cubicle conditions and lameness showed that there was an association between good conditions and less lameness, an effect partially mediated through increased lying time. Further studies with heifers in overcrowded conditions indicated that only a severe reduction in lying time (5 hours per 24 hours) was associated with increases in clinical lameness and it was concluded that reduced lying time acts as an exacerbating factor in the development of claw lesions.

These studies of lying behaviour of dairy cattle provide useful information for improved management, housing and welfare of cattle over the winter period.

Introduction

This chapter gives an overview of the findings of a series of studies of cow behaviour in cubicle housing systems. The results presented concentrated principally on lying time as this is considered a useful index of cow comfort. Firstly, lying behaviour patterns at pasture and in winter housing are compared and, in the next section, various findings are presented on management practices which encourage or discourage lying behaviour in cubicles. An evaluation of various cubicle designs is reported under the heading 'Cubicle designs for dairy cows' and this is followed by a section discussing the merits of various methods for training young animals to use cubicles. The two final parts of the chapter deal with the role of cubicle design and lying behaviour in the development of claw lesions (injuries to the horny part of the foot) and lameness in cattle.

The behaviour of cattle falls into various activity patterns (Hafez & Schein, 1969), including ingestion, resting, care-giving and seeking, sexual, investigatory, agonistic behaviour and other social interactions. For dairy cows lying and resting are important behavioural activities as they are important for restorative processes (Oswald, 1980). Suss and Andreae (1984) summarised the available literature and found that dairy cows lie down for approximately 9 to 12 hours daily. This variation in the time spent lying may be due to individual variation between cows caused by various factors (e.g., age and social factors), and also partly due to the housing and management of the animals (Wierenga & Hopster, 1990).

Deprivation experiments (Metz, 1985; Wierenga & Metz, 1986) showed that when lying space and food were restored to cows who had previously been simultaneously deprived of both, a priority for lying over eating occurred at certain times of the day. Krohn and Konggaard (1982) found a marked increase in cortisol concentration in the blood of cows whose daily lying time was restricted by 75%. This finding indicates that cows have great difficulty in coping with rest deprivation which lasts for many hours. In addition to lying time being necessary for restorative processes, a number of authors have also found a relationship between poor lying times and lameness (Colam-Ainsworth, Lunn, Thomas, & Eddy 1989; Galindo & Broom 1993; Leonard, O'Connell, & O'Farrell, 1994).

The objectives of the present study were twofold: we sought to establish (i) the relationship between cubicle design and bedding material and the lying behaviour of dairy cows in winter housing; (ii) the relationship between lying behaviour in different cubicle types at different cow to cubicle ratios and lameness of dairy cows.

Lying behaviour at pasture and in winter housing

The research programme commenced with an examination of the behaviour of cows at pasture and in winter housing through the construction of two separate ethograms. Lying behaviour only is considered in the present paper, for full details see O'Connell, Giller, & Meaney (1989a). There was considerable similarity in the temporal distribution of lying behaviour at pasture and in winter housing. However, more time was spent lying down by the cows at pasture (p<0.01). The herd showed two main periods of lying down: (a) before the evening milking and (b) from sunset to sunrise. During the latter period, up to 90% of the cows were lying down at any one time, with highest levels between 03:00 hours and sunrise. The remaining cows were restless and engaged in more active behaviour.

Management practices and cubicle refusal in dairy cows

In the 1960s, two farmers, one in the UK and one in the USA, developed a cubicle system for the housing of dairy cows (Harper, 1983). This was a simple but revolutionary development and has been widely accepted by dairy farmers. In Ireland, the vast majority of cows are overwintered in cubicle houses. The aim of cubicle housing is to allow cows to be undisturbed with minimal risk of injury, in clean comfortable conditions needing only moderate amounts of bedding (Ministry of Agriculture and Fisheries and Food [MAFF], 1983). When used correctly, cubicles should not adversely affect cow health, milk production or cleanliness. However, cubicle housing systems are not without their problems and continue to be the source of considerable discussion (Cermak, 1987; Harper, 1983; Suss & Andreae, 1984; Wierenga, 1983).

A survey of dairy herds in Belgium showed that 5% of cows refused to use cubicles (Daelemans, Maton, & Lambrecht, 1981). Cows refusing to lie in cubicles tend to lie in passageways and become dirty and as a result udders need extra cleaning at milking. This behaviour adversely affects the quality of milk (Daelemans *et al.*, 1981). A preliminary investigation into the extent of the problem and the possible links between cubicle types, dimensions, management practices and cubicle refusal levels in Ireland was undertaken in a survey of 60 farms (O'Connell, Giller, & Meaney, 1993a). In this survey a mean of 8.5% of cows on each farm refused to use cubicles with a range from zero to 47%. The present recommended dimensions for cubicles are 2130 mm × 1160 mm for body weight 475–575 kg (Cermak, 1984; Kelly, 1983). The survey showed that 45% of farms had cubicles which were too short and 63% had cubicles which were too narrow. Most (88.5%) had a cubicle to cow ratio of greater than 0.8, and there was no correlation between cubicle refusal and cubicle to cow ratio. This ratio has been shown to be adequate based on experimental evidence which indicates that the maximum number of cows occupying cubicles during peak time (03:00–07:00 hours) is 75–85% (Albright & Timmons, 1984; Gebremedhin, Cramer, & Larsen, 1981, 1985; O'Connell, Giller, & Meaney, 1992). Bedding materials used in cubicles also seem to play a role in cubicle refusal levels. The majority of farms with no cubicle refusal problems used mats as bedding. These farms also provided cubicle accommodation for their weanling heifers and had more efficient slurry removal systems, for example automatic scrapers or slats.

Cubicle designs for dairy cows

Design, construction and dimensions of dairy cattle cubicles affect the overall success of cubicle housing systems. The major features of the cubicles are the nature and dimensions of the bed and cubicle frames which divide one cubicle from another. Cubicle frames have been developed and changed over a number of years and there is now a large choice of designs. The objectives of the frames are to align the cow properly in her own cubicle, to prevent cows interfering with or injuring their neighbours and to minimise the risk of injury to limbs or teats as the cow changes position (Webster, 1987). Cubicle length, width and the condition of the cubicle bed are important for lying comfort (Graves, 1977; Irish & Martin, 1983; O'Connell, Giller, & Meaney, 1989b, 1992; O'Connell, Meaney, & Giller, 1991). Small cubicles are an important cause of injuries (Bell, 1986). According to Westendorp (1973), the type of partition influences the 'available' lying space. With open frames, cows can use more space laterally.

In order to evaluate the relative merits of different designs, the monitoring of cattle behaviour has been shown as a useful method of obtaining direct evidence of cow comfort and responses to various cubicle types (Gwynn, Wilkinson, & Thomas, 1991; Metz & Wierenga, 1987; O'Connell *et al.*, 1989b, 1992; O'Connell et al., 1991). Lying time by individual cows in cubicles is considered as a comfort index of the housing environment (Irish & Martin, 1983). Preliminary studies demonstrated differences in behaviour and occupancy levels between two cubicle designs, Dutch Comfort and Newton Rigg (O'Connell *et al.*, 1989b). Manipulation of longitudinal space within the less used design (Newton Rigg) could only partially overcome such differences (O'Connell *et al.*, 1992) and although the addition of bedding (mats) increased the occupancy of the Newton Rigg cubicle, the relative difference in utilisation of the two designs was retained.

In the research presented here behavioural studies were used to assess the effectiveness of five cubicle designs, Newton Rigg and four relatively new designs, Dutch Comfort, Super Dutch Comfort, Dutch Cantilever and Dorsdunn (Figure 1). All cubicles measured 2130 mm × 1160 mm, with a floor slope of 100 mm and a kerb height of 225 mm over the dunging passage. All experiments were conducted with a cubicle space per cow. Cubicle acceptability and comfort was measured by calculating (i) total percentage occupancy per cubicle type (lying and standing in the cubicle) and also (ii) lying only occupancy. Occupancy was measured using the formula

Occupancy = $T(y)/P \times 100$

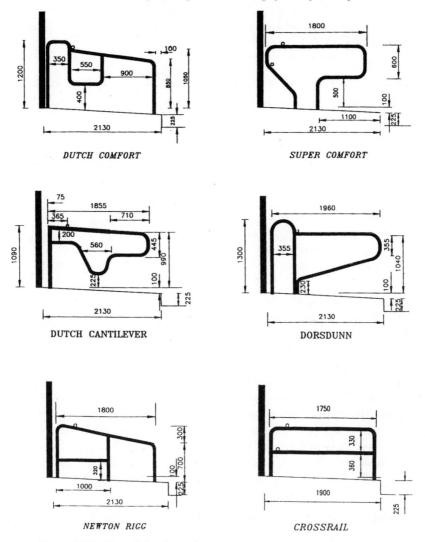

Figure 1.   Dimensions (mm) of Dutch Comfort, Super Comfort, Dutch Cantilever, Dorsdunn, Newton Rigg and Crossrail type cubicles

T = the sum of the number of cubicles of type (y) occupied at each 30-minute scan; P = the number of cubicles of type (y) multiplied by the number of 30-minute observation periods.

   In order of occupancy, the Dutch Cantilever cubicles were preferred to the other designs (Table 1) and both Dutch Comfort cubicle types were next. Both these cubicle types were selected in greater proportion to their availability

Table 1 *Total occupancy (lying and standing) and occupancy based on lying only for each cubicle type in three experiments.*

		% Occupancy/Cubicle	
Expt. Number	Cubicle Design	Lying & Standing	Lying Only
1	Dutch Comfort	58.03	41.82
	Super Dutch Comfort	63.88	44.31
2	Newton Rigg	45.51	32.41
	Super Dutch Comfort	71.13	52.93
3	Dutch Cantilever	66.94	39.95
	Dutch Comfort	53.54	32.90
	Dorsdunn	51.52	29.98

than the Newton Rigg cubicles. The Newton Rigg which has been on the market for over twenty years performed badly against the four new types. The Dorsdunn performed poorly in comparison to the three Dutch types.

One of the main causes of low cubicle selectivity is the lack of space at the front of the cubicle. Cows lunge forward on rising and a large cow needs 700–1000 mm of lunging space to rise with reasonable ease (Cermak, 1987; MAFF, 1983; Rogerson, 1972). The success of the Dutch Cantilever and of both Dutch Comfort type cubicles appears to be associated with the availability of sufficient head room to enable cows to rise without difficulty. The open frame design also allowed cows to share space laterally, for stretching their legs. In conclusion, this set of experiments indicated that cows (i) lay longer in some designs than in others and (ii) chose cubicle designs that allowed more space sharing.

Weanling experience and cubicle usage by heifers

Changes in dairy practices as a result of increasing herd size and new housing facilities have caused problems in rearing herd replacements. Acceptance of cubicles by heifers joining the milking herd has been a serious problem for many dairy farmers. Few farms have smaller cubicles to suit these animals. Other farmers prefer to winter their heifers in straw bedded loose houses (Grout & Guss, 1973; Harper & Hodgson-Jones, 1983). According to Webster (1987), heifers in their second winter should be housed in groups well matched for size and preferably in accommodation similar to that which they are likely to experience as adult cows. Thus, if they are to spend the winters of their adult lives in cubicles then they should gain experience of cubicles before calving. This should help to minimise the confusion and stress that they experience when entering the adult world of cubicles, milking parlour and dominant cows (Webster, 1987) and also help to reduce cubicle refusals.

A series of experiments by O'Connell, Giller, and Meaney (1993b) examined (i) the comparative success of training weanlings to use cubicles; and (ii) a follow-up of these weanlings to establish their reaction to adult cubicles as pregnant heifers in comparison to heifers with no previous experience of cubicles. Two weanling experiments were set up in which weanling heifers were housed in a weanling cubicle shed. The weanling cubicles were of Crossrail design (Figure 1), and measured 1820 mm × 910 mm. In the first experiment (non-training), the cubicles were simply available to the animals. In a second experiment (training), the weanlings were trained to use cubicles through the introduction of mats and/or feed blocks onto the cubicle beds. Sixty-one per cent of the weanlings in the non-training experiment used the cubicles in contrast to 95% in the training experiment. In the training experiment, the cubicles with mats attracted greater occupancy than the cubicles without mats. All animals that had previously used cubicles as weanlings consistently used the adult cubicles the following winter, but those animals who refused cubicles as weanlings initially refused the adult cubicles. However, about 50% of these could be enticed to use the adult cubicles when a mat was placed on the bed. In a final experiment, eleven heifers housed in a slatted unit as weanlings were introduced to cubicles. Only one animal consistently used the cubicles. The results of these three experiments indicated that training animals to use cubicles at the weanling stage was an effective method of preparing pregnant heifers for entry into the main milking herd. The provision of mats appeared to be the most successful method of training young stock to use cubicles.

The effect of cubicle design on behaviour and foot lesions in a group of in-calf heifers

Lameness is a major cause of economic loss to the cattle industry and is also of concern due to welfare considerations (Esselmont, 1990; Metz & Wierenga, 1987). It is a multifactorial condition and genetic, nutritional and environmental factors are considered important in the aetiology of lameness. Housing conditions can be important in the development of lameness (David, 1986; Murphy, Hannan, & Monaghan, 1987; Schlichting, 1987). Bee (1986) described a high incidence of sole ulcer and white line disease in herds fed low levels of concentrates but with poor concrete surfaces and low cubicle utilisation. A number of studies were set up to investigate the role of behavioural and traumatic factors under different housing conditions on lameness development. Three groups of animals were studied, two groups of spring-calving and one group of autumn-calving animals. First-calving animals were used in all trials in order to eliminate the confounding effects of parity and previous foot lesion development. Having established that dairy cows display distinct preferences for cubicle types, the purpose of the first experiment was to investigate the effect of cubicle design and bedding on the behaviour of heifers and possible influences on the development of foot lesions (Leonard *et al.*, 1994).

Twenty-two heifers were housed in a bay fitted with Dutch Comfort cubicles (2160 mm × 1160 mm; Figure 1) and 21 heifers in a bay fitted with Newton Rigg cubicles (2960 mm × 1090 mm; Figure 1). There was a 1:1 cow to cubicle ratio. The Dutch Comfort cubicles were fitted with mats whereas the Newton Rigg cubicles had no mats. The animals in the bay fitted with the Dutch Comfort cubicles and mats spent significantly more time lying down than their counterparts in the Newton Rigg bay. There was a significant increase in the mean haemorrhage score following housing in both groups of heifers, however, claw health deteriorated significantly more by one month post-partum in the animals housed in the Newton Rigg cubicles. This study showed that heifers in cramped unbedded cubicles showed more foot lesions than animals housed in spacious cubicles bedded with rubber mats. This study showed no consistent correlation between lying time and foot lesions.

The effect of overcrowding on claw health in first-calved heifers

Two additional studies were set up using overcrowding to induce a wide range of lying times in an attempt to clarify the influence of time spent lying down on foot lesion development pre- and post-calving. Claw health was monitored monthly, and behavioural activities such as lying/standing were observed every 15 minutes for five consecutive days and nights each month of the housing season, in two studies on overcrowding and foot lesion development. In the first experiment, 35 autumn-calving heifers were housed in a 2:1 heifer to cubicle ratio immediately after calving. In the second, 40 spring-calving heifers were housed at a ratio of 2:1 for two months before calving and with one cubicle each after calving. Lying time was reduced to five hours per 24 hours in some of the autumn-calving animals and these animals had significantly worse foot lesion scores and clinical lameness than animals lying for seven or 10 hours per 24 hours. The spring-calving animals did not show such a severe reduction in lying time and no significant correlation between haemorrhage score and lying time was detected (Leonard, O'Connell, & O'Farrell, 1996a).

In a further study, Leonard, O'Connell, and O'Farrell (1996b) carried out an observational study of the relationships between foot lesions and herd risk factors in 14 herds in North Cork. This study showed that herds where cows lay for longer developed less foot lesions than herds where cows had poor lying times. Herds where cubicle comfort was good (at least two of the following parameters: cubicle size, design and bedding satisfactory) tended to show longer lying times.

Conclusions

It is important to have a clear understanding of an animal's behaviour under various environmental conditions for a more informed analysis of research results on physiology, nutrition, breeding and management. This study of the lying behaviour of dairy cattle, has been shown to be valuable in the management of cattle over winter and in improving winter housing conditions. This was achieved by (i) identifying how the lying behaviour of the cows was modified in winter housing, (ii) identifying factors important to cattle in their use of cubicles, (iii) establishing the fact that reduced lying time acts as an exacerbating factor in the development of claw lesions, and (iv) developing techniques to manipulate behaviour to improve utilisation of cubicles.

References

Albright, L. D. & Timmons, M. B. (1984). Behaviour of dairy cattle in free stall housing. *Transactions of the ASAE, 27H*, 1119–1126.

Bee, D. J. (1986). Observations on lameness in a Hampshire (UK) practice. *Proc. Vth Intl. Symposium on Disorders of the Ruminant Digit, August 1986, Dublin*, 74–78.

Bell, E. H. (1986). Dairy cattle. *Farm Building Progress, 86*, 2–4.

Cermak, J. (1984). Housing. *CIGR Section II, Working Group Cattle Housing*, 34–65.

Cermak, J. (1987). The design of cubicles for British Friesian dairy cows with reference to body weight and dimensions, spatial behaviour and upper leg lameness. In: H. K. Wierenga & D. J. Peterse (Eds), *Cattle Housing Systems, Lameness and Behaviour* (pp. 119–129). Dordrecht, The Netherlands: Martinus Nijhoff.

Colam-Ainsworth, P., Lunn, G. A., Thomas, R. C., & Eddy, R. G. (1989). Behaviour of cows in cubicles and its possible relationship with laminitis in replacement dairy heifers. *Veterinary Record, 125*, 573–575.

Daelemans, J., Maton, A., & Lambrecht, J. (1981). An appraisal of some cubicle floors by cows. *CIGR Section II Seminar, Aberdeen*, 231–235.

David, G. (1986). Cattle behaviour and lameness. The influence of the animal building interaction on the incidence of lameness in dairy cattle. *Proc. Vth Intl. Symposium on Disorders of the Ruminant Digit, August 1986, Dublin*, 79–86.

Esselmont, R. (1990). The costs of lameness in dairy herds. *Proc. Vith Intl. Symposium on Diseases of the Ruminant Digit, July 1990, Liverpool*, 237–251.

Galindo, F. A. & Broom, D. M. (1993). The relationship between social behaviour of dairy cows and the occurrence of lameness. *Cattle Practice, 1*, 360–364.

Gebremedhin, K. G., Cramer, C. O., & Larsen, H. J. (1981). *Behavioural responses in selection of stalls in confinement* (ASAE Paper No. 81–4542). Michigan, USA: ASAE.

Gebremedhin, K. G., Cramer, C. O., & Larsen, H. J. (1985). Preference of dairy cattle for stall options in free stall housing. *Transactions of the ASAE, 28*(5), 1637–1640.

Graves, R. E. (1977). *Free stall design and construction criteria* (ASAE Paper No. 74–4503). Michigan, USA: ASAE.

Grout, R. G. & Guss, S. B. (1973). Requirements for heifer rearing. *Dairy Housing Conference, Michigan State University, 6–8 Feb.*, 315–320.

Gwynn, P. E. J., Wilkinson, R., & Thomas, T. P. (1991). Modifying timber cow cubicle divisions to improve cow acceptability. *Applied Animal Behaviour Science, 28*, 311–319.

Hafez, E. S. E. & Schein, H. W. (1969). *The Behaviour of Cattle* (2nd ed.). London: Bailliere, Tindall & Cassel.

Harper, A. D. (1983). Cow cubicles – 20 years on. *Farm Building Progress, 72*, 5–9.

Harper, A. D. & Hodgson-Jones, L. (1983). Adjustable width 'trombone' cubicles for heifers at Langhill. *Farm Building Progress, 73*, 3–4.

Irish, W. W. & Martin, R. O. (1983). Design considerations for free stalls. *ASAE Proceedings of the 2nd National Dairy Housing Conference, Madison*, 108–121.

Kelly, M. (1983). Good dairy housing design – a form of preventive medicine. *Veterinary Record, 113*, 582–586.

Krohn, C. C. & Konggaard, S. P. (1982). Investigations concerning feed intake and social behaviour among group fed cows under loose housing conditions. *Beret Stalens Husdyrbrugs Forsog.*

Leonard, F. C., O'Connell, J. M., & O'Farrell, K. J. (1994). Effect of different cubicle housing conditions on behaviour and foot lesions in Friesian heifers. *Veterinary Record, 134*, 490–494.

Leonard, F. C., O'Connell, J. M., & O'Farrell, K. J. (1996a). Effect of overcrowding on claw health in first-calved Friesian heifers. *British Veterinary Journal, 152*, 459–472.

Leonard, F. C., O'Connell, J. M., & O'Farrell, K. J. (1996b). Possible housing risk factors associated with lameness in Irish dairy herds. *Proc. IXth Intl. Symposium on Diseases of the Ruminant Digit, April, 1996, Israel.* (Abstract).

Metz, J. H. M. (1985). The reaction of cows to a short-term deprivation of lying. *Applied Animal Behaviour Science, 13*, 301–307.

Metz, J. H. M. & Wierenga, H. K. (1987). Behavioural criteria for the design of housing systems for cattle. In H. K. Wierenga & D. J. Peterse (Eds), *Cattle Housing Systems, Lameness and Behaviour* (pp. 14–25). Dordrecht, The Netherlands: Martinus Nijhoff.

Ministry of Agriculture and Fisheries and Food. (1983). *Design and Management of Cubicles for Dairy Cows (Booklet No. 2432)*. Northumberland, U.K.: MAFF Publications.

Murphy, P. A., Hannan, J., & Monaghan, M. (1987). A survey of lameness in beef cattle housed on slats and on straw. In H. K. Wierenga & D. J. Peterse (Eds), *Cattle Housing Systems, Lameness and Behaviour* (pp. 67–72). Dordrecht, The Netherlands: Martinus Nijhoff.

O'Connell, J. M., Giller, P. S., & Meaney, W. J. (1989a). A comparison of dairy cattle behaviour patterns at pasture and during confinement. *Irish Journal of Agricultural Research, 28*, 65–72.

O'Connell, J. M., Giller, P. S., & Meaney, W. J. (1989b). A comparison of dairy cattle utilisation of Dutch Comfort and Newton Rigg cubicles in winter housing. *Irish Journal of Agricultural Research, 28*, 123–132.

O'Connell, J. M., Giller, P. S., & Meaney, W. J. (1992). Factors affecting cubicle utilisation by cattle using stall frame and bedding manipulation experiments. *Applied Animal Behaviour Science, 35*, 11–21.

O'Connell, J. M., Giller, P. S., & Meaney, W. J. (1993a). A survey of cubicle refusal in dairy cows and implications for management. *Irish Journal of Agricultural Research, 32*, 83–86.

O'Connell, J. M., Giller, P. S., & Meaney, W. J. (1993b). Weanling experience and cubicle usage as heifers. *Applied Animal Behaviour Science, 37*, 185–195.

O'Connell, J. M., Meaney, W. J., & Giller, P. S. (1991). An evaluation of four cubicle designs using cattle behaviour criteria. *Irish Veterinary Journal, 44*, 8–13.

Oswald, I. (1980). Sleep as a restorative process: Human clues. *Progr. Brain Research, 53*, 279–288.

Rogerson, P. D. (1972). The size of cattle and their requirements for space. *Farm Buildings R and D Studies, 3*, 3–18.

Schlichting, M. C. (1987). Adaptation of cattle to different floor types. In H. K. Wierenga & D. J. Peterse (Eds), *Cattle Housing Systems, Lameness and Behaviour* (pp. 87–97). Dordrecht, The Netherlands: Martinus Nijhoff.

Suss, M. & Andreae, U. (1984). Rind. In H. Bogner & A. Grauvogl (Eds), *Verhalten Landwirtschaftlicher Nutztiere* (pp. 149–246). Stuttgart: Verlag Eugen Ulmer.

Webster, J. (1987). *Understanding the Dairy Cow*. Oxford: BSP Professional Books.

Westendorp. (1973). Ligboxen-en voer ligboxstallen. *ILB Publication, 62*, 6–37.

Wierenga, H. K. (1983). The influence of the space for walking and lying in a cubicle system on the behaviour of dairy cattle. In S. H. Baxter & J. A. C. McCormack (Eds), *Farm Animal Housing and Welfare* (pp. 171–180). The Hague: Martinus Nijhoff.

Wierenga, H. K. & Hopster, H. (1990). The significance of cubicles for the behaviour of dairy cows. *Applied Animal Behaviour Science, 26*, 309–337.

Wierenga, H. K. & Metz, J. H. M. (1986). Lying behaviour of dairy cows influenced by crowding. In: M. Nichelmann (Ed.), *Ethology of Domestic Animals* (pp. 61–66). Toulouse: Privat, I.E.C.

PART 3

EXPERIMENTAL ISSUES

11

Relational frame theory and the experimental analysis of human sexual arousal: Some interpretive implications[1]

Dermot Barnes and Bryan Roche

Abstract

Experimental analyses of human sexual arousal have been decidedly sparse. Recent relational frame research, however, has opened the way for a modern behaviour-analytic treatment of human sexual arousal. The current paper outlines relational frame theory, describes recent relational frame research that has examined the acquisition of sexual stimulus functions in human adults, and finally presents relational frame interpretations of a variety of human sexual phenomena. A number of important caveats are also considered.

Introduction

There are many reasons why behaviour analysts have not been recently active in the experimental analysis of human sexual behaviour. One reason is that the use of aversive therapeutic techniques by behaviour therapists has generated a degree of controversy. For example, the use of electric shock treatment to 'change homosexuals into heterosexuals' (see McGuire & Valance, 1964) is no longer considered to be an ethically acceptable practice (see Makay, 1976; Teal, 1971). Furthermore, these aversive conditioning techniques have not proved to be entirely successful in the permanent eradication of unwanted sexual behaviour (Barlow, Abel, & Blanchard, 1977; Barlow, Abel, & Blanchard, 1979; Maletzky, 1991; Masters & Johnson, 1979; Rimm & Masters, 1979). Finally, many researchers have had difficulty explaining the entire range of human

---

[1] Address correspondence concerning this chapter to Dermot Barnes, BACS Unit, Department of Applied Psychology, University College, Cork, Ireland.

sexual activities using the traditional principles of behaviour analysis (e.g., Gelder, 1979; McConaghy, 1987).

Perhaps for these reasons, a behavioural approach to human sexuality has attracted little support amongst the sex research community. Nevertheless, we would argue that recent behaviour-analytic research into verbal behaviour, conducted under the rubric of relational frame theory, has laid the groundwork for important experimental and conceptual analyses of those behavioural processes that generate specific sexual response patterns (e.g., fetishism). In the current paper we will: (*a*) briefly outline the conceptual underpinnings of relational frame theory, (*b*) describe recent relational frame research that has examined the acquisition of sexual stimulus functions in human adults, and (*c*) construct relational frame interpretations of a variety of human sexual behaviours based upon these recent experimental investigations.

Relational frame theory, stimulus equivalence, and transfer of function

To appreciate fully the conceptual underpinnings of relational frame theory, and its implications for the analysis of verbal and sexual behaviour, we must first consider the phenomenon of stimulus equivalence. Many studies have shown that non-human subjects can demonstrate conditional discriminations in a matching-to-sample context using arbitrary stimuli (i.e., stimuli that are not consistently related to each other along any consistent physical dimension/s). The simplest example involves two separate trial types. For one trial type, a particular sample (A1) is presented with two choice or comparison stimuli (B1 and B2). For the second trial type, a different sample (A2) is presented, but with the same choice stimuli (i.e., B1 and B2). These tasks are normally presented in random order for a large number of trials, and on each trial reinforcers are delivered contingent upon the subject choosing B1 in the presence of A1, or B2 in the presence of A2 (choosing B2 in the presence of A1, or B1 in the presence of A2, is either not reinforced or is explicitly punished). When a subject reliably chooses B1 given A1, and B2 given A2, this response pattern is considered to be an example of conditional discriminative control insofar as the pattern is produced by an explicit history of differential reinforcement. Recent developments in stimulus equivalence research, however, have indicated that certain properties of human discrimination are not readily predicted by the traditional concept of conditional discriminative control. Specifically, when verbally-able humans are trained on a series of conditional discriminations, the stimuli often become related to each other in untrained or derived ways. For example, when a subject is taught to match stimulus A to stimulus B and then to match A to C, it is likely that the subject will also match B to A, C to A (symmetry), B to C, and C to B (combined symmetry and transitivity) without further training. Following such a derived performance, the stimuli are said to participate in an equivalence relation (Barnes, 1994; Sidman & Tailby, 1982). The important point here is that the equivalence test outcomes are not readily predicted by the traditional concept of conditional discrimination, since neither B nor C has a *direct* history of differential reinforcement with regard to the other, and therefore neither stimulus should control selection of the other (remember also that the stimuli are not related to each other along any consistent physical dimension/s).

Interestingly, other novel or derived performances have also been generated using stimulus equivalence procedures. For example, when a simple discriminative function is trained to one stimulus in an equivalence relation, the function will often transfer to the other stimuli participating in that relation, without further reinforcement. This derived transfer of function effect in accordance with equivalence relations has been demonstrated with discriminative (Barnes & Keenan, 1993; Barnes, Browne, Smeets, & Roche, 1995; de Rose, McIlvane, Dube, Galpin, & Stoddard, 1988; Gatch & Osborne, 1989; Kohlenberg, Hayes, & Hayes, 1991; Wulfert & Hayes, 1988), consequential (Hayes, Devany, Kohlenberg, Brownstein, & Shelby, 1987; Hayes, Kohlenberg, & Hayes, 1991), and respondent stimulus functions (Dougher, Augustson, Markham, Greenway, & Wulfert, 1994; Roche & Barnes, 1997). In the study conducted by Hayes *et al.* (1987), for example, adults were first trained in four matching-to-sample tasks (i.e., if sample A1, select comparison B1 and not B2; if A2, select B2 and not B1; if A1, select C1 and not C2; if A2, select C2 and not C1). Subjects were then tested for the formation of two equivalence relations (A1–B1–C1, A2–B2–C2). Next, a stimulus from each equivalence relation was given a distinct, simple discriminative function; in the presence of B1 clapping was reinforced, and in the presence of B2 waving was reinforced. During testing, the discriminative functions assigned to the B1 and B2 stimuli were seen to transfer through equivalence to the C1 and C2 stimuli, in the absence of differential consequences for either clapping or waving (i.e., B1→clap transferred to C1→clap, and B2→wave transferred to C2→wave).

According to relational frame theory, stimulus equivalence and the derived transfer of function are both considered to be products of the same behavioural process of arbitrarily applicable relational responding. In effect, emergent performances such as equivalence and derived transfer are normally produced, in part, by the subject's history of arbitrarily applicable relational responding that is brought to bear by various contextual cues on the matching-to-sample test (see Barnes & Holmes, 1991; Barnes, 1994; Barnes; 1996; Barnes & Roche, 1996; Hayes, 1991, 1994; Hayes & Hayes, 1989; Roche & Barnes, 1996). From this perspective, learning to name objects and events in the world represents one of the earliest and most important forms of arbitrarily applicable relational responding. For instance, parents often utter the name of an object in the presence of their young child and then reinforce any orienting response that occurs towards the named object. This interaction may be described as, hear name A → look at object B. Parents also often present an object to their young child and then model and reinforce an appropriate 'tact' (Skinner, 1957). This interaction may be described as see object B → hear and say name A (see Barnes, 1994, for a detailed discussion). Initially each interaction may require explicit reinforcement for it to become firmly established in the behavioural repertoire of the child, but after a number of exemplars have been trained, derived 'naming' may be possible. Suppose, for example, a child with this naming history is told 'This is your shoe'. Contextual cues, such as the word 'is' and the naming context more generally, may establish symmetrical responding between the name and the object. Without further training, for example, the child will now point to the shoe when asked 'Where is your shoe?' (name A → object B) and will utter 'shoe' when presented with the shoe and asked 'What is this?' (object B → name A).

Arbitrarily applicable relational responding may be brought to bear on any stimuli, given appropriate contextual cues. Relational frame theory therefore explains equivalence and derived transfer in terms of a training history applicable to a given situation. In effect, when a young child is taught a number of name–object and object–name relations and is then exposed to a matching-to-sample procedure, contextual cues provided by this procedure may be discriminative for equivalence responding. In fact, the matching-to-sample format itself may be a particularly powerful contextual cue for equivalence responding insofar as it is often used in preschool education exercises to teach picture-to-word equivalences (see Barnes, 1994, for a detailed discussion).

Relational frame theory views stimulus equivalence and derived transfer as having very important implications for a behaviour analysis of human language. Consider the following example. Suppose that a young child on hearing that she must attend a 'dentist' (Stimulus A), experiences a painful tooth extraction. The child may then learn at school that an 'orthodontist' (Stimulus B) is a type of dentist. Later, on hearing that she must attend an 'orthodontist', the child may show signs of anxiety despite having had no direct experience with an orthodontist. This transfer of function effect is based on the behavioural function of A and the derived relation between A and B. In effect, the child does not need to experience the possibly aversive consequences of attending an orthodontist in order to show signs of anxiety.

This dentist example illustrates one of the core assumptions of the relational frame account of verbal events. *That is, a stimulus is rendered verbal by its participation in an equivalence or other type of derived relation* (see Hayes & Hayes, 1989, 1992; Hayes & Wilson, 1993, pp. 286–289). As we shall see, this functional definition of verbal events has important implications for the experimental and conceptual analysis of human sexual behaviour.

Before we return to the issue of sexual behaviour, however, we should first explain that relational frame theory incorporates derived relations other than equivalence such as opposition, difference, and comparison. For example, if an arbitrary stimulus, A, is the opposite of another arbitrary stimulus, B, then A and B are said to participate in a relational frame of opposition. This relation has the property that if A is the opposite of B and B is the opposite of C, then A and C are the same, not opposite. Similarly, if an arbitrary stimulus A is better than an arbitrary stimulus B, then A and B are said to participate in a relational frame of comparison. This relation has the property that if A is better than B, then B is worse than A. In the same way that terms such as, 'This is a . . . (name)' set the occasion for equivalence responding, a history of interaction with terms such as 'pick the opposite one' and 'show me the better one' form part of the historical context that gives rise to relational responding in accordance with the frames of opposition and comparison, respectively. Evidence that human subjects can respond to arbitrarily applicable relations is limited but growing (e.g., Dymond & Barnes, 1994, 1995; Roche & Barnes, 1996; Steele & Hayes, 1991). In the Steele and Hayes (1991) study, for example, teenage subjects were trained to relate same stimuli (e.g., a large line with a large line) in the presence of one contextual cue, opposite stimuli (e.g., a large line with a small line) in the presence of a second contextual cue, and different stimuli (e.g., a circle with a cross) in the presence of a third contextual cue. Subsequently, subjects were trained in an extensive network of conditional discriminations, with each discrimination being made in the presence of one of the three contextual cues. To understand the procedures involved in this complex experiment, consider the following six training trials; [S] A1/B1–B2–B3, [S] A1/C1–C2–C3, [O] A1/B1–B2–B3, [O] A1/C1–C2–C3, [D] A1/B1–B2, [D] A1/C1–C2. The letters S, O, and D represent the SAME, OPPOSITE, and DIFFERENT contextual cues, respectively. A1 represents the sample, and the B and C stimuli represent the comparisons. Choosing B1 and C1 was always reinforced in the presence of the SAME stimulus, choosing the B3 and C3 stimuli was always reinforced in the presence of the OPPOSITE stimulus, and choosing the B2 and C2 stimuli was always reinforced in the presence of the DIFFERENT stimulus. Now consider the following three test trials; [S] B1/C1–C2–C3, [S] B3/C1–C2–C3, [D] C1/B1–B2–N3. Subjects chose C1, C3, and B2, respectively on these tasks, indicating that the relational frames of co-ordination, opposition, and distinction had been brought to bear. More specifically, if B1 and C1 are the same as A1, then B1 and C1 are the same, and if B3 and C3 are opposite to A1 then B3 and C3 are the same. Finally, if B2 is different from A1, and C1 is the same as A1, then B2 is also different from C1. These data, and more recent findings (e.g., Barnes & Hampson, 1993; Dymond & Barnes, 1995; Roche & Barnes, 1996), support the view that certain patterns of human derived relational responding cannot readily be viewed simply as equivalence responding. A detailed discussion of the relationship between relational frame theory and Sidman's mathematical set theory of stimulus equivalence is beyond the scope of the current paper, but this issue has been examined in detail elsewhere (see Barnes, 1994; Barnes & Roche, 1996; Saunders, 1996).

Having briefly outlined the relational frame view of verbal events, and some relevant data, we will now turn to the issue of sexuality.

The experimental analysis of human sexuality

Early research

During the 1960s, behaviour-analytic sex research was more or less confined to the identification of the processes by which sexual stimulus functions might be established in visual stimuli (such as the human form) in the world outside the laboratory. It was hoped that analyses of 'laboratory induced fetishes' would help produce a behaviour-analytic account of human sexual orientation (see McGuire, Carlisle, & Young, 1965). This early sex research normally employed respondent conditioning techniques to establish sexual stimulus functions in a range of stimuli such as abstract symbols (Lovibond, 1963), a pair of female boots (Rachman, 1966; Rachman & Hodgson, 1968), or red circles (McConaghy, 1970). Although these early basic experimental analyses appeared promising, after a decade of research Bancroft (1969) and McConaghy (1969) concluded that conditioned sexual responses to experimental stimuli were simply too weak to serve as a realistic experimental analogue of fetishistic behaviour, or sexual behaviour more generally, in the world outside the laboratory. Indeed, it is now generally accepted that good analogues of deviant arousal, such as fetishism, cannot be created through traditional laboratory conditioning procedures (LoPiccolo, 1994). Perhaps for this reason, amongst others (e.g., ethical constraints), little has been done to supplement this early research (Laws & Marshall, 1990; Quinsey & Marshall, 1983). Even the analysis of operant processes in sexual behaviour has been studied rarely, with only a handful of relevant studies published over the past twenty years (see Earls & Castonguay, 1989; Marshall & Barbaree, 1988). Finally, the clinical studies that have been conducted under the rubric of behaviour analysis have largely been concerned with altering already-established unwanted sexual behaviours, rather than examining how sexual responses are established in the first instance. In summary, therefore, there has been no detailed experimental analysis of the basic behavioural processes of human sexual arousal since the preliminary investigations conducted in the 1960s.

Recent research

As outlined earlier, relational frame theory defines all forms of arbitrarily applicable relational responding as quintessentially verbal. Consequently, *instances of sexual behaviour that are arbitrarily applicable (i.e., transfer according to relational frames) constitute instances of verbal behaviour.* This basic assumption forms the bedrock of the recent sex research conducted at the Cork laboratory. We take the view that stimuli may acquire their sexual functions through a history of differential reinforcement and respondent conditioning, *and also* via the arbitrary relations in which those stimuli participate. We would expect, therefore, that an individual's sexual behaviour should depend, in part, on the way in which their verbal culture is organised. Consider, for example, two stimuli A and B that participate in a relational frame of equivalence, such that A is *equivalent to* B. Upon the establishment of a sexual arousal function in B, stimulus A should, without further training, actualise some of the sexual arousal functions of B. In more concrete terms, suppose the individuals John (A) and Roger (B) are both considered by many women to be physically attractive. Now consider a woman who is told that she is soon to go on a blind date with John (A), who looks very similar to her close friend Roger (B). It is likely, that for this verbally-able adult, hearing of meeting John (A) will actualise sexual arousal functions based on the explicitly-established functions of Roger (B) and the equivalence relation between Roger and John (i.e., B's sexual arousal functions transfer to A without direct experience of A).

The foregoing idea has been tested empirically at the Cork laboratory. In one study, seven subjects were seated comfortably before a microcomputer on which a series of related conditional discrimination tasks were presented (i.e., see A1 pick B1, see B1 pick C1, see A2 pick B2, see B2 pick C2, see A3 pick B3, see B3 pick C3, where all stimuli were nonsense syllables). For four subjects, training on these tasks led to the emergence of the following equivalence relations during testing; A1–B1–C1, A2–B2–C2, and A3–B3–C3. The remaining three subjects were not tested for equivalence relations at this stage. Using a respondent conditioning procedure, sexual and non sexual functions were then established for the C1 and C3 stimuli, respectively. Specifically, a short sexually explicit film taken from a popular sex instruction video followed quasi-random presentations of C1 on 80 percent of trials whereas a short non sexual film depicting scenic landscapes followed quasi-random presentations of C3, again on 80 percent of trials. A 45–60 second interval separated the conditioning trials.

We probed for respondent conditioning by measuring skin resistance responses (SRRs) during the 5-s nonsense syllable/film clip interval on the 12 final conditioning trials (i.e., six responses to either stimulus were recorded). Within approximately 18 conditioning trials, subjects generally showed differential conditioning (i.e., C1 produced significantly greater SRRs than C3). Subsequently, these differential respondent conditioning functions transferred through equivalence relations to the A1 and A3 stimuli, respectively. Specifically, five of seven subjects showing significantly greater SRRs to C1 over C3 also showed a significant response differential to A1 over A3. (The response differential to A1 and A3 was *derived*, in that A1 and A3 were not paired with film clips at any stage (see Roche & Barnes, 1995; 1997).

Further research at the Cork laboratory has provided empirical evidence that sexual stimulus functions can transfer in accordance with relations other than equivalence. In one study, six subjects were exposed to Same and Opposite relational pre-training similar to that used during the Steele and Hayes (1991) study (outlined previously). Subjects were then trained to relate the arbitrary stimuli B1 and C1 to A1 in the presence of the SAME contextual cue, and to relate the arbitrary stimuli B2 and C2 to A1 in the presence of the OPPOSITE contextual cue (where all stimuli were nonsense syllables). The emergence of the derived relations; [S] B1–C1 and [S] B2–C2 was predicted (i.e., A1 is the same as B1, A1 is the same as C1, therefore B1 is the same as C1; A1 is the opposite of B2, A1 is the opposite of C2, therefore B2 is the same as C2). Using a respondent conditioning procedure, sexual arousal and emotionally neutral functions were also established for the two nonsense syllables, B1 and B2, respectively (for some subjects the functions of these stimuli were reversed). The test for a transfer of sexual functions involved the presentation of the C1 and C2 stimuli alone. Four of six subjects showed significant respondent conditioning (i.e., a response differential to B1 and B2) and a subsequent transfer of sexual arousal functions in accordance with sameness and opposition (i.e., a transfer of the response differential from B1 and B2 to C1 and C2, respectively).

Relational frame interpretations

Having examined relational frame theory and its primary concepts, and having outlined recent data gathered at the Cork laboratory, we will now offer relational frame interpretations of a number of human sexual phenomena. Although the following sections explore the application of relational frame theory to a wide range of sexual behaviours in a somewhat speculative manner, the interpretations presented are firmly grounded in functional-analytic terms. In the same way that astrophysicists interpret cosmic events in terms of variables that are manipulable on a smaller scale (e.g., the activity of particles in a particle accelerator), we will interpret highly complex behaviour in terms of the types of behavioural variables that we have manipulated in our empirical studies.

Learning in the absence of a direct training history

A common finding reported in the sex research literature is that individuals often report a predilection for a sexual activity in the absence of an explicit or direct experience that would readily account for that predilection (e.g., most cross-dressers report that they had never seen or heard of another individual cross-dress before they first engaged in transvestism (McConaghy, 1987; personal communication)). Relational frame theory suggests, however, that given a history of arbitrarily applicable relational responding, phrases such as 'this is the same as . . .' and 'this is the opposite of . . .' may establish relational frames through which sexual functions transfer. Consider, for example, the following personal account of sexual development recorded by Zilbergeld (1979);

> The most interesting thing, though, is that for many months after I started masturbating, I never connected what I was doing with girls or what little I knew about sex. Masturbation – 'whacking off' is what my room-mates called it – was just an enjoyable activity that boys did alone or in darkness. Only after I heard that one could put his penis in a vagina and experience similar sensations did I begin to put together what I was doing with what I might someday do with a girl and start developing sexual fantasies to accompany my solo ministrations. (p. 22)

In order to clarify the sequence of events reported in the above account, examine the relational network in Figure 1. This network indicates that, for this individual, sexual arousal functions did not transfer from actual masturbation and the word 'masturbation' (or 'whacking off') to the word 'vagina' and perhaps pictures of vaginas (if this individual had been exposed to pornography) until both participated in a *derived* relational frame of coordination. For this individual, the derived frame of coordination was established, in part, through verbal interactions with his peers. In effect, the establishment of sexual arousal functions in the word 'vagina' in the absence of an explicit stimulus pairing or response reinforcement history, can be conceptualised as a derived transfer of sexual arousal functions in accordance with a derived relational frame of coordination.

The foregoing also suggests that it is not necessary that a sexual behaviour, such as cross-dressing, be directly paired with sexual arousal or a conditioned sexual stimulus in order for transvestism to emerge. To appreciate this point, consider a boy who learns verbally (e.g., is told by his classmates) that 'bizarre' behaviours are often considered sexually arousing (see Figure 2, upper section). For this boy, sexual arousal and bizarre behaviour will then participate in a relational frame of coordination. If this boy is then told at another time (e.g., a week or a month later) that it is 'weird' or 'bizarre' to dress in the clothes of the opposite sex (it would be fair to argue that many children learn this), the behaviour of cross-dressing may become related to bizarre behaviours, in general, through a relational frame of coordination. In a suitable context, therefore, the *words* 'sexual arousal' may be related to the *words* 'cross-dressing' in accordance with the frame of coordination. Perhaps of greater interest here, however, is the fact that the words 'sexual arousal' and the words 'cross-dressing' also participate in socially established frames of coordination with actual sexual arousal and actual cross-dressing, respectively. The operation of these types of frames makes it likely that, in some contexts, the functions of actual sexual arousal will transfer to actual cross-dressing according to the extended relational frame presented in Figure 2. In effect, the operation of this relational network may facilitate the emergence of transvestism as a form of 'novel' behaviour.

Sexual fantasy

Another common finding in the sex research literature is that sexual behaviour is often related, and even emerges from the subjective content of sexual fantasies. Some researchers, for example, have had success 'reorienting sexual deviants who had no normal sexual interest by instructing them that whatever the initial stimulus to masturbation the fantasy in the five seconds just before orgasm must be of normal sexual intercourse' (McGuire, Carlisle, & Young, 1965, p. 187; see also Bancroft, 1970; Barlow *et al.*, 1977; Rachman & Hodgson, 1968).

Interestingly, relational frame theory allows for the transfer of covert and overt response functions, and thus it provides a conceptual framework for the experimental analysis of covert perceptual functions, such as sexual imagery. In the words of Hayes (1991):

The transfer of stimulus functions includes not just discriminative or reinforcement functions, but also such things as perceptual functions. As a network of relational events becomes organized, the person may, for example, see one stimulus given another. Consider the following phrase and do what it says: 'Picture a car'. Many readers presumably did in fact see a car. This perceptual event can be thought of as a transfer of the visual functions of cars to the verbal name symmetrically related to it. (p. 24)

This relational frame view helps us to account for the dynamic relationship between sexual fantasising and overt behaviour (see Figure 3). Consider a young boy, for example, who becomes sexually aroused while listening to the sexual conquests of an older schoolmate (Public Story → Arousal). When this boy becomes sexually aroused in suitable contexts on future occasions (e.g., in the privacy of his bedroom) he may 'remember' or fantasise about the sexual conquests of his friend (Arousal → Private Story). In effect, the relationship between the sexual story and sexual arousal has become bidirectional or symmetrical (i.e., either can now produce the other by virtue of the bidirectional transfer of response functions). Thus, when sexual arousal produces fantasising, this may lead to a further increase in sexual arousal (i.e., a type of feedback loop is in operation whereby arousal leads to fantasising which in turn leads to

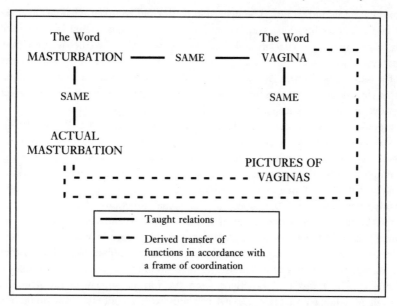

Figure 1. A set of taught and derived relations according to which sexual functions might transfer from masturbation to pictures of vaginas.

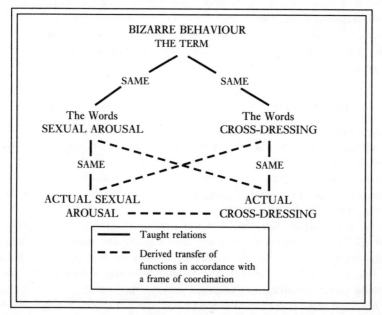

Figure 2. A set of taught and derived relations according to which sexual functions might transfer to produce the 'novel' sexual behaviour of transvestism.

more arousal, and so on). The operation of this bidirectional relationship makes it likely that on future occasions sexual arousal will produce fantasising that will, in turn, increase sexual arousal, and so on. In effect, this behavioural interpretation can account for the covert strengthening of sexual fantasising in terms of a bidirectional (symmetrical) transfer of fantasy/arousal functions. Although this view is somewhat speculative within the context of sexual behaviour, recent evidence suggests that symmetrical relations *can* emerge between two different response patterns produced by the same individual (Dymond & Barnes, 1994).

Another important feature of relational responding is that ongoing interactions with the verbal community allow sexual functions to transfer in increasingly complex ways. For example, the verbal nature of sexual fantasising makes it likely that sexual fantasies will participate in a relational frame of coordination with each other, and thus some of the sexual functions of one fantasy may transfer to another. Consider an individual who on some occasions (i.e., contexts) sexually fantasises about a colleague at their place of work, and on other occasions fantasises about having sexual relations in a public place. Under these circumstances, both acts of fantasising may become related via the *term* sexual fantasy. The transfer of functions from the former fantasy to the later may result in a fantasy involving sexual relations with a colleague in a public area (see Figure 4). An individual may, therefore, 'imagine' novel and, apparently original sexual images and scenarios. Although researchers have long been aware that composite sexual fantasies may emerge (e.g., Laws & Marshall, 1990), relational frame theory provides a set of functional-analytic terms with which to discuss the behavioural process by which this phenomenon occurs. In effect, a relational control view of sexual behaviour explains, at least potentially, the occurrence of novel or unique sexual fantasies in non-mentalistic terms.

The impermanence of aversive therapeutic effects

A third finding in the sex research literature is that conditioned responses and the effects of behaviour therapy are relatively short-lived (Gosselin & Wilson, 1984; Masters & Johnson, 1979; Rimm & Masters, 1979). Some researchers, therefore, have suggested that the process by which sexual behaviours initially arise is not one best described using behavioural principles (e.g., Gosselin & Wilson, 1984; McConaghy, 1987).

We would argue, however, that the complexity of verbal behaviour, as defined by relational frame theory, may explain the difficulty behaviou therapists have in permanently eradicating unwanted sexual behaviour. Before we consider this idea in greater detail it may be useful to look briefly at the types of verbal contingencies that might give rise to deviant sexual behaviour.

Although men, at least in Western culture, are not explicitly reinforced for deviant behaviour such as rape, they are, however, exposed to social/verbal

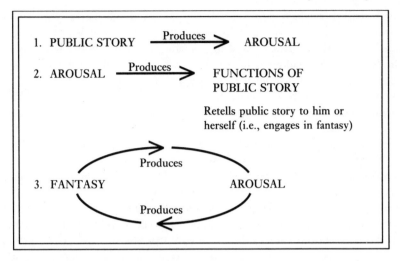

Figure 3. The covert strengthening of a sexual fantasy resulting from the bidirectional transfer of functions between fantasy and sexual arousal.

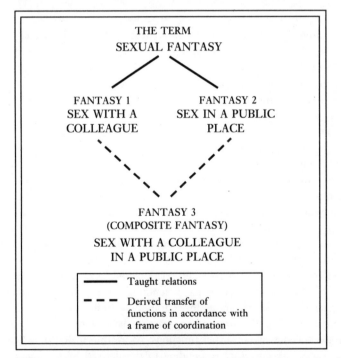

Figure 4. The derivation of a composite and novel sexual fantasy by virtue of the bidirectional transfer of functions between two sexual fantasies.

contingencies in which caring, gentle, helpless, and submissive women often participate in a relational frame of coordination with sexual attraction (e.g., a beautiful damsel in distress saved by a knight in shining armour is a common theme in the fairy stories told to young children). Males are also exposed to contingencies in which women participate in a frame of coordination with 'not knowing their own minds' and 'meaning "yes" even when they say "no"' (see Beloff, 1992). Thus women may fall into a frame of coordination with 'weakness' and 'must be controlled for their own good' and into a frame of opposition with 'strength' and 'must be taken seriously'.

To appreciate how this analysis may help us to understand the act of rape, consider the relational network in Figure 5. The lower section of the diagram (indicated by brackets) represents one possible set of taught and derived relations according to which members of our culture might respond in the context of gender and sexuality. For example, it is fair to say that most members of Western cultures are explicitly taught that, in the context of gender relations, males and females are 'opposite' (e.g., members of 'opposite' sexes). Many children also learn, through interaction with popular culture (i.e., television, magazines, 'pop' music) that women are submissive, whereas men are dominant (see Biglan, 1995, pp. 353–358; Guerin, 1994, pp. 283–287). Furthermore, the words 'dominant' and 'submissive' often participate in frames of coordination with the terms 'a lot of control' and 'lacking control', respectively. Given that many members of our culture respond according to the foregoing relational network, we might expect to find that many men are sexually attracted to submissive women or women that lack control. Similarly, we might expect to find that many women are sexually attracted to powerful men, or men that possess a lot of control.

Although the foregoing analysis refers only to sexual activities that fall within what we might call the 'normal' range of sexual behaviours, the relational frame interpretation offered here makes its most significant contribution to our understanding of less widespread sexual activities, such as rape. Consider, for instance, the upper right-hand section of Figure 5. This extended relational frame indicates that, in a suitable context, men may respond to the term 'lack of control' as related to the term 'no control' through a relational frame of comparison (i.e., greater than). Also, in an appropriate context, the term 'no control' may be related to the term 'victim' according to a frame of coordination. This extended relational network represents one of the processes by which terms pertaining to femininity (e.g., woman, female) may become related to those pertaining to victimisation. In most contexts, of course, (e.g., that of reading the present paper) the derivation of such a relation involves the transfer of nonsexual functions. More informally, it is likely that you, the reader, are currently responding to the derived relation between the terms 'female' and 'victim' at a purely intellectual level. In some limited

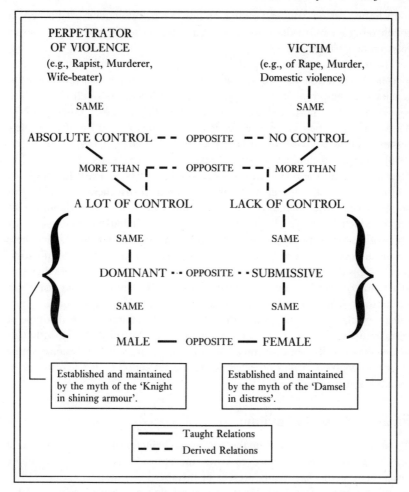

Figure 5. An extended relational network according to which sexual arousal functions might transfer to produce rape.

contexts, however, the sexual arousal functions that have been socially established for terms pertaining to femininity will transfer according to this extended relational frame to terms pertaining to victimisation. Under these circumstances, verbal descriptions of powerless, submissive or victimised women (e.g., in pornography) will actualise sexual arousal.

Of course the particular historical and current contexts in which sexual functions transfer according to such extended relational networks, have yet to be identified. Although this issue certainly deserves further empirical attention, the relational frame interpretation offered here makes an immediate theoretical contribution to our understanding of how verbal functions established in childhood (e.g., by media images and fairy stories) might give rise to sexual coercion or violence in later life.[2]

The foregoing analysis suggests that using aversive conditioning techniques to counter-condition deviant sexual responses may leave the verbal contingencies governing rape in tact (e.g., the rapist still lives in a culture in which women are often portrayed as submissive; see Biglan, 1995; Guerin, 1994). Thus, traditional behaviour therapeutic methods may not lead to the complete cessation of sexual violence (Maletzky, 1991; Marshall, Laws, & Barbaree, 1990). In order to eliminate unwanted sexual behaviour completely, it would be necessary to alter the relational frames according to which sexual functions are transferring. Perhaps, therefore, future research in sexual therapy should focus on identifying efficient methods for the manipulation of verbal relations. One way in which a rapist's 'deviant frames' might be altered, for example, is by confronting him with rape victims in a nonsexual clinical setting. Under these circumstances, the rape victim may shift from a frame of coordination containing 'submission', 'needing to be controlled', or 'deserving what they got' to a frame of coordination containing 'a women like my mother or sister' (or any platonic female friend or relative who is held in high esteem) or 'a human being just like me'. In fact, some therapists have had success with this type of perpetrator/victim confrontation technique (e.g., Murphy, 1990), although success has usually been attributed to mentalistic processes. Relational frame theory, in contrast, makes no reference to mental concepts in its treatment of complex sexual behaviour.

Bizarre sexual behaviour

A fourth claim often made in the sex research literature is that behavioural principles cannot be extended to cover the entire range of highly complex sexual behaviours that clients present in therapy. For example, Gelder (1979; see also Bourget & Bradford, 1987) pointed out that it is difficult to account for the emergence of a fire fetish,[3] in terms of respondent or operant processes (e.g., it is difficult to imagine a situation in which fire reliably predicts the onset of a sexual stimulus or in which contact with fire is sexually reinforced). Indeed, although we may account for many instances of fetishistic behaviour in terms of respondent processes (e.g., common fetish objects appear frequently in

---

[2]   Although we refer to rape as possessing sexual stimulus functions, we do not mean to say that the act of rape is purely sexual in nature (see also LoPiccolo, 1994). Rather, the foregoing interpretation serves merely to help us understand how sexual stimulus functions might combine with acts of violence and power to produce rape.

[3]   Although rare, fire fetishism (also known as pyrolangia or sexual arson) has not gone unreported. Cox (1979) stated that, having set a fire, the fire fetishist 'will claim that he has had his best ever orgasm as he watched the flames leap up . . .' (p. 343).

pornography; see Rosengrant, 1986), it is difficult to interpret unusual fetishes, such as a fire fetish (Bourget & Bradford, 1987; Cox, 1979), in these terms (see Gelder, 1979; McConaghy, 1987).

A relational frame interpretation of sexual fetishism, however, suggests that the cultural/verbal relations according to which individuals respond may account for the emergence of highly unusual fetishes for which there appears to be no explicit reinforcement history. For example, we might account for the emergence of a fire fetish by pointing to the significant overlap between 'sexual frames' and 'fire frames'. More specifically, both sexual arousal and fire are spoken of as 'explosive' and 'hot'. In popular romantic literature lust is often referred to as 'burning desire' and love as a 'flame'. In popular music, lyrics have contained phrases such as 'Come on baby light my fire (The Doors)' and 'Come on and stand next to my fire' (Jimi Hendrix). Indeed a European porno-graphic television channel is known as 'Red Hot Dutch'. Furthermore, the *Collins English Dictionary and Thesaurus* lists the terms 'ardour', 'excitement', 'lustre', and 'passion' under the reference term 'fire'. Thus, given that terms pertaining to fire and sexual behaviour often participate in frames of coordi-nation with each other, we would expect to observe occasionally a transfer of functions from sexual arousal to fire, even though prevailing physical contin-gencies make such a transfer unlikely (i.e., exposure to 'sexually attractive' fire is painful).[4] In effect, relational frame theory suggests that the specific arbitrarily applicable relations to which the fetishist responds are of primary importance in the control of sexual behaviour. Thus, relational frame theory may account for a wide range of human fetishistic behaviours.[5]

As an aside, the formal properties of fire and sex are likely to play some role in establishing the arbitrarily applicable relation between these two events (i.e., physiological changes caused by close proximity to fire may be physically similar to the physiological changes that occur during sexual arousal, such as increased blood flow, oxygen intake, and perspiration). The idea that the formal properties of events in the natural world help establish arbitrarily applicable relational responding is entirely consistent with the relational frame account. Consider the following passage from Hayes (1994):

Select two concrete nouns – anything – before reading the next sentence. Now, we will call the first noun 'A' and the second noun 'B'. How are 'A' and 'B' alike? Different?

---

[4]   Given that direct sexual contact with fire is certainly painful (and that repeated contact is life-threatening), it is not surprising that so few people ever develop a fire fetish, even though relational frames obviously support the emergence of such behaviour. Nevertheless, the fact that fire fetishes *do* occasionally emerge, despite the immediate physical contingencies that make it unlikely, is testimony to the power that relational framing may exert over sexual behaviour.

[5]   Interestingly, psychoanalysts have also noted the overlap between terms pertaining to fire and sex. Cox (1979), for example, identified the phrases 'my best flame' and 'you set me on fire' as possible sources of fire fetishism. From a psychoanalytic perspective, however, the emergence of the fetishism is mediated by ill-defined subconscious processes.

Why is 'A' better? How is 'A' the father of 'B'? My guess is that every one of these relational questions, or a myriad like them, will lead to a sensible answer justified by supposed formal properties of the related events. But often these same formal properties would hardly control the nonarbitrary capabilities of nonverbal organisms. In other words, the formal properties used to 'justify' such relational activities are themselves abstracted as a result of these same relational activities. If it is always possible to answer such questions we must either suppose that all objects are related in all ways to each other, or that such relations are arbitrarily applicable and that formal properties are context for such activities but not the source of them. (pp. 23–24)

According to relational frame theory, therefore, although the equivalence relation between fire and sex may be based to some extent on the formal properties of these events, it seems unlikely that the formal properties are in themselves sufficient to account for the equivalence relation between fire and sex.

Conclusion

In the present paper, we have examined the limited empirical evidence in support of a behavioural approach to human sexuality and suggested that further basic research is required. We have also briefly outlined empirical findings from our own research and used them to develop relational frame interpretations of specific human sexual phenomena.

Some readers may dismiss the relational frame interpretation of human sexuality presented here, on the grounds that it is to some degree speculative. It is important to remember, however, that the terms and concepts of relational frame theory are firmly attached to a set of experimental procedures (see Dymond & Barnes, 1995; Dymond & Barnes, 1986; Lipkens, 1992; Roche & Barnes, 1996; Steele & Hayes, 1991). Insofar as these procedures allow for the prediction and control of human behaviour, the relational frame interpretation offered here brings us closer to producing the prediction and control of human sexual activity.

Other readers may argue that the investigation of complex human (sexual) behaviour should progress more cautiously, pointing to the fact that many basic questions regarding the equivalence effect, as one form of relational responding, remain unanswered (see Markham & Dougher, 1994; Stromer, McIlvane, & Serna, 1993). However, speculation is not necessarily counterproductive to scientific progress. It may be, that casting a wide net by applying relational frame theory to highly complex behaviours in a range of social settings will result in the successful application of behavioural principles to a whole host of complex human behaviours.

Finally, the current paper and the interpretations offered herein, have focused on a small range of human sexual phenomena that lend themselves readily to 'molecular' and laboratory-based analyses. Alternative and supplementary behaviour-analytic approaches may be found in recent works by

Guerin (1994) and Biglan (1995). It is our hope that these socially-based 'molar' analyses, combined with the approach offered in the current paper, will eventually provide a more complete behaviour-analytic account of human sexuality.

References

Bancroft, J. (1969). Aversion therapy of homosexuality. *British Journal of Psychiatry, 115*, 1417–1432.

Bancroft, J. (1970). A comparative study of aversion and desensitization in the treatment of homosexuality. In L. E. Burns & J. L. Worsley (Eds), *Behaviour therapy in the 1970s* (pp. 1–22). Bristol: John Wright & Sons.

Barlow, D. H., Abel, G. G., & Blanchard, E. B. (1977). Gender identity change in a transsexual: An exorcism. *Archives of Sexual Behavior, 6*, 387–395.

Barlow, D. H., Abel, G. G., & Blanchard, E. B. (1979). Gender identity change in transsexuals. *Archives of General Psychiatry, 36*, 1001–1007.

Barlow, D. H., Agras, W. S., Leitenberg, H., & Callahan, E. F. (1972). The contribution of therapeutic instructions to covert sensitization. *Behavior Research and Therapy, 10*, 411–415.

Barnes, D. (1994). Stimulus equivalence and relational frame theory. *The Psychological Record, 44*, 91–124.

Barnes, D. (1996). Sacrificing behavior analysis at the altar of popularity: A reply to Horne & Lowe (Commentary). *Journal of the Experimental Analysis of Behavior 65*, 264–267.

Barnes, D. Browne, M., Smeets, P., & Roche, B. (1995). A transfer of functions and a conditional transfer of functions through equivalence relations in three- to six-year old children. *The Psychological Record, 45*, 405–430.

Barnes, D. & Hampson, P. J. (1993). Stimulus equivalence and connectionism: Implications for behavior analysis and cognitive science. *The Psychological Record, 43*, 617–638.

Barnes, D. & Holmes, Y. (1991). Radical behaviorism, stimulus equivalence, and human cognition. *The Psychological Record, 41*, 19–31.

Barnes, D. & Keenan, M. (1993). A transfer of functions through derived arbitrary and non-arbitrary stimulus relations. *Journal of the Experimental Analysis of Behavior, 59*, 61–81.

Barnes, D. & Roche, B. (1996). Relational frame theory and stimulus equivalence are fundamentally different: A reply to Saunders' commentary. *The Psychological Record, 46*, 489–508.

Beloff, H. (1992). Mother, father and me: Our I.Q. *The Psychologist, 5*, 309–311.

Biglan, A. (1995). *Changing cultural practices: A contextualistic framework for intervention research*. Reno, NV: Context Press.

Bourget, D. & Bradford, J. M. (1987). Fire fetishism, diagnostic and clinical implications: A review of two cases. *Canadian Journal of Psychiatry, 32*, 459–462.

Collins English Dictionary and Thesaurus. (1992). London: HarperCollins.

Cox, M. (1979). Dynamic psychotherapy with sex-offenders. In I. Rosen (Ed.), *Sexual deviation* (pp. 306–350). Oxford: Oxford University Press.

de Rose, J. C., McIlvane, W. J., Dube, W. V., Galpin, V. C., & Stoddard, L. T. (1988). Emergent simple discrimination established by indirect relation to differential consequences. *Journal of the Experimental Analysis of Behavior, 50*, 1–20.

Dougher, M. J., Augustson, E., Markham, M. R., Greenway, D. E., & Wulfert, E. (1994). The transfer of respondent eliciting and extinction functions through stimulus equivalence classes. *Journal of the Experimental Analysis of Behavior, 62,* 331–352.

Dymond, S. & Barnes, D. (1994). A transfer of self-discrimination response functions through equivalence relations. *Journal of the Experimental Analysis of Behavior, 62,* 251–267.

Dymond, S. & Barnes, D. (1995). A transformation of self-discrimination response functions in accordance with the arbitrarily applicable relations of sameness, more-than, and less-than. *Journal of the Experimental Analysis of Behavior, 64,* 163–184.

Dymond, S. & Barnes, D. (1996). A transformation of self-discrimination response functions in accordance with the arbitrarily applicable relations of sameness and opposition. *The Psychological Record, 46,* 271–300.

Earls, C. M. & Castonguay, L. G. (1989). The evaluation of olfactory aversion for a bisexual paedophile with a single-case multiple baseline design. *Behavior Therapy, 20,* 137–146.

Feldman, M. P. & MacCulloch, M. J. (1971). *Homosexual behaviour: Therapy and assessment.* Oxford: Pergamon.

Gatch, M. B. & Osborne, J. G. (1989). Transfer of contextual stimulus function via equivalence class development. *Journal of the Experimental Analysis of Behavior, 51,* 369–378.

Gelder, M. (1979). Behaviour therapy for sexual deviations. In I. Rosen (Ed.), *Sexual deviation* (pp. 351–375). Oxford: Oxford University Press.

Gosselin, C. & Wilson, G. (1984). Fetishism, sadomasochism and related behaviours. In K. Howells (Ed.), *The psychology of sexual diversity* (pp. 89–110). Blackwell.

Guerin, B. (1994). *Analyzing social behavior. Behavior analysis and the social sciences.* Reno, NV: Context Press.

Hayes, S. C. (1991). A relational control theory of stimulus equivalence. In L. J. Hayes & P. N. Chase (Eds), *Dialogues on verbal behavior* (pp. 19–41). Reno, NV: Context Press.

Hayes, S. C. (1994). Relational frame theory: A functional approach to verbal events. In S. C. Hayes, L. J. Hayes, M. Sato, & K. Ono (Eds), *Behavior analysis of language and cognition* (pp. 9–30). Reno, NV: Context Press.

Hayes, S. C., Devany, J. M., Kohlenberg, B. S., Brownstein, A. J., & Shelby, J. (1987). Stimulus equivalence and the symbolic control of behavior. *Revista Mexicana de Analisis de la Conducta, 13,* 361–374.

Hayes, S. C. & Hayes, L. J. (1989). The verbal action of the listener as a basis for rule-governance. In S. C. Hayes (Ed.), *Rule-governed behavior: Cognition, contingencies, and instructional control.* (pp. 153–190). New York: Plenum.

Hayes, S. C. & Hayes, L. J. (1992). Verbal relations and the evolution of behavior analysis. *American Psychologist, 47,* 1383–1395.

Hayes, S. C., Kohlenberg, B. S., & Hayes, L. J. (1991). The transfer of specific and general consequential functions through simple and conditional equivalence relations. *Journal of the Experimental Analysis of Behavior, 56,* 119–137.

Hayes, S. C. & Wilson, K. G. (1993). Some applied implications of a contemporary behavior-analytic view of verbal events. *The Behavior Analyst, 16,* 283–301.

Kohlenberg, B. S., Hayes, S. C., & Hayes, L. J. (1991). The transfer of contextual control over equivalence classes through equivalence classes: A possible model of social stereotyping. *Journal of the Experimental Analysis of Behavior, 56,* 505–518.

Laws, D. R. & Marshall, W. L. (1990). A conditioning theory of the etiology and maintenance of deviant sexual preference and behavior. In W. L. Marshall, D. R. Laws, & H. E. Barbaree (Eds), *Handbook of sexual assault* (pp. 209–229). New York: Plenum.

Lipkens, R. (1992). A behavior analysis of complex human functioning: Analogical reasoning. Unpublished doctoral thesis, University of Nevada, Reno. NV.

LoPiccolo, J (1994). Acceptance and broad spectrum treatment of paraphilias. In S. C. Hayes, N. S. Jacobson, V. M. Follette, & M. J. Dougher (Eds), *Acceptance and change: Content and context in psychotherapy* (pp. 149–170). Reno, NV: Context Press.

Lovibond, S. H. (1963). Conceptual thinking, personality and conditioning. *British Journal of Social and Clinical Psychology, 2*, 100–111.

Makay, D. (1976). Modification of sexual behaviour. In S. Gown (Ed.), *Psychosexual problems: Psychotherapy, counselling and behavioural modification* (pp. 89–102). London: Academic Press.

Maletzky, B. M. (1991). *Treating the sexual offender*. Newbury Park, California: Sage.

Markham, M. R. & Dougher, M. J. (1994). Compound stimuli in emergent stimulus relations: Extending the scope of stimulus equivalence. *Journal of the Experimental Analysis of Behavior, 60*, 529–542.

Marshall, W. L. & Barbaree, H. E. (1988). An outpatient treatment programme for child molesters. *Annals of the New York Academy of Sciences, 528*, 205–214.

Marshall, W. L., Laws, D. R., & Barbaree, H. E. (1990). *Handbook of sexual assault*. New York: Plenum. Press.

Masters, W. H. & Johnson, V. E. (1979). *Homosexuality in perspective*. Boston: Little, Brown.

McConaghy, N. (1969). Subjective and penile plethysmograph responses following aversion-relief and apomorphine aversion therapy for homosexual impulses. *British Journal of Psychiatry, 115*, 723–730.

McConaghy, N. (1970). Penile response conditioning and its relationship to aversion therapy in homosexuals. *Behavior Therapy, 1*, 213– 221.

McConaghy, N. (1987). A learning approach. In J. H. Geer & W. T. O'Donohue (Eds), *Theories of human sexuality* (pp. 282–333). New York: Plenum.

McGuire, R. J., Carlisle, J. M., & Young, B. G. (1965). Sexual deviations as conditioned behavior: A hypothesis. *Behavior Research and Therapy, 2*, 185–190.

McGuire, R. J. & Valance, M., (1964). Aversion therapy by electric shock: A simple technique. *British Medical Journal, 1*, 151–153.

Murphy, W. D. (1990). Assessment and modification of cognitive distortions in sex. In W. L. Marshall, D. R. Laws & H. E. Barbaree (Eds), *Handbook of sexual assault* (pp. 331–361). New York: Plenum.

Quinsey, V. L. & Marshall. W. L. (1983). Procedures for reducing inappropriate sexual arousal: An evaluation review. In J. G. Geer & I. R. Stuart (Eds), *The sexual aggressor: Current perspectives on treatment* (pp. 267–289). New York: Van Nostrand Reinhold.

Rachman, S. (1966). Sexual fetishism: An experimental analogue. *The Psychological Record, 16*, 293–296.

Rachman, S. & Hodgson, R. J. (1968). Experimentally-induced 'sexual fetishism': Replication and development. *The Psychological Record, 18*, 25–27.

Rimm, D. C. & Masters, J. C. (1979). *Behavior therapy: Techniques and empirical findings*. (2nd Edition). New York: Academic Press.

Roche, B. & Barnes, D. (1995). Technical Information: The establishment and electrodermal assessment of conditioned sexual responses. *The Experimental Analysis of Human Behavior Bulletin, 13*, 26–29.

Roche, B. & Barnes, D. (1996). Arbitrarily applicable relational responding and sexual categorization: A critical test of the derived difference relation. *The Psychological Record, 46*, 451–476.

Roche, B. & Barnes, D. (1997). A transfer of respondently conditioned sexual arousal functions through derived arbitrary relations. *Journal of the Experimental Analysis of Behavior, 67*, 275–301.

Rosengrant, J. (1986). Contributions to psychohistory: Fetish symbols in *Playboy* centerfolds. *Psychological Reports, 59*, 623–631.

Saunders, R. (1996). From review to commentary on Roche & Barnes: Towards a better understanding of stimulus equivalence in the context of relational frame theory. *The Psychological Record, 46*, 477–487.

Sidman, M. & Tailby, W. (1982). Conditional discrimination vs. matching to sample: An expansion of the testing paradigm. *Journal of the Experimental Analysis of Behavior, 37*, 5–22.

Skinner, B. F. (1957). *Verbal behavior.* New York: Appleton-Century-Crofts.

Steele, D. & Hayes, S. C. (1991). Stimulus equivalence and arbitrarily applicable relational responding. *Journal of the Experimental Analysis of Behavior, 56*, 519–555.

Stromer, R., McIlvane, W. J., & Serna, R. W. (1993). Complex stimulus control and equivalence. *The Psychological Record, 43*, 585–598.

Teal, D. (1971). *The gay militants.* New York: Stein and Day.

Wulfert, E. & Hayes, S. C. (1988). Transfer of a conditional ordering response through conditional equivalence classes. *Journal of the Experimental Analysis of Behavior, 50*, 125–144.

Zilbergeld, B. (1979). *Men and sex.* London: Souvenir Press.

12

Rules and rule-governance: New directions in the theoretical and experimental analysis of human behaviour

Ken P.J. Kerr and Michael Keenan

Abstract

From the seminal work of B. F. Skinner (1957) to recent publications on rule-governance and instructional control (e.g., Baron & Galizio, 1983; Hayes, 1989) behaviour analysis has offered a thorough and systematic approach to the area of language. The present chapter introduces this work by reviewing recent research into verbal behaviour, rule-governed behaviour, and instructional control on schedules of reinforcement. We conclude by discussing the possibility of extending the stimulus equivalence paradigm to deal with the emergence of rule-following.

What is verbal behaviour?

Skinner (1957) defined verbal behaviour as 'behavior reinforced through the mediation of other persons. . . . Any movement capable of affecting another organism may be verbal' (p. 14). This definition recognises that one of the important functions of language is that it can lead to other people changing their behaviour. In this context, language and verbal behaviour are not considered interchangeable. Rather, language is considered as a set of signs or symbols utilised within the wider class of verbal behaviour (cf. Guerin, 1994). The concept of 'verbal behaviour' breaks with tradition in not bestowing a special quality on speaking and listening, preferring instead to treat such instances like any other behaviour. Furthermore, the adoption of a natural science perspective means that just like any other behaviour an explanation for verbal behaviour is formulated by referring to the relations between the conditions under which the behaviour occurs, the actual behaviour itself, and its consequences. The important role played by the context, both historical and current, is emphasised in the following quotation from Hayes (1986):

In a behavior-analytic approach, all 'causes' are ultimately restricted to environmental events. Behavioral causes are not ultimately acceptable because no one can change behavior without changing its context (e.g., through instructions, drugs, consequences, settings). Behavioral influences are often thought to be important aspects of an overall causal chain, but for philosophical reasons the search is never ended until sources of environmental control are established. (p. 361)

The analysis of verbal behaviour

The focus of this chapter concerns the manner in which verbal behaviour and rule-governed behaviour are accommodated within behaviour analysis. To start with we will concentrate on an area which is of utmost importance to the analysis of verbal behaviour, namely the 'meaning' of a word or a sentence. *The Concise Oxford Dictionary* (1994) defines meaning as 'what is meant by a word, action, idea'. Also, the word 'mean' is partly defined as 'design or destine for a purpose; have as one's purpose or intention; intend to convey or indicate or refer to (a particular thing or notion)'. These definitions illustrate that meaning is often considered as a tangible entity which a person purposively expresses by choosing certain words which subsequently determines their actions. To show the difficulty with this view consider a basic example. Imagine you hear a person say 'Water'. What does this word mean? Expanding the example by telling the person to imagine that you are located in the desert may make things clearer. The call for water could be said to mean that the person calling is extremely thirsty or has just found water. Without the context the meaning is very vague. An analysis of meaning from a behaviour-analytic perspective represents an analysis of the context, the behaviour, and the consequences of the behaviour (cf. Skinner, 1945; Zuriff, 1985). For example, imagine you stand up in a room and shout '*plimth*'. This nonsense word has no meaning, as can be seen by consulting any dictionary. However, if every time you shouted the nonsense word plimth you received water it would be quite reasonable to assume that plimth means that you want some water. Rather than supposing any intrinsic quality of a stimulus, meaning is made apparent by studying the interactions between context, behaviour, and consequences.

Skinner's (1957) original definition of verbal behaviour as operant behaviour considered meaning only from one side of the interaction in a verbal episode, namely the speaker. The rationale for this was that the analysis of the speaker is considered to be complete on its own with any further analysis based on the listener deemed unproductive. In justifying this Skinner suggested that 'the behaviour of a man as listener is not to be distinguished from other forms of his behaviour' (Skinner, 1957, p. 34). As such, the behaviour of the listener was not considered verbal. The analysis of verbal behaviour, however, is not complete until its context is defined. In a verbal episode, the listener provides part of this context by shaping and maintaining the behaviour of the speaker (Hayes & Wilson, 1993). Any account of verbal behaviour that does not recognise the importance of the speaker and the listener is, therefore, incomplete (see Hayes & Hayes, 1989). Before a more complete account of the control exerted by verbal behaviour can be offered it is important to be clear on what constitutes a 'verbal stimulus' in behaviour analysis.

To illustrate the concept of a verbal stimulus Hayes (1989) employed the example of a person walking in a forest with the wind blowing gently through the trees. At some point they mistake the sound for someone whispering their name and they turn around. Is this an instance of verbal behaviour? According to Skinner (1957) verbal behaviour requires the mediation of another person, so by definition the behaviour of turning around on hearing the wind is not verbal. If we remove the natural event from the example and include another person calling their name we would all readily agree that the interaction is verbal in nature. The only difference is the source of the verbal stimulus, whether it comes from a person or a natural event. In the example the natural event has seemingly adopted the function of a verbal stimulus which results in the person turning around to see who is calling (Hayes, 1989). The example illustrates clearly that a natural, supposedly non-verbal event, can adopt a certain function but should we call this function a verbal stimulus? Hayes (1989) argued that the source of a stimulus was not of key importance as to whether the label 'verbal' was employed. He said 'it seems that the concept of verbal stimuli makes sense only if the listener *as listener* can respond verbally' (p. 356). This serves to emphasise the importance of the person as 'listener' in the verbal episode. The role of the listener is of utmost importance when you consider how an individual comes to change their behaviour due to a verbal exchange with another person, action, event, or stimulus. One context which has provided an abundance of research into how the behaviour of the listener is both established and maintained due to verbal interactions is that of 'rule-governed behaviour' (see Hayes, 1989 for a review of current research on rule-governed behaviour).

Rule-governed behaviour

Although many authors consider the term rule-governed behaviour to be inappropriate (Buskist & DeGrandpre, 1989; Guerin, 1994) it appears to be sufficiently well established to justify its continued use. Recent research in the area of rule-governed behaviour has affirmed the positive contribution of behaviour analysis to the study of human behaviour. A coherent theory of how and why people respond to rules is emerging, though there is still much work to be done.

Vaughan (1989) noted that experimentally the role of instructions, whether experimenter-generated or self-generated, became a fashionable area of study in the 1980s. During this time instructions and instruction-following began to be equated with rules and rule-governed behaviour. Before we can fully appreciate the importance of rule-governed behaviour, a brief discussion of the role of contingency-shaped behaviour is required. Contingency-shaped behaviour is behaviour under the control of certain environmental contingencies, including the consequences of behaviour (Skinner, 1966, 1969). For example, a person can learn not to go too near a fire by being too close on occasion and getting burned. The consequence of 'getting burnt' will probably act as a punisher resulting in a decrease in the probability of sitting too close to the fire in the future. Whilst this represents one type of learning process, namely contingency-shaped learning, another process results in learning whereby the direct acting consequences of behaviour do not have to be experienced. That is, human behaviour can be controlled by verbal statements in the form of either a rule or an instruction. The verbal statement, as an antecedent to behaviour, may result in either the generation or the maintenance of behaviour without the actual contingencies being experienced. One of the primary tasks of the experimental analysis of human behaviour is, therefore, to determine the relative effects of contingency control and rule-governance in establishing and maintaining behaviour (Catania, Shimoff, & Matthews, 1989).

Skinner (1969) noted that whilst behaviour produced by either rule-governance or contingency-shaping often appears to be similar, the controlling variables are different. For example, a person who has received no tuition may have a good golf swing due to many hours spent practising on the range. Another person may have received tuition from an expert in forming the 'perfect' swing. Whilst the end result, the swing, may be similar it is obvious that different variables have come into play. In the latter, the tutored swing, a history of social compliance between the learner and the coach is an important part of the training history related to rule-governed behaviour.

Zettle and Hayes (1982) provided a conceptual framework within which to study rule-governed behaviour and the role of additional contingencies arranged by the social community. Rule-governed behaviour was defined as 'behaviour in contact with two sets of contingencies, one of which includes a verbal antecedent' (p. 78). The significant feature of this definition is that it emphasises that behaviour is still a function of contingencies, although the analysis may be somewhat more complex than that which relies on the notion of contingency-shaped behaviour. Thus rule-governed behaviour is behaviour that can be modified by altering the verbal antecedents, that is the rule, or by modifying the consequences of the behaviour specified, or both (Cerutti, 1989). Whilst the definition above is valuable as it emphasises the extra layer of complexity due to contingencies arranged by the social community, the task of clearly defining the word 'rule' has not been attempted. The starting point in defining the word rule is to differentiate 'rule' as a technical term from that of its vernacular usage so that a clear understanding of the term is possible.

What is a rule?

Consider a basic action such as an apple falling from a tree. When the apple becomes detached from the tree it would be quite common to assume that the cause for such an action is the effect of gravity. Skinner (1969) noted that the scientific translation of the natural phenomena of gravity as 's=1/2gt does not govern the behavior of falling bodies' (p. 141). Instead the scientific formulation of gravity is merely a description of a natural event, not the explanation for the event. The apple will fall regardless of whether the Law of Gravity has been formulated in verbal terms or not. Reese (1989) proposed that a description of an event in the natural world, and the event itself, could be described as a 'normal rule', referring to 'the way the world is'. The normal rule refers to regularity in nature and does not control behaviour, it is merely a description of regularity (see Figure 1 for a diagrammatic representation of the key elements of a normal rule).

If a person's behaviour comes under the control of a description of an event the categorisation of the rule changes (Reese, 1989). By introducing a person into the above example the control by a verbal statement can be illustrated. Imagine that a person is told 'If you climb the tree and shake the branches the apples will fall' and they subsequently climb the tree. In this instance the concept of rule appears to have subtly changed whereby the rule has adopted a causal role. Such an example illustrates that behaviour can be controlled by a description of the contingencies. This may be seen in terms of a 'normative rule' prescribing the way in which one ought to proceed (Reese, 1986). The person climbing the tree could say to himself, or have been instructed by another person, that if you shake the branch, the apples will fall. Such a verbalisation is considered to be a normative rule if it at *least implicitly* specifies the three-term contingency: in the presence of a specified antecedent stimulus (the tree), occurrence of a certain behaviour (climbing and shaking the tree) will produce a specific consequence (falling apples). The inclusion of the qualifier 'at least implicitly' allows for the inclusion of vague or incomplete statements as normative rules despite the fact that they do not include the antecedent conditions necessary or the consequences of the specified behaviour. For example, on hearing the shout of 'Fore!' on the golf course we all know to be careful of a wayward shot. We do not need to hear a complete specification of the three-term contingency in this context before we act appropriately.

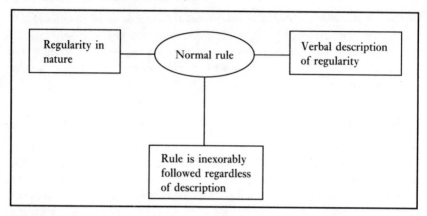

Figure 1. The key elements of a normal rule.

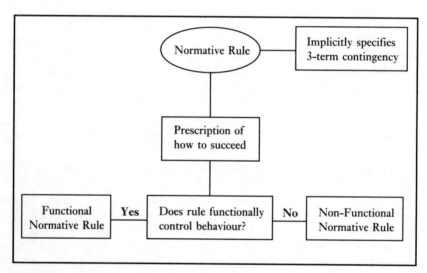

Figure 2. The key elements of a normative rule.

The analysis to date needs to be elaborated further because a normative rule can be either functional or non-functional depending on whether it effects behaviour (Reese & Fremouw, 1984). The normative rule given above may have the effect that the person climbs the tree and shakes the branch. Alternatively, the person may disregard the rule and engage in a different behaviour. The former instance of compliance would point to a functional normative rule, the latter non-compliance would point to a non-functional normative rule. Within such a paradigm the normative rule is merely a prescription of how to proceed or succeed, no more no less. Normative rules are therefore optional in the sense that they can be followed or ignored (see Figure 2 for a description of the key elements of a normative rule).

The conceptualisation of rules as either normal or normative is also comparable with Glenn's (1987) suggestion that 'as objective environmental events, rules must be specifiable without reference to the events that enter into functional relations with them' (p. 30). Glenn's analysis defines the term rule in the traditional terms of Skinner (1966, 1969) with:

the further stipulation that the object called a rule be a verbal, contingency-specifying stimulus, sets the parameters for emission of the verbal response 'rule' and limits the instances of behavior we might call 'rule-governed behavior' to those instances where a functional relation between a rule and a response can at least be reasonably hypothesized. (p. 31)

Basically, from this perspective rules can be identified as objects in the environment which may subsequently enter into a functional relations controlling behaviour. One difficulty with this suggestion is that the class of stimuli called 'rules' would be so large that it consists of everything, thereby rendering the classification redundant. However, the final sentence in the quotation above is important as it emphasises that rule-governed behaviour is shorthand for the functional relation between a verbal stimulus (often referred to as a rule) and responding. If the verbal stimulus does functionally control behaviour it is then, and only then, that we can talk about rule-governed behaviour. The quotation above also introduces a concept considered by many researchers to epitomise the control exerted by verbal stimuli, namely 'contingency-specifying stimuli' (cf. Skinner, 1969; Blakely & Schlinger, 1987).

Contingency-specifying stimuli (CSS)

Hayes and Hayes (1989) note that to 'specify a contingency' presumably involves constructing a regularity in verbal terms. According to Skinner (1969) a CSS is a *verbal* description of the contingency between antecedent stimuli, behaviour, and consequences. For example, the CSS must name at least two members of this set (e.g., two stimuli, or an antecedent stimulus and a response, or a response and a consequence; Blakely & Schlinger, 1987). Using such a classification a command such as 'Be quiet!' would not be considered a CSS as it does not fully specify the contingencies, although it may still have its desired effect. On the other hand, using the classification of rules mentioned earlier, the command 'Be quiet!' may be considered as *implicitly* specifying the contingency and thus function as a normative rule. The categorisation of rules as being normative appears to represent a more general (i.e., higher level) type of analysis in that the complete specification of the rule in terms of CSSs can be considered as only one type of normative rule.

How does a rule function?

The traditional view of the function of a rule is that '[a]s a discriminative stimulus, a rule is effective as part of a set of contingencies of reinforcement' (Skinner, 1969, p. 148). This raises the question of whether CSSs, or more generally, normative rules, function as discriminative stimuli? This is not easily answered because, as we shall see, there is inconsistency in the use of the term 'discriminative stimulus'.

The term 'discriminative stimulus' (S^D) first originated from a set of procedures used in nonhuman experiments to control certain behaviours. For example, once lever pressing has been established it might then be reinforced only in the presence of a light (Stimulus A in Figure 3). The light is deemed a discriminative stimulus when it is said to 'set the occasion for' or 'evokes' a certain type of behaviour because of the higher probability of reinforcement in its presence than in its absence. One definition of an S^D, therefore, implies a trained history of differential reinforcement *in the presence* of the stimulus (see Michael, 1993).

Whilst the idea of an S^D appears straightforward problems have arisen with its usage in the experimental analysis of human behaviour. A simple example may help the discussion. Consider a coach telling his players that if the opposition score they should change their defensive strategy (Instruction X). The effect of this instruction (a normative rule in prescribing the way to suc-ceed) is to bring the behaviour of changing defence under the control of the opposition scoring at a later point in time. The traditional analysis of this would be that the rule works as a discriminative stimulus. The general defini-tion of an S^D, however, implies a trained history of differential reinforcement *in the presence* of the stimulus. In the example above, the normative rule stated by the coach does not evoke an immediate changing of strategies nor is it present when the strategies are subsequently changed (see Figure 4 for a diagrammatic representation of the difference between an S^D and an instruction). This would imply that the coach's instruction is not an S^D.

The normative rule stated by the coach, according to the definition above, is therefore not an S^D (see Ribes, 1992, pp. 213–214). If any aspect of the example is to be considered an S^D perhaps the opposition scoring would be more appropriate as it evokes the change. If the opposition scoring is an S^D, the question remains as to where this function came from. There appears to be no history of trained differential reinforcement to justify the use of the term S^D. Ribes (1992) argued in a similar vein that although the topography of certain behaviours may be similar, the behaviours may in fact be related functionally to different variables.

Various interpretations of functional S^D-like stimuli have been offered using the traditional language of the discriminative control. For example, Cerutti and others (e.g., Catania, Matthews, & Shimoff, 1990) do not consider the history of training to be crucial to the definition of a stimulus as an S^D:

To the extent that the elementary discriminations in instructions are generalized classes they can be recombined in novel instructions that produce novel complex responses. (Cerutti, 1989, p. 261)

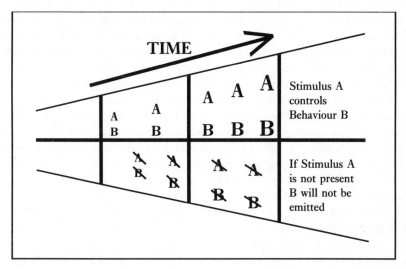

Figure 3. The training of a discriminative relationship between a stimulus (A) and behaviour (B) across time.

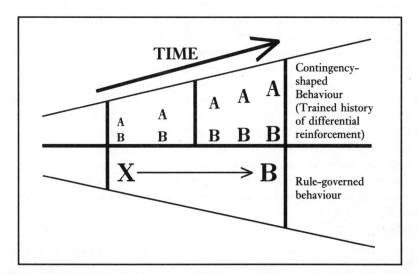

Figure 4. The relation between a trained discriminative stimulus (A) and an instruction (X) both of which enter into a controlling relation with behaviour (B).

Such an analysis suggests that the discriminative units in a rule can maintain their integrity outside the context of the specific rule. Imagine a child learns through discrimination training to 'Lift their arms and cheer' whenever their favourite basketball team scores. In this context, a specific functional relation may be identified between 'favourite team scoring' and 'cheering'. A few years later on going to a football match similar behaviour may be observed. That is, a team scores a goal and the person cheers. The specific elements within the rule 'see favourite team score, cheer' have maintained control over behaviour outside the original context in which it was learned. Whilst the scoring in the new untrained football context may be classed as an S^D for cheering, the history of the stimulus acquiring the function is largely ignored. Thus generalized discrimination, rather than explicit discrimination learning in the presence of the stimuli, is said to occasion new and complex behaviours. Whilst accepting the plausibility of discriminative units breaking and subsequently reforming, Schlinger (1993) stated that this does not mean that the function of rules be best described as a discriminative one. Alessi (1992) also recognised the possibility that rules might mimic the effects of operant discrimination training and he suggested the use of the phrase 'analogue discrimination training'. Although the analysis is consistent with that of Schlinger, the terminology used may be too similar to that of traditional discrimination language which may result in confusion over how one should conceptualise the variables controlling behaviour.

Schlinger, Blakely, Fillhard, and Poling (1991) conducted a survey of how behaviour analysts use the term discriminative stimulus and found that there was no universal acceptance of one definition. Differences existed in the attitude towards the element of temporal proximity. For example, most researchers considered a command such as *'Please leave now!'* to be a verbal discriminative stimulus. If the required action was temporally extended, that is, the action was required to occur in two hours time problems arose. If the instruction was 'when the bell rings *in two hours* please leave' a sizeable minority did not consider this to be an S^D. If there is some disagreement as to the context in which the label discriminative stimuli can be used it is difficult to imagine a specific context in which the terms 'generalized discriminative stimuli' or even 'analogue discrimination training' would be appropriate. Perhaps before concepts such as generalized discrimination are unequivocally accepted as accounting for the function of stimuli labelled as 'rules', a precise definition of an S^D should be agreed upon. Schlinger *et al.* (1991) proposed a three-step definition of an S^D:

(1) a stimulus in whose presence a response is highly probable (2) because in the past, that response has been differentially reinforced in the presence of the stimulus [and] . . . (3) the increase in response probability must have occurred because of the stimulus and the history of differential reinforcement, *and for no other reason.* (p. 159, italics added)

Because the definition of an S^D offered here emphasises the importance of the training history in the presence of the stimulus, its use does not appear to be appropriate to the analysis of verbal events. That is, many instances of verbal control over behaviour do not meet the specific criteria of the S^D. Indeed, instead of advancing our understanding of human behaviour it may well be the case that the reliance on the traditional language of discrimination only serves to impede the search for other behavioural processes (see Blakely & Schlinger, 1987). If this is the case what type of categorisation would account for the control exerted by verbal events or rules over behaviour? One suggestion put forward by Schlinger and Blakely (1987) is that of function-altering operations.

Function-altering operations

The term *function-altering operations* (FAO) denotes environmental operations that alter the behavioural functions of other stimuli (Schlinger, 1993; Schlinger & Blakely, 1987; see Michael, 1982, 1983, for a discussion of environmental operations). In the example given above using a coach telling his players to change defences whenever the opposition scores, the function-altering operation is easy to see. The oppositions scoring has been endowed with an evocative function which appears to be like that of an S^D. Schlinger (1993) suggested that the function-altering stimuli 'must specify the events to be related; in other words to borrow a term from Skinner (1969), they must be *contingency-specifying stimuli* (CSSs)' (p. 12, italics added). Indeed, Blakely and Schlinger (1987) went as far as coining the term 'function-altering contingency-specifying stimuli'. The present discussion has, however, gone beyond the limited nature of CSSs by adopting the classification of normative rules. The term 'function-altering normative rule' whilst suggesting a greater range of control is, however, cumbersome. It is therefore suggested that the shorter term, 'function-altering stimulus' is used to deal with the control exerted by verbal stimuli. An additional advantage of this classification is that problems associated with masking other behavioural processes due to the misclassification of stimuli as S^D's are avoided. As Blakely and Schlinger (1987) note:

Rules can alter the function of stimuli in many ways, and these function-altering effects would be more evident if the interpretation of rules focused on such effects. Furthermore, for greater precision and simplicity, stimuli that function only as S^{D}s should be described as S^{D}s. (p. 186)

Whilst the refinement of key definitions in behaviour analysis has provided a more extensive analysis of the function of verbal stimuli than the traditional language of discrimination, it remains to be seen how these re-definitions and proposed new terms will influence the nature of the experimental analysis of rule-governed behaviour.

Experimental analysis of rule-governed behaviour

A full review of the issues concerning the experimental analysis of rule-governed behaviour is beyond the scope of the present chapter. Instead, we will address those awkward questions that are important to the theoretical issues discussed so far. One of the most prominent areas of research on rule-governed behaviour has been on the issue of instructions resulting in 'insensitivity' of behaviour to contingencies (Baron, Kaufman, & Stauber 1969; Catania, Shimoff, & Matthews, 1989; Galizio, 1979; Joyce & Chase, 1990; Kaufman, Baron, & Kopp, 1966; LeFrancois, Chase, & Joyce, 1988; Matthews, Catania, & Shimoff, 1985; Shimoff, Catania, & Matthews, 1981; Wulfert, Greenway, Farkas, Hayes, & Dougher, 1994; Zettle & Hayes, 1982). Insensitivity refers to the fact that behaviour is not under control by the programmed contingencies in the experimental setting. Caution is required at this point, however, so that it is recognised that behaviour may not be under the control of the programmed contingencies yet it is still under the control of a possibly unidentified set of contingencies. Perhaps a more constructive view of the effect of instructions is that insensitivity to one set of contingencies can be due to additional contingencies brought into play by instructional control. Insensitivity would therefore be better defined as the effect of competing contingencies rather than insensitivity to contingencies per se (Hayes, Rosenfarb, Wulfert, Munt, Korn, & Zettle, 1985; Hayes & Wolf, 1984; Rosenfarb & Hayes; 1982; Zettle & Hayes, 1982).

This is of the utmost importance in comparing contingency-shaped and rule-governed behaviour. By definition behaviour which is contingency-shaped is sensitive to its consequences, that is, the behaviour is under the control of its consequences. Where does this leave rule-governed behaviour? Does this mean that the behaviour of following a rule is not under the control of its consequences? Probably not, as rule-following is itself typically shaped by certain contingencies. For example, if you are told 'Don't sit out in the midday sun' two actions are possible. If you sit out and get badly burnt you will be less likely to sit out at that time again. If, however, the sun is relaxing for you and you go nicely tanned, you would be less likely to follow such a rule in the future. The consequences of following rules are therefore important in determining whether the rule will be followed in the future (Skinner, 1984).

Generally, findings on the apparent insensitivity of behaviour under the control of rules to consequences suggest that responding will be insensitive to the contingencies whenever there is little or no cost to the person (cf. Galizio, 1979). The type of instruction, that is the nature of the description involved, has been shown to be a key factor in determining whether responding is insensitive to the programmed contingencies (cf. Matthews, Catania, & Shimoff, 1985). Insensitivity to contingencies is considered to be one of the biggest advantages of following rules where people are considered to be buffered from the world as contact with every contingency is not required (cf. Skinner, 1966). People do not have to be exposed to aversive or punishing contingencies before they learn to avoid them. Similarly, people can contact more favourable contingencies without having to be explicitly exposed to them. Instead, a description of the contingencies can be written so that others follow these instructions.

Researchers have adopted an approach whereby they evaluate 'sensitivity' to changes in the programmed consequences of responding by firstly developing a steady state responding on a given schedule, followed by a change in the parameters of the schedule. One variable which has been identified as influencing the extent to which responding is sensitive to the programmed contingencies is that of the type of instructions employed. Instructions which generate high rates of responding or low rates generally result in behaviour which is insensitive (Baron, Kaufman, & Stauber 1969; Shimoff, Catania, & Matthews, 1981). The reason for this appears to be that excessively high or low rates may result in responding which does not contact the scheduled contingencies. This suggests that the question of insensitivity is also related to the extent to which the schedule reinforces the rate of responding. Subjects instructed on a variety of schedules (e.g., LeFrancois, Chase, & Joyce, 1988) or given instructions stating that variable responding is best (e.g., Joyce & Chase, 1990) also tend to respond in a fashion which is sensitive to changes in the contingencies.

The teasing apart of the role of rule-following in the generation of either rigid (i.e., insensitive) or variable behaviour is one area which has drawn special interest. One theory is that a history of compliance with instructions can reduce behavioural variability due to the competitive effect of the social consequences for rule-following (Wulfert *et al.*, 1994). Zettle and Hayes (1982) considered the role of social contingencies in their distinction of the functional units in a listener's behaviour in regards to rule-following, namely pliance and tracking. Pliance, derived from compliance, was defined as rule-governed behaviour primarily under the control of apparent speaker-mediated consequences for a correspondence between the rule and behaviour. Therefore, pliance is considered as behaviour under strict instructional control. For example, if a robber states 'Stand and Deliver' the victim's behaviour in giving up his money is under the control of the apparent threat offered by the assailant. Such compliance may lead to generalised compliance of instructions given by those perceived as being in power to basically stay on the 'safe' side. The production of 'safe' behaviours (Wulfert *et al.*, 1994) in itself may, therefore, be perceived as a type of rigidity. Tracking – suggesting a path – is rule-governed behaviour under the control of the apparent correspondence between the rule and the way the world is arranged. A person is said to track a rule whenever the contingencies specified in the rule adopt a reinforcing function. For example, a child is told 'Don't go too near the fire'. If the child subsequently touches the fire and is exposed to aversive stimuli, the probability of similar behaviour in the future decreases. People with a history of contacting the actual contingency specified in the instruction may behave in a more flexible manner due to the lack of strict enforcement of rule-following through social contingencies.

The issue of insensitivity is central to our understanding of rules and rule-governed behaviour. That is, we must recognise that the function of rules, resulting in rule-governed behaviour, is determined by the nature of the control exerted by the contingencies. This can be re-phrased to pose the question 'under what circumstances do verbal stimuli enter into functional controlling relations?' One assumption so far, however, is that rules have already acquired a certain function. We have talked of rules mainly as antecedents to behaviour studied within the context of schedules of reinforcement which organise and maintain behaviour. However, with the development of the stimulus equivalence paradigm to study behaviour which has no apparent reinforcement history, it is possible that a new theoretical and experimental context for the study of rule-following is available.

Stimulus equivalence

Stimulus equivalence offers behaviour analysis the opportunity to study behaviour which emerges without any explicit previous history of reinforcement (see Dougher & Markham, 1994 for a review of important issues in stimulus equivalence). The typical experimental procedure in stimulus equivalence involves the training of related conditional discriminations (see Sidman, 1994). For example, a person is trained to select the arbitrary comparison Stimulus 'B' in the presence of the sample Stimulus 'A' (i.e., reinforcer delivery is available for the appropriate selection). Similarly, the person may be trained to select comparison Stimulus 'C' in the presence of sample Stimulus 'B'. In a test situation (i.e., reinforcer delivery is no longer available) the person is likely to select Stimulus 'A' given Stimulus 'B' as the sample (i.e., symmetrical relation) and to select Stimulus 'A' given Stimulus 'C' as the sample (i.e., combined symmetry and transitivity relation). In the test situation relations emerge between stimuli despite there being the absence of a history of explicit training.

Of particular interest to the present paper, researchers have found that when a discriminative function is trained to one of the stimuli in an equivalence class, this can have the effect of altering the function of other members of the same class (see Barnes & Keenan, 1993; Dymond & Barnes, 1994; Hayes & Hayes, 1989; Markham & Dougher, 1993). This finding has important implications for an understanding of one property of language, namely symbolic control. It is commonplace to talk about one word 'standing for' or 'representing' another word, object, or event despite there being no physical similarity between the two (cf. Sidman, 1994). For example, a person may be taught the conditional relation between MADRA and CHIEN. That is, see CHIEN

(French word for Dog), choose MADRA (Irish word for Dog). Similarly, they may be taught the conditional relation between MADRA and DOG. In certain test situations, the person may show the ability to form the derived relations between MADRA–CHIEN, DOG–MADRA (both symmetrical relations), MADRA–CHIEN (transitive relation), DOG–CHIEN (equivalence relation) despite the absence of a trained history of responding in this way (see Sidman & Tailby, 1982 for a discussion of the defining relations between stimuli in an equivalence class).

The equivalence phenomenon, and the associated transformation of stimulus function, offers a context whereby the origin and nature of the control exerted by verbal stimuli can be studied. Consider an equivalence class of stimuli consisting of three members, A, B, C. The transformation of function procedure usually involves the training of a function (e.g., clapping) onto the 'A' stimuli. Subsequently, the conditional relations between the A–B and B–C stimuli are established. The test for the transformation of function involves testing the 'C' stimulus to determine if the transfer has occurred from the A stimulus (see Dougher & Markham, 1994; Dube, McDonald, & McIlvane, 1991; Markham & Dougher, 1993). That is, when presented with the 'C' stimulus does the person also clap?

If clapping does occur, Stimulus 'C' can certainly be considered to be 'verbal' in lines with the definition offered by Hayes and Wilson (1993). Barnes (1991) commented that:

a word or symbol may control human behaviour through equivalence relations to other words, objects, or actual events. *It is important to understand that an actual object, or event, also functions as a verbal stimulus when it controls behaviour through its participation in an equivalence class.* (p. 196, italics added)

In the clapping example above, Stimulus 'C' is verbal as it exerts its control because of its membership of an equivalence class. In terms of the earlier discussion on normative rules, it can be said that the 'C' stimulus certainly prescribes the way to proceed. That is, the presentation of the 'C' stimulus may be viewed as a 'rule' which may ultimately result in rule-governed behaviour (i.e., the 'C' stimulus functions as a normative rule in controlling responding). Although the stimulus equivalence paradigm appears to offer a new context in which rules and rule-following could be studied very little progress has been made in terms of empirical research connecting this area to the notion of rule-governance.

One study by Hayes, Thompson, and Hayes (1989) considered the relation between stimulus equivalence and rule-following. They reasoned that if equivalence relations are a model of various linguistic phenomena it may be possible to construct a 'rule' out of different members of an equivalence class. Their experiments employed two independent sets of equivalence relations, both pertaining to musical stimuli (i.e., Set 1 was relevant to musical timing and Set 2 was relevant to placement). The aim of their research was to assess the extent that the combination of stimuli from each independent set was possible. If the two sets combined, a series of new compound stimuli could be created which may determine novel patterns of responding. The data suggested that novel patterns of responding could be produced through the combination of stimulus functions from different classes of stimuli.

Dougher and Markham (1994) also considered the function of a combination of stimuli in the context of stimulus equivalence. They suggested that the use of compound stimuli better represents the natural stimulus relations which result in complex stimulus control. A flexible definition of a compound was employed whereby the compound stimulus was considered to consist of interchangeable elements (see Markham & Dougher, 1993; Strommer, McIlvane, & Serna, 1993). Briefly, the idea is that in training conditional relations, separable and interchangeable compound elements are trained. Following from this, match-to-sample training can be conceptualised as training compounds such as A1B1, A2B2, B1C1, and B2C2. The emergence of the derived relation of equivalence (e.g., C1A1, C2A2) and transitivity (e.g., AC) therefore are the result of compounds separating and reforming through their relations with other stimuli (e.g., B1 and B2). Strommer *et al.*(1993) suggested that the 'control by separable compound stimuli may therefore be the basic context in which stimulus equivalence relations emerge' (p. 593).

The analysis of the role of the combination of stimuli from different equivalence classes (e.g., Hayes, Thompson, & Hayes, 1989) or in terms of the compounding of stimuli (e.g., Dougher & Markham, 1994) may have interesting implications for the study of rule-governed behaviour and rule-following. Perhaps one question that can be posed is 'to what extent can the equivalence test itself be considered as a rule governing subjects' behaviour?' That is, if the configuration of stimuli in an equivalence test was translated into a verbal statement would the result be a string of words that we could label a rule? Kerr (1996) answered this question by investigating the emergence of complex behaviours through the integration of previously trained functions and response type. Briefly, the basic procedure involved loading different functions via instructions onto four stimuli during discrimination training. Specifically, subjects were instructed to 'Make one response' on the centre key of a response pad when the 'A1' stimulus was presented, and 'Make five responses' on the centre key of a response pad when the 'A2' stimulus was presented. Similarly, subjects were instructed to 'Make one response on the left key' on the response pad when the 'C1' stimulus was presented, and to 'Make one response on the right key' on the response pad when the 'C2' stimulus was displayed. Subjects were subsequently trained on a match-to-sample task with subjects instructed to 'point to' the appropriate stimuli on the screen in the presence of a 'green strip'. The main test was of the equivalence relations between the stimuli. That is, the screen configuration was either 'C1' or 'C2' (sample) with 'A1' and

'A2' acting as the comparison stimuli. Subjects were given this test a number of times with either the response pad present, the green strip present, or both the pad and the strip present. Results generally showed that when responding on the response pad alone, subjects responded to the function of the appropriate comparison stimuli. For example, when **C2**: A1, **A2** (with the equivalence relation marked in bold for discussion purposes) was presented, subjects generally responded five times on the centre key (i.e., A2 controlled five responses on the centre key). When the green strip was displayed, subjects always responded by pointing to the appropriate equivalence relation on the screen. When both response options were presented, response pad and green strip, subjects generally pointed to the equivalence relation on the screen and then responded to the function of the experimentally-related comparison stimuli. The results were interesting in that a sequence of responses was produced with no real integration in terms of the trained response options or the placement of responding. Assuming that a rule in the form of verbal statement would be read in sequence from left to right it may have been expected that a subject would verbalise the configuration of stimuli **C2**:A1, **A2** as 'Make one response on the right key, make one response on the centre key, and make five responses on the centre key'. Alternatively, assuming that equivalence formation results in the creation of a specific 'rule' in terms of the combination of stimuli, it may also have been expected that the subjects would attend to the **C2–A2** stimuli. That is, subjects may have responded to the function of the sample stimulus followed by a response to the function the comparison stimulus in the equivalent relation. So given **C2**:**A2**, A1 subjects may have responded once on the right key (i.e., the function of C2) and five times on the centre key (i.e., the function of A2) when the response pad was present. Such patterns were not apparent with no subject responding to the function of the sample stimulus. This in itself was interesting as it suggested that the control exerted by the configuration of equivalence stimuli proved to be stronger than the control exerted by the trained function of the individual stimuli.

In a subsequent experiment, Kerr (1996) employed the same basic procedure except one additional test presented the 'B' stimuli (nonsense stimuli) individually after the equivalence classes were trained and tested. Subjects were asked to 'respond as they considered appropriate'. Two subjects responded sequentially, that is they responded to the function controlled by the A stimulus followed by the function controlled by the 'C' stimulus. That is, when presented with B1 (ZIM) these subjects responded once on the centre key (i.e., function controlled by A1) followed by once on the left key (i.e., function controlled by C1). One subject, however, responded by integrating the functions of the A and C stimuli. That is, when presented with B1 (ZIM) she responded once on the left button. When presented with B2 (VEK) she responded *five times on the right button* (i.e., the functions of the A2 and C2 stimuli merged in terms of number of responses and location of responses). This finding marks a shift from focusing on the transformation of one function in an equivalence class to the integration of multiple functions.

To place these findings into the general context of issues raised in this chapter, it is useful to consider the function of the 'B' stimuli in terms of rule-governance. The important question is 'can the B stimuli be considered to be verbal stimuli in controlling a subject's behaviour?' It was noted previously that a stimulus is considered verbal if it controls behaviour through its participation in an equivalence class. Also, the behaviour of the listener is considered verbal if it is in response to a stimulus function which is derived rather than trained (cf. Barnes, 1991; Hayes & Wilson, 1993). The responding by the subjects to the 'B' stimuli meet these criteria and the control by the stimuli is properly considered verbal. In these terms, the experiment shows a verbal relation between the stimulus function and the behaviour of the subject.

An added question may be 'to what extent do the B stimuli function as rules in controlling behaviour?' A rule has previously been defined as normative if it prescribes the way to proceed, and normal, if it describes a regularity in nature. The function of the 'B' stimuli can be considered as a functional normative rule whereby the stimuli control responding on certain locations. Note that the function of the rule does not lie in any intrinsic quality of the stimulus. Instead, the derived function controlled by the 'B' stimuli is the result of the training of individual functions that have become integrated. If the 'B' stimuli are considered as a normative, in prescribing how the subject should respond, where exactly did this function come from?

To answer this question, consider again the experimental procedure. The original functions of the 'A' and 'C' stimuli were initially changed by a verbal instruction before a trained history of differential reinforcement in the presence of the stimuli was implemented. Although the instruction and the training are virtually temporally contiguous, the resulting control exerted by the stimuli may not be like that of the discriminative control shown with nonhumans. That is, an extra layer of control by a history of 'rule-following' enters into the equation. It is possible that by temporally separating the instruction and the actual stimulus endowed with a certain function, that other types of control may ensue (see Schlinger, 1993). Regardless of the type of control exerted, the function would not properly be conceived of as being discriminative in the traditional sense. As for the 'B' stimuli in the present experiment, the control exerted by them is merely discriminative-like. Hayes and Wilson (1993) make a similar point in stating that:

the transformation of discriminative functions through equivalence classes is dependent upon relating as a learned process. *The resultant stimulus function is not discriminative in the normal sense, but is only discriminative-like.* (p. 290, italics added)

One way to conceptualise the type of control over responding in the present experiment is to consider the 'A' and 'C' stimuli as being function-altering (cf. Schlinger, 1993). In these terms, the 'B' stimuli have been endowed with an evocative function which appears to be like that of an S^D, although the functions of the 'B' stimuli have been derived rather than directly trained. The 'A' and 'C' stimulus functions would then be perceived as overlapping in the sense that both stimuli alter the function of the previously neutral 'B' stimuli.

Hayes *et al.* (1989) also tested for the integration of behavioural functions across stimulus classes and offered a working definition of rule-following where:

rule-following involves acting with respect to verbal stimulation at one point in time and, at a later point, acting in some other way with respect to other stimulus conditions. The two instances must be related . . . an uncontaminated instance of rule-following implies a novel pattern of activity. (p. 275)

It appears from this definition of rule-following that the stimulus equivalence paradigm can be useful in studying rule-governed behaviour. In Hayes *et al.*'s terms the emergence of the integrated behaviour onto the 'B' stimuli is an example of an uncontaminated instance of rule-following implying a novel pattern of activity. In summary, the experiments by Kerr (1996) show the development of a procedure within the stimulus equivalence paradigm which can be used to study rule-following.

Summary and conclusions

The present chapter highlights the difficulties in trying to pin down specific definitions of technical terms within behaviour analysis. In particular definitions of key terms such as verbal behaviour, verbal stimuli, discriminative stimuli, rule-governed behaviour, and contingency-specifying stimuli are examined. Rather than accepting previous definitions of key terms as inherently correct, the present analysis has refined old definitions in providing an explanation of the functional control exerted by verbal stimuli. Two types of rules, namely a normal rule which describes natural phenomena and a normative rule which prescribes the way in which one ought to proceed, are also defined. Normative rules were shown to encompass a wider range of verbal control than the commonly accepted indicator of rule-governance, contingency-specifying stimuli.

Rule function was discussed firstly in terms of discriminative stimuli. The traditional language of discrimination was, however, shown to be inappropriate in accounting for verbal control. Instead the use of the term 'function-altering stimulus' was advocated as an alternative which encompasses the nature of verbal control over behaviour. In expanding the study of rule-governance to stimulus equivalence the role of function-altering stimuli was demonstrated. Of particular interest was the transformation of a stimulus function as a result of training two different functions on to related stimuli in the same class. The development of this procedure stems from the detailed theoretical analysis described in this chapter and furthers a recent way of thinking in the experimental analysis of human behaviour.

References

Alessi, G. (1992). Models of proximate and ultimate causation in psychology. *American Psychologist, 47*, 1359–1370.

Barnes, D. (1991). Schedules of reinforcement and human behaviour: A contextualistic Perspective. Unpublished doctoral thesis, University of Ulster.

Barnes, D. & Keenan, M. (1993). A transfer of function through derived arbitrarily and nonarbitrary stimulus relations. *Journal of the Experimental Analysis of Behavior, 59*, 61–81.

Baron, A. & Galizio, M. (1983). Instructional control of human operant behavior. *The Psychological Record, 33*, 495–520.

Baron, A., Kaufman, A., & Stauber, K. A. (1969). Effects of instructions and reinforcement-feedback on human operant behavior maintained by fixed-interval reinforcement. *Journal of the Experimental Analysis of Behavior, 12*, 701–712.

Blakely, E. & Schlinger, H. (1987). Rules: Function-altering contingency-specifying stimuli. *The Behavior Analyst*, 10, 183–187.

Buskist, W. F. & DeGrandpre, R. J. (1989). The myth of rule-governed behavior. *Experimental Analysis of Human Behavior Bulletin*, 7, 4–6.

Catania, A. C., Matthews, B. A., & Shimoff, E., (1990). Properties of rule-governed behavior and their implications. In D. E. Blackman & H. Lejeune (Eds), *Behavior analysis in theory and practice: Contributions and controversies*. Hillsdale, NJ: Erlbaum.

Catania, A. C., Shimoff, E., & Matthews, B. A. (1989). An experimental analysis of rule-governed behavior. In S. C. Hayes (Ed.), *Rule-governed behavior: Cognition, contingencies, and instructional control* (pp. 119–1150). New York: Plenum.

Cerutti, D. T. (1989). Discrimination theory of rule-governed behavior. *Journal of the Experimental Analysis of Behavior, 51*, 259–276.

Dougher, M. J. & Markham, M. R. (1994). Stimulus equivalence, functional equivalence, and the transfer of function. In S. C. Hayes, L. J. Hayes, M. Sato, & K. Ono (Eds), *Behavior analysis of language and cognition* (pp. 71–91). Reno, NV: Context Press.

Dube, W. V., McDonald, W. J., & McIlvane, W. J. (1991). A note on the relationship between equivalence classes and functional classes. *Experimental Analysis of Human Behavior Bulletin, 9*, 7–11.

Dymond, S. & Barnes, D. (1994). A transfer of self-discrimination response functions through equivalence relations. *Journal of the Experimental Analysis of Behavior, 62*, 251–267.

Galizio, M. (1979). Contingency-shaped and rule-governed behavior: Instructional control of human loss avoidance. *Journal of the Experimental Analysis of Behavior, 31*, 53–70.

Glenn, S. S. (1987). Rules as environmental events. *The Analysis of Verbal Behavior, 5*, 29–32.

Grant, L. & Evans, A. (1994). *Principles of behavior analysis*. New York HarperCollins.

Guerin, B. (1994). *Analyzing social behavior: Behavior analysis and the social sciences*. Reno, NV: Context Press.

Hayes, S. C. (1986). The case of the silent dog – Verbal reports and the analysis of rules: A review of Ericson & Simon's protocol analysis: Verbal reports as data. *Journal of the Experimental Analysis of Behavior, 45,* 351–363.

Hayes, S. C. (Ed.) (1989). *Rule-governed behavior: Cognition, contingencies, and instructional control.* New York: Plenum.

Hayes, S. C. & Hayes, L. J. (1989). The verbal action of the listener as a basis for rule-governance. In S. C. Hayes (Ed.), *Rule-governed behavior: Cognition, contingencies, and instructional control* (pp. 191–220). New York: Plenum.

Hayes, S. C., Rosenfarb, I., Wulfert, E., Munt, E. D., Korn, Z., & Zettle, R. D. (1985). Social reinforcement effects – an artefact of social standard setting. *Journal of Applied Behavior Analysis, 18,* 201–214.

Hayes, L. J., Thompson, S., & Hayes, S. C. (1989). Stimulus equivalence and rule-following. *Journal of the Experimental Analysis of Behavior, 52,* 275–292.

Hayes, S. C., Zettle, R. D., & Rosenfarb, I. (1989). Rule-following. In S. C. Hayes (Ed.), *Rule-governed behavior: Cognition, contingencies, and instructional control* (pp. 191–220). New York: Plenum.

Hayes, S. C. & Wilson, K. G. (1993). Some applied implications of a contemporary behavior-analytic account of verbal events. *The Behavior Analyst, 16,* 283–301.

Hayes, S. C. & Wolfe, M. R. (1984). Cues, consequences, and therapeutic talk – Effects of social-context and copying statements of pain. *Behavior Research and Therapy, 22,* 385–392.

Joyce, J. H. & Chase, P. N. (1990). Effects of response variability on the sensitivity of rule-governed behavior. *Journal of the Experimental Analysis of Behavior, 54,* 251–262.

Kaufman, A., Baron, A., & Kopp, R. E. (1966). Some effects of instructions on human operant behavior. *Psychonomic Monograph Supplements, 1,* 243–250.

Kerr, K. (1996). Schedules of reinforcement and stimulus equivalence: An integrative approach to rule-governed behaviour. Unpublished Doctoral Thesis, University of Ulster.

LeFrancois, J. R., Chase, P. N., & Joyce, J. H. (1988). The effects of a variety of instructions on human fixed-interval performance. *Journal of the Experimental Analysis of Behavior, 49,* 383–393.

Markham , M. R. & Dougher, M. J. (1993). Compound stimuli in emergent stimulus relations – Extending the scope of stimulus equivalence. *Journal of the Experimental Analysis of Behavior, 60,* 529–542.

Matthews, B. A., Catania, A. C., & Shimoff, E. (1985). Effects of uninstructed verbal behavior on nonverbal responding: Contingency descriptions versus performance descriptions. *Journal of the Experimental Analysis of Behavior, 27,* 453–467.

Michael, J. (1982). Distinguishing between discriminative and motivational functions of stimuli. *Journal of the Experimental Analysis of Behavior, 37,* 49–55.

Michael, J. (1983). Evocative and repertoire-altering effects of an environmental event. *The Analysis of Verbal Behavior, 2,* 21–23.

Michael, J. (1993). Establishing operations. *The Behavior Analyst, 16,* 191–206.

Reese, H. W. (1986). On the theory and practice of behavior analysis. In H. W. Reese & L. J. Hayes (Eds), *Behavior science: Philosophical, methodological, and empirical advances* (pp. 157–195). Hillsdale, NJ: Erlbaum.

Reese, H. W. (1989). Rules and rule-governance: Cognitive and behavioristic views. In S. Hayes (Ed.), *Rule-governed behavior: Cognition, contingencies, and instructional control* (pp. 3–84). New York: Plenum.

Reese, H. W. & Fremouw, H. J. (1984). Normal and normative ethics in behavioral sciences. *American Psychologist, 39,* 863–876.

Ribes, E. (1992). Effects of visual demonstration, verbal instructions, and prompted verbal descriptions on the performance of human subjects in conditional discriminations. *The Analysis of Verbal Behavior, 10,* 23–36.

Rosenfarb, I. S. & Hayes, S. C. (1982). Social standard setting – The Achilles heel of informational account of therapeutic change. *Behavior Therapy, 15,* 515–528.

Schlinger, H. (1993). Separating discriminative and function-altering effects of verbal stimuli. *The Behavior Analyst, 16,* 9–23.

Schlinger, H. & Blakely, E. (1987). Function-altering effects of contingency-specifying stimuli. *The Behavior Analyst, 10,* 41–45.

Schlinger, H., Blakely, E., Fillhard, J., & Poling, A. (1991). Defining terms in behavior analysis: Reinforcer and discriminative stimulus. *The Analysis of Verbal Behavior, 9,* 153–161.

Shimoff, E., Catania, A. C., & Matthews, B. A. (1981). Uninstructed human responding: Sensitivity of low-rate performance to schedule contingencies. *Journal of the Experimental Analysis of Behavior, 36,* 207–220.

Sidman, M. (1994). *Equivalence relations and behavior: A research story.* Boston, MA: Authors Co-operative Inc.

Sidman, M. & Tailby, W. (1982). Conditional discrimination vs matching to sample: An expansion of the testing paradigm. *Journal of the Experimental Analysis of Behavior, 37,* 5–22.

Skinner, B. F. (1945). The operational analysis of psychological terms. *Psychological Review, 52,* 270–277.

Skinner, B. F. (1957). *Verbal behavior.* New York. Appelton-Century-Crofts.

Skinner, B. F. (1966). The phylogeny and ontogeny of behavior. *Science, 153,* 1205–1213.

Skinner, B. F. (1969). *Contingencies of reinforcement: A theoretical analysis.* New York. Appelton-Century-Crofts.

Skinner, B. F. (1984). The evolution of behavior. *Journal of the Experimental Analysis of Behavior, 41,* 217–221.

Strommer, R., McIlvane, W. J., & Serna, R. W. (1993). Complex stimulus control and equivalence. *The Psychological Record, 43,* 585–598.

Vaughan, M. (1989). Rule-governed behavior in behavior analysis: A theoretical and experimental analysis. In S. C. Hayes (Ed.), *Rule-governed behavior: Cognition, contingencies, and instructional control* (pp. 97–118). New York: Plenum.

Wulfert, E., Greenway, D. E, Farkas, P., Hayes, S. C., & Dougher, M. J. (1994). Correlation between self-reported rigidity and rule-governed insensitivity to operant contingencies. *Journal of Applied Behavior Analysis, 27,* 659–671.

Zettle, R. D. & Hayes, S. C. (1982). Rule-governed behavior: A potential theoretical framework for cognitive-behavioral therapy. In P. C. Kendall (Ed.), *Advances in cognitive-behavioral research and therapy* (Vol. 1, pp. 73–118). San Diego, CA: Academic Press.

Zuriff, G. E. (1985). *Behaviorism: A conceptual reconstruction.* New York: Columbia University Press.

Notes on contributors

Donald M. Baer, Roy A. Roberts Distinguished Professor of Human Development and Family Life and a Senior Scientist in the Life Span Institute at the University of Kansas, obtained his doctorate from the University of Chicago in 1957, where he was advised by Jacob Gewirtz. At his first teaching position at the University of Washington, he collaborated frequently with Sidney Bijou. Since 1965 he has been at the University of Kansas and has held many visiting appointments. He has served as editor and associate editor for over ten journals including the *Journal of Applied Behavior Analysis* and the *American Journal on Mental Deficiency*. His research interests have centred on language, early education, social control, imitation, self-regulation and retardation.

Leo J. V. Baker taught behaviour analysis at Trinity College Dublin for nearly 30 years and introduced Keller-Plan teaching to the Department of Psychology. He was one of the founding members of the Behaviour Analysis in Ireland group and has been a member of the UK Experimental Analysis of Behaviour Group since the mid-1960s. Leo Baker is now retired.

Dermot Barnes is a lecturer in Psychology and Director of the Behaviour Analysis and Cognitive Science Unit at University College Cork. His long-standing research interests include the experimental analysis of human behaviour and conceptual and philosophical issues in behavioural psychology. More recent interests include applied behaviour analysis in clinical and industrial settings.

Samuel D. Cromie did his doctoral research on the self-control of study in third-level students. He is currently a postdoctoral researcher at Trinity College Dublin, and a member of the Aerospace Psychology Research Group. His current research is largely in aviation psychology

Karola Dillenburger has worked in statutory and voluntary child care agencies in Germany and Northern Ireland over the past twenty years and is currently lecturing in the Social Work Department at The Queen's University of Belfast. Her main research interests include human development, attachment and loss, bereavement, child sex abuse, social work education and equal opportunities.

Michael Keenan is a lecturer in the Department of Psychology at the University of Ulster at Coleraine. His research interests include equivalence responding, biofeedback, imitation learning, the analysis of social behaviours, schedules of reinforcement, community psychology, autism, hypnosis, and child sex abuse.

Ken P. J. Kerr is at present a teaching assistant at the University of Ulster, where he obtained his doctorate. His main interests in behaviour analysis are in schedules of reinforcement and stimulus equivalence research, rule-governed behaviour and sport psychology.

Finola Leonard qualified from the Faculty of Veterinary Medicine at University College Dublin in 1983. After three years in private practice, she joined Teagasc, the Agriculture and Food Development Authority. She is currently working on dairy cow and pig health and welfare. Her particular interests are the influence of behaviour on the development of lameness in dairy cows and the welfare of sows in the furrowing house.

Julian C. Leslie completed a DPhil in psychology in the area of behaviour analysis at the University of Oxford. Since 1974 he has mostly worked in Northern Ireland and is now Professor of Psychology at the University of Ulster at Jordanstown. He has published extensively in the areas of the experimental analysis of behaviour, behaviour pharmacology and, more recently, applied psychology and research ethics.

Janet O'Connell graduated from University College Cork in zoology and worked as an animal behaviour specialist in Teagasc, Moorepark, Co. Cork for nine years. She is currently farming in Co. Wicklow and continuing to work on animal behaviour with her husband, John Kent.

Dermot O'Reilly is a Senior Social Worker with the Lucena Clinic Child Guidance Service, Bray, Co. Wicklow. He is enrolled as a doctoral research student with the Department of Social Work, The Queen's University of Belfast.

Mark F. O'Reilly is a lecturer in psychology at University College Dublin. His research interests include applied behaviour analysis, the experimental analysis of behaviour, and the assessment and treatment of behaviour disorders in children with severe developmental disabilities.

Bryan Roche is a lecturer in psychology at the University of Bath. His doctoral research at University College Cork concerned verbal behaviour and its relation to complex sexual functioning. Brian Roche's research interests also include behaviour-analytic epistemology and conceptual and methodological issues in psychophysiological assessment.

John A. Smith graduated in psychology at the University of Ulster in 1985 and has since trained as a clinical psychologist.

Ian Taylor is in the final stages of completing his PhD in psychology at University College Dublin. He has been involved in applied behaviour analysis with people with developmental disabilities. His interests in behaviour analysis include verbal behaviour, private events and functional analysis techniques.

Kevin J. Tierney has a PhD from Trinity College Dublin and trained in Dublin as a clinical psychologist. He is now a lecturer in psychology at the University of Ulster. He served as President of the Psychological Society of Ireland (1995–96) and chaired the Scientific Committee for the Fifth European Congress of Psychology. He has published in the areas of behaviour analysis and applied behaviour analysis.

Peter Walsh is a clinical psychologist working in Galway with people with learning disabilities. He obtained a doctorate from University College Galway for his work investigating the use of differential reinforcement as a means of reducing stereotypical behaviour. He has co-authored a book for the Wiley Series in Clinical Psychology on stereotyped movement disorders.

Index